22/06/02.

# Montreal Memories

# Montreal Memories

of the

Century

from the

Sketchbooks

of

John Collins

Shoreline

**Montreal Memories of the Century**
**from the Sketchbooks of John Collins**



Published by Shoreline,
23 Ste-Anne, Ste-Anne-de-Bellevue,
Quebec H9X 1L1. Phone/fax: 514-457-6733.
bookline@total.net www.total.net/~bookline

Printed in Canada by AGMV Marquis

Dépôt légal: Bibliothèque nationale du Québec and
The National Library of Canada



**Cataloguing in Publication Data**

Collins, John 1917-
Montreal memories of the century:
from the sketchbooks of John Collins

ISBN 896754-11-2

1. Collins, John, 1917- 2. Montreal (Québec)—in art. I. Title.

NC143.C63A42999 741.971 C00-900508-0

My thanks

to Shoreline;

to Edgar Andrew Collard,
who set me out to hunt illustrations for his *Gazette* column,
"All Our Yesterdays";

to the people at *Senior Scene,*
who re-awakened my interest in what we did
when we were so much younger;

and finally, to my wife,
who has put up with my love affair with a sketchbook
all these years

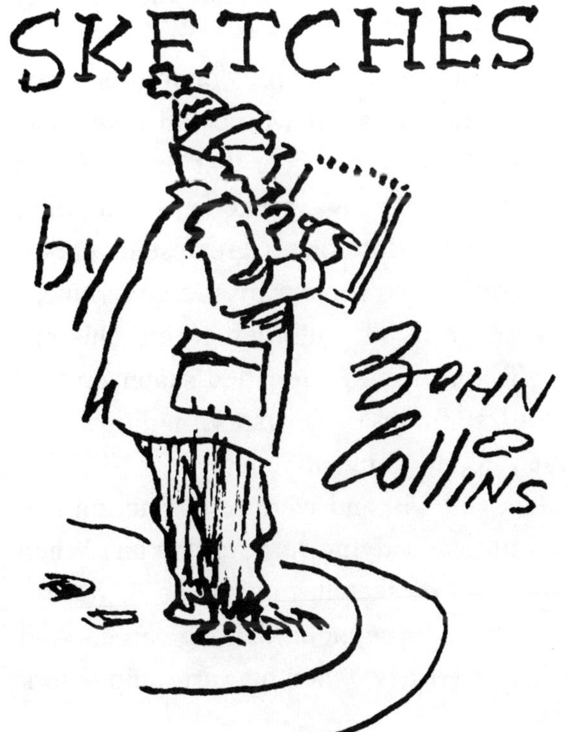

## FOREWORD

Seeing the proofs of this splendid book inspired me to seek out a microfilm machine and scan issues of *The Montreal Gazette* of half a century ago. I found the ads of 1949 particularly fascinating, with Eaton's offering elevator shoes that would make short men taller and corsets that would make stout women slimmer. But I wasn't looking for curiosities like these as I wound my way through the microfilmed pages. What I wanted to do was refresh my memory of the John Collins of those long-ago days, when he used to draw political cartoons for the editorial page.

I was a young reporter on *The Gazette* in 1949 and I remember sitting at my desk and watching John step out of the elevator and sweep through the newsroom on his way to another part of the building. There, in an office near that of the publisher, he would be far from the tumult and chattering typewriters of the newsroom (those being the days before computers). And it was there that John executed the next day's cartoon.

Although he was only about ten years older than I was, John Collins was to me an august personage. We reporters were, at best, craftsmen, but this man was an *artist.* We recorded, but he created. We conveyed facts - or at least tried to - but he was allowed to make it all up, out of his head. After work, most of us ink-stained wretches trudged up the hill to Dorchester Street, to Slotkin and Slitkin's bar and grill, where we drank beer and denounced our editors. But John Collins went home, obviously a man with better things to do.

Going through the 1949 *Gazette,* I found many examples of John's virtuosity as a political cartoonist. Was there ever another artist who could give us as many versions of the face of Joseph Stalin? Here was a face that leapt off the page, sometimes scowling, sometimes grinning, frowning, menacing, ingratiating - each expression more malevolent than the last. But John's greatest invention was Mr. Canadian Taxpayer, a miserable creature so robbed by the government that he was often depicted as being deprived of his very clothes: to hide his nakedness he wore a barrel. Sometimes Mr. Taxpayer was a terrified skater on thin ice or a petrified skier about to crash into a tree. In his 43 years as a political cartoonist, John Collins seemed never to have run out of inventiveness.

His cartoons were fueled by sarcasm and wit, and were full of action and absurd characters staggering, tumbling, sliding, and flying through the air. When you compare them with the serenity of most of the sketches in this book you realize what a versatile artist John Collins has been throughout his long career. And we should be grateful that he found time, day after day, when his cartooning work was done, to roam the city and record its life.

This book has given me great pleasure and has evoked long dormant memories, as it will for any Montrealer who has been around for a while. John's observations about the days when cars were "put up" in the winter reminded me of my father telling me how he would not only put his Chevy up on blocks in some unheated storage space, but he would take the battery home and put it under his bed to keep it warm. And he insisted that in the early 1920s, when there weren't many cars in Montreal, there was only one No Parking sign in the whole city. It was on Sherbrooke Street and it said, "Please do not park in front of the horse trough."

I can vouch for the authenticity of many of John's observations about people like the "floorwalkers" in department stores, who helped customers find what they were looking for (and, I might add, discouraged shoplifters). "To little children accompanying their mothers," John writes, "the towering floorwalker in Eaton's was an awe-inspiring sight...." Indeed he was. On more than one occasion I told my mother that this bald-headed giant in his cutaway coat was God, and she had a hard time persuading me that he wasn't.

When you go through these pages, you will not only see the Montreal of bygone days but you will also hear it - sounds of the city that were once familiar but have now vanished, sounds like the peculiar music, on St. Catherine Street, from the hurdy-gurdy man's barrel organ; the rattle of tire chains on the snow in the days before snow tires; the sleigh bells in winter; the vegetable man on his wagon calling out "Fresh tomatoes!"; the clang of the streetcar bell; the steam whistle from the chip wagon down the street, beckoning you to buy French fries. If the city's landscape has changed, the music of its soundscape has also changed and, to my mind, we've lost some fine melodies.

As John Collins says, all you need is "a little nudge to bring back a happier, simpler time." As for younger people, whose memories don't go all that way back, this book should be a revelation about the splendid, curious, shabby, elegant place Montreal used to be.

*William Weintraub*

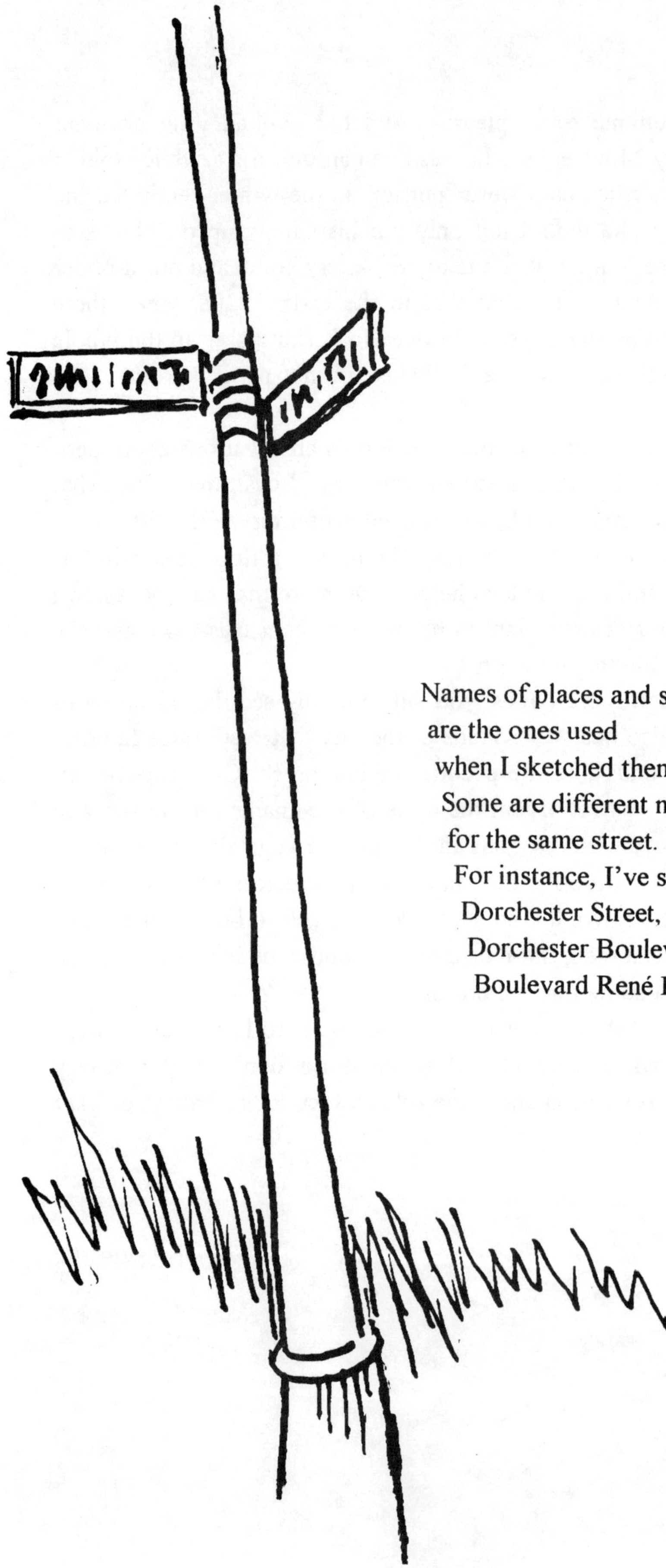

Names of places and streets
are the ones used
when I sketched them.
Some are different names
for the same street.
For instance, I've sketched on
Dorchester Street,
Dorchester Boulevard and
Boulevard René Lévesque.

What is an Old Montrealer? No, don't give me that "somebody now living in Toronto" line. This book is dedicated to anyone who has lived, maybe even grown up, in Montreal, no matter where they now reside. The sketches are to jog your memories as the pages of my sketchbooks jogged mine. Perhaps you remember sports, the baseball Royals at Delorimier Park or the Expos at Jarry, with its crazy fans. Everybody must remember hockey at the Forum, not only Les Canadiens but the Maroons who won a Stanley Cup, too. The exciting days at Molson Stadium with Sam Etcheverry and Hal Patterson should linger in a lot of memories. Your own childhood games and activities should need only a little nudge to bring back a happier, simpler time.

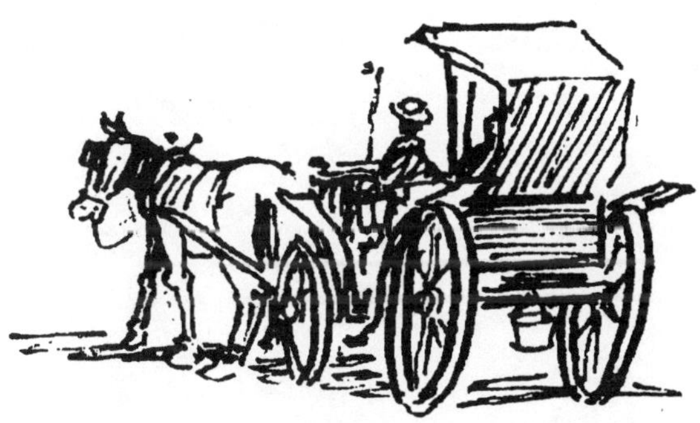

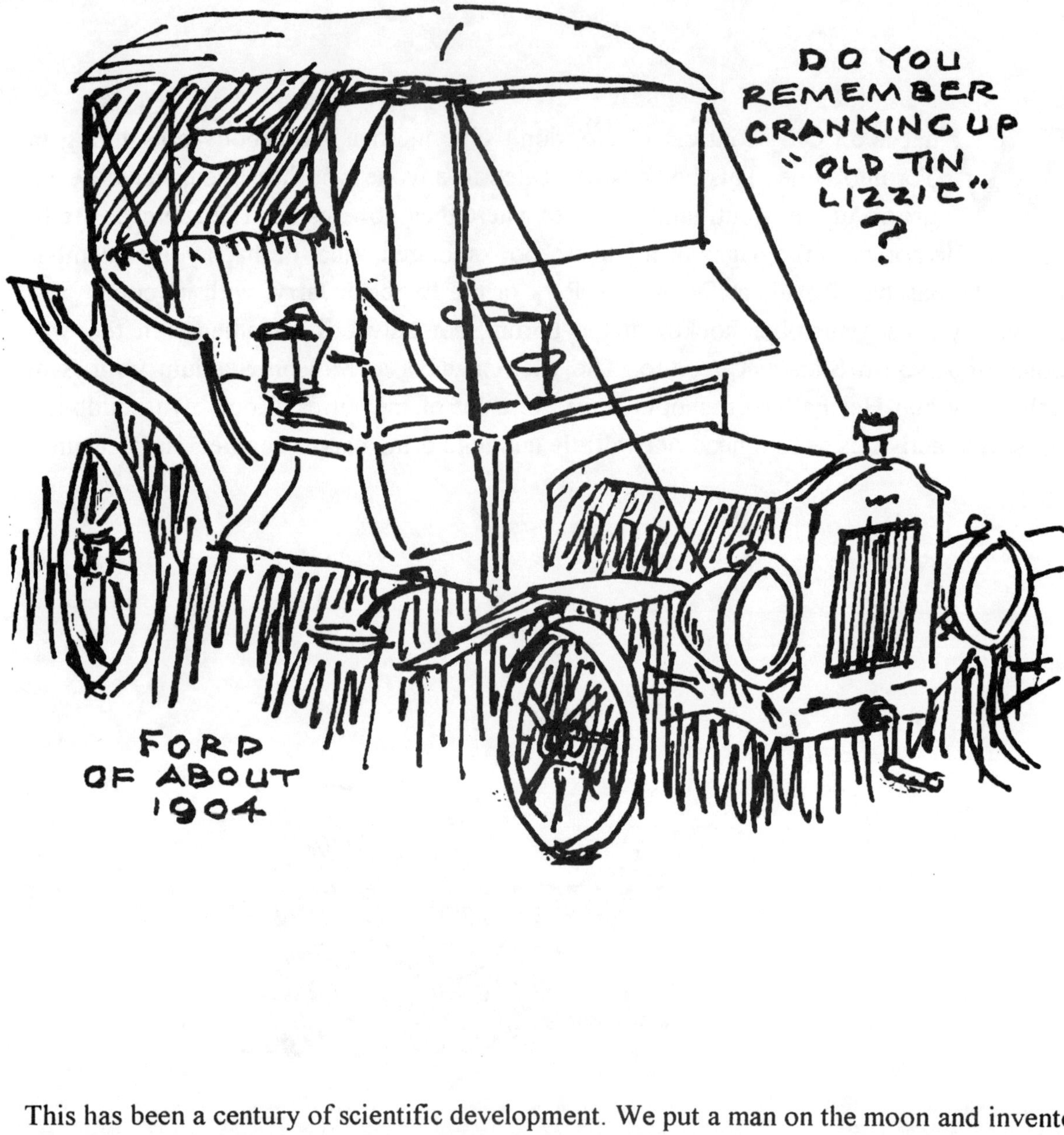


This has been a century of scientific development. We put a man on the moon and invented radio, TV, the computer and other "miracles" of science. But the invention that affected people the most was probably the automobile. We entered the century as a horse-drawn society, and exited as a motor-driven one. Early in this century, the island of Montreal outside the city proper was largely a land of farms. Now it is crisscrossed by autoroutes, highways and traffic interchanges, the farms having been replaced by shopping centers, strip malls, suburban housing, and office space. My sketches show some of what the highways have paved over.

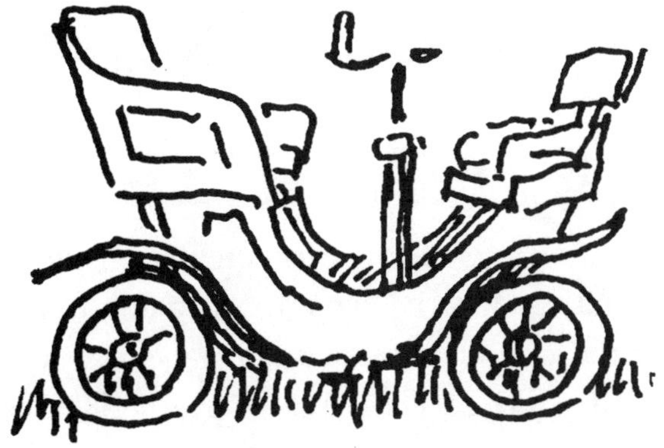

# The FIRST AUTOMOBILE IN MONTREAL

A DE DION BOUTON PHAETON OWNED BY U.H. DANDURAND

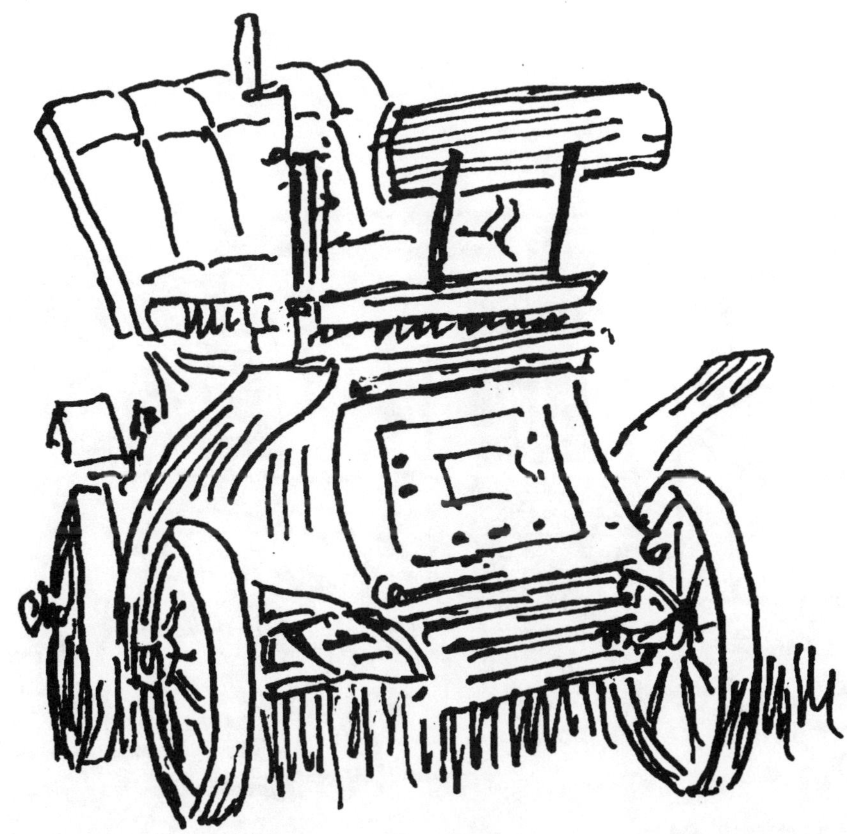

If you can remember this one, you should recall running boards and isinglass windows you snapped on the old touring car when it rained. And how about those old songs, "Get Out and get Under" or "In My Merry Oldsmobile," or the early comic strip, "Gasoline Alley."

In the early days of the century when a farmer came to town to conduct business, visit a doctor, or purchase supplies, tools and clothes, he would rent a room and leave his rig and horses at a stable run for the convenience of such travellers. The farmer would go uptown, do his business and return to his room for the night. The next day he would pick up rig and horses and return home. One of the stables, the "Griffintown Horse Palace," is still going strong on Ottawa Street, catering to the needs of the carriages that carry tourists on sightseeing trips.

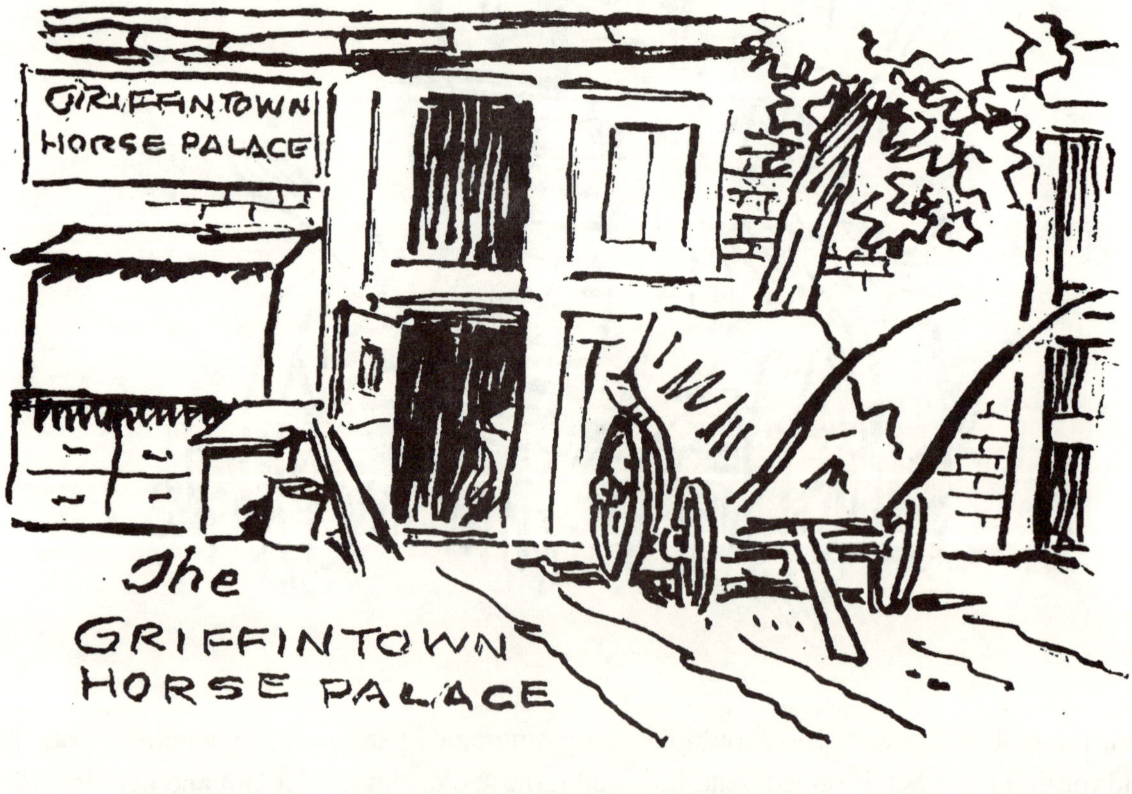

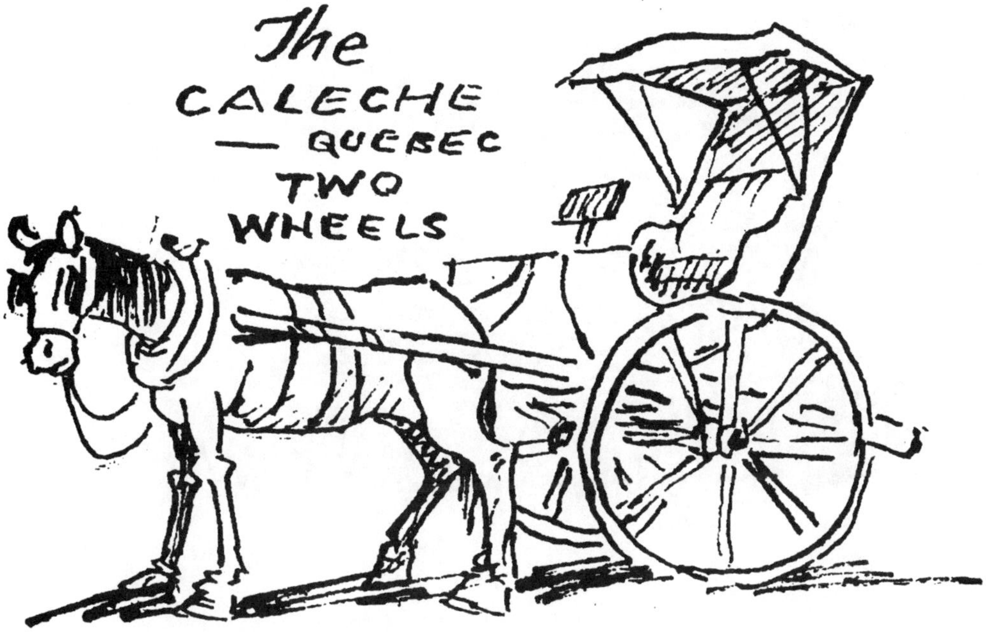
The
CALECHE
— QUEBEC
TWO
WHEELS

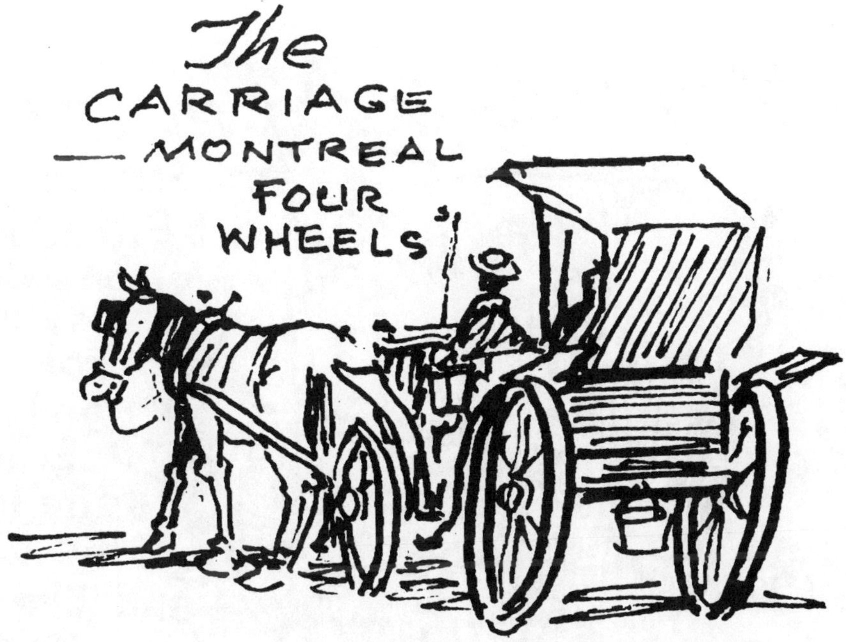
The
CARRIAGE
— MONTREAL
FOUR
WHEELS

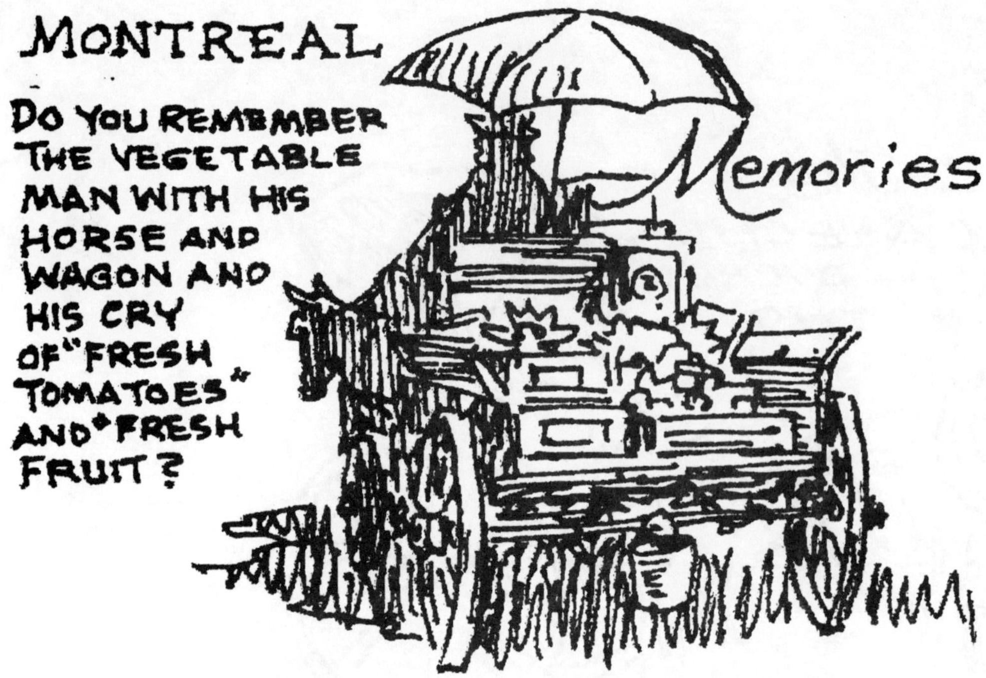


Horse-drawn delivery carts with the vegetable, milk and bread delivery men calling out their wares to housewives, played a big part in street life during the first half of the century. Does anyone remember "Piggly Wiggly" stores? Their American inventor claimed them to be the first self-service grocery stores. I remember one in Monkland and my wife says there was one in Montreal West.

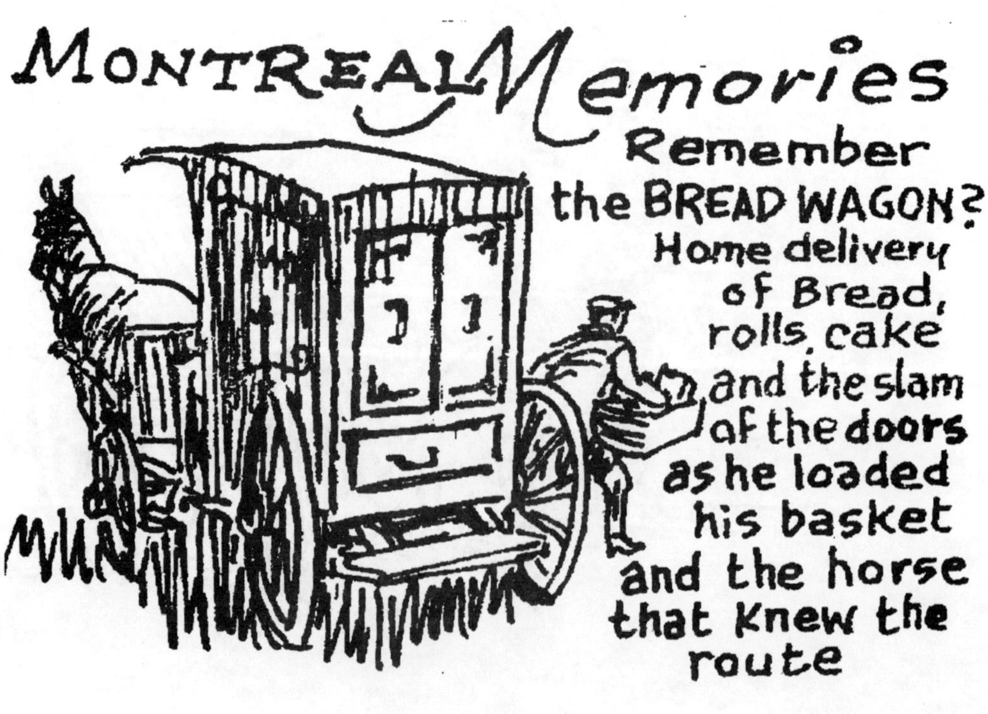

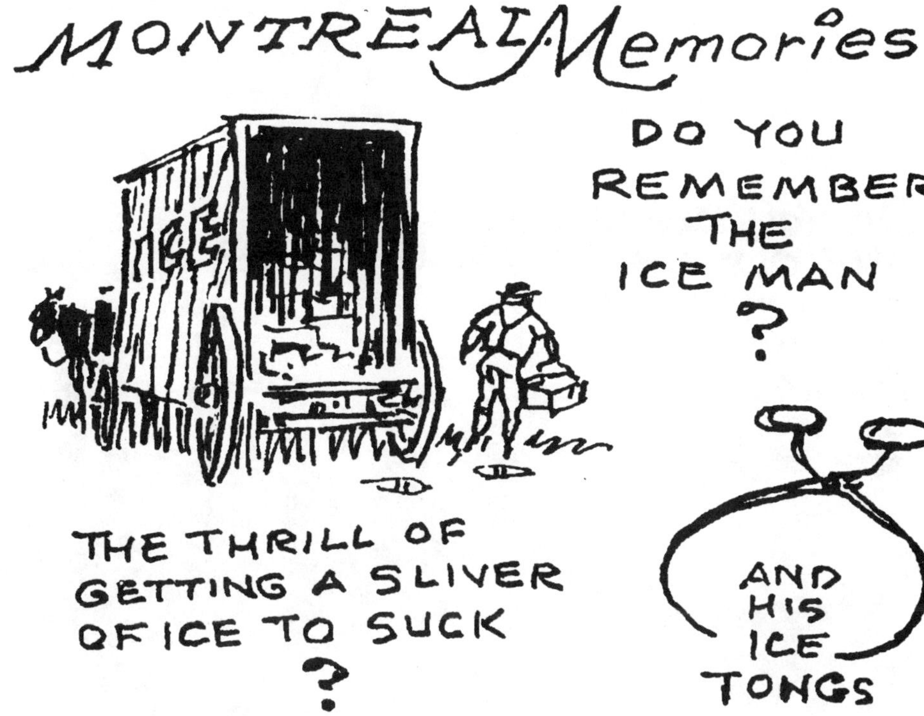


On a long hot summer day in a Montreal neighborhood, nothing was more welcome than the ice wagon. Before electric refrigerators, you had an icebox and regular visits from the iceman. Clad in a rubber apron, he would head for your kitchen carrying a block of ice with his ice tongs. Youngsters loved to peer into the black cool depths of the wagon and steal chips of ice to suck. Often they would follow the ice wagon and, during deliveries of the blocks of ice, would sneak up to seize the hot weather treats.

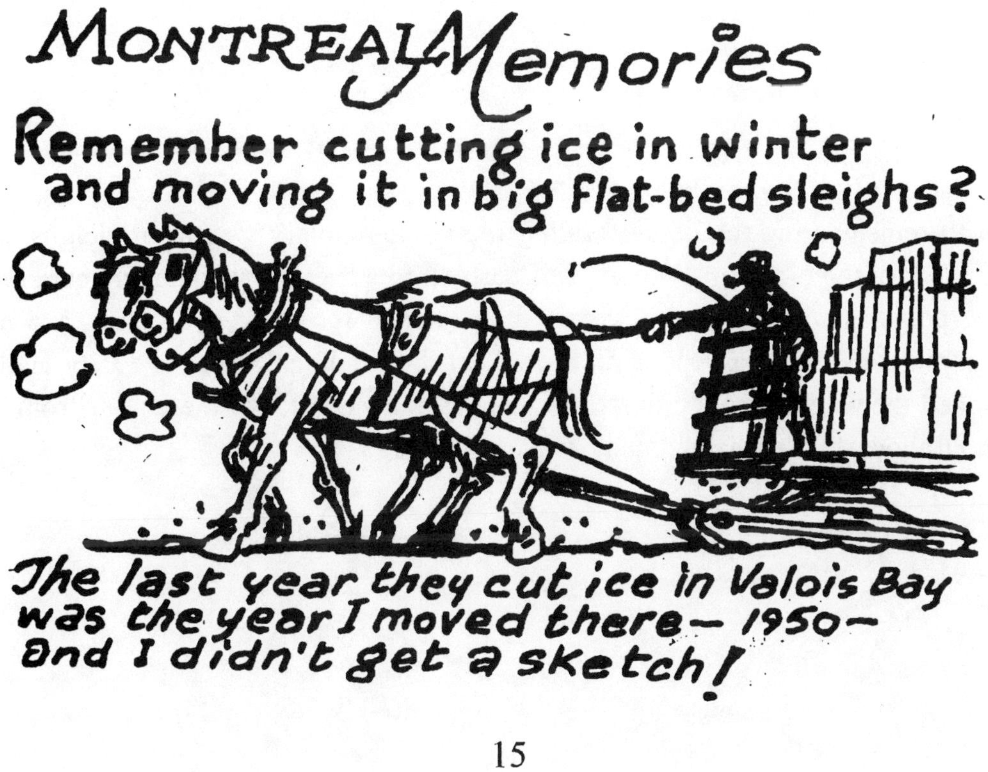

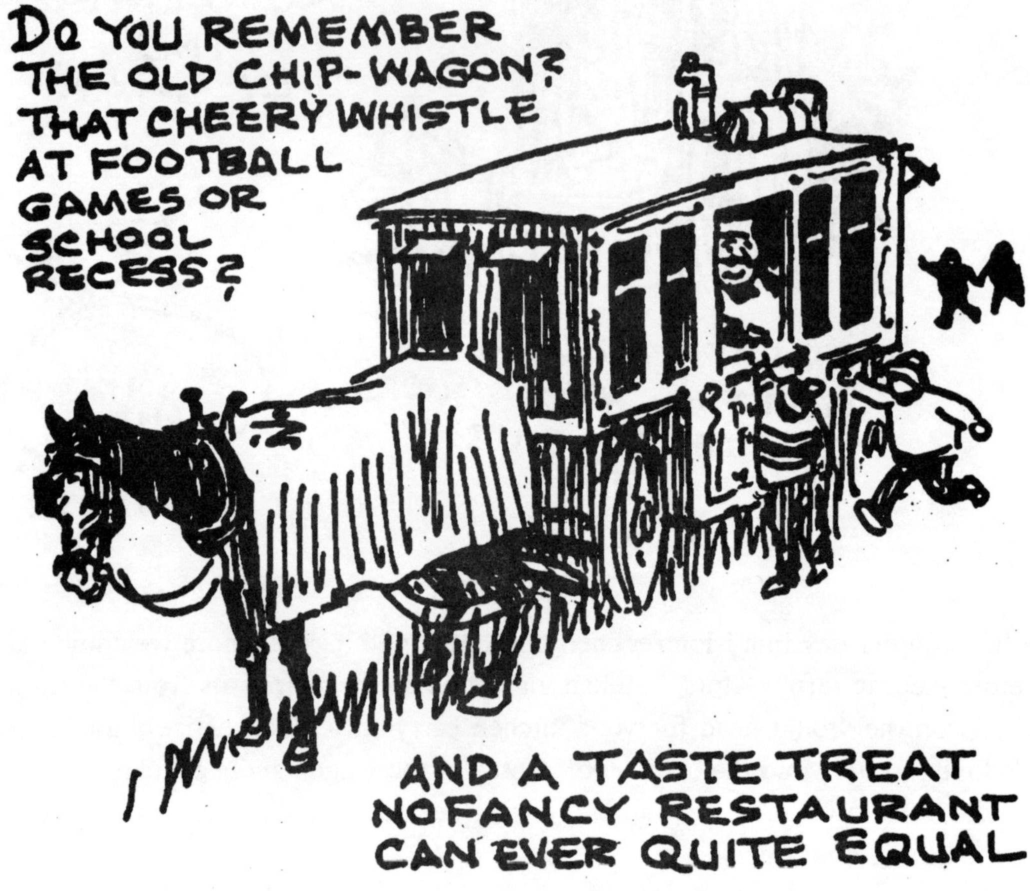


In addition to remembering the horses pulling the home-delivery wagon or sleighs, a lot of us will fondly think of the old Chip Wagon. This cart with its friendly whistle and enticing smell of French fried potatoes was a welcome visitor at schools at recess or noon hour, and no football game was complete without a vendor of "Fries" on the sidelines. When the City Hall Planning Experts banned the wagons from city streets, they took away a lot of the colour from our Montreal neighbourhoods, but left happy memories.

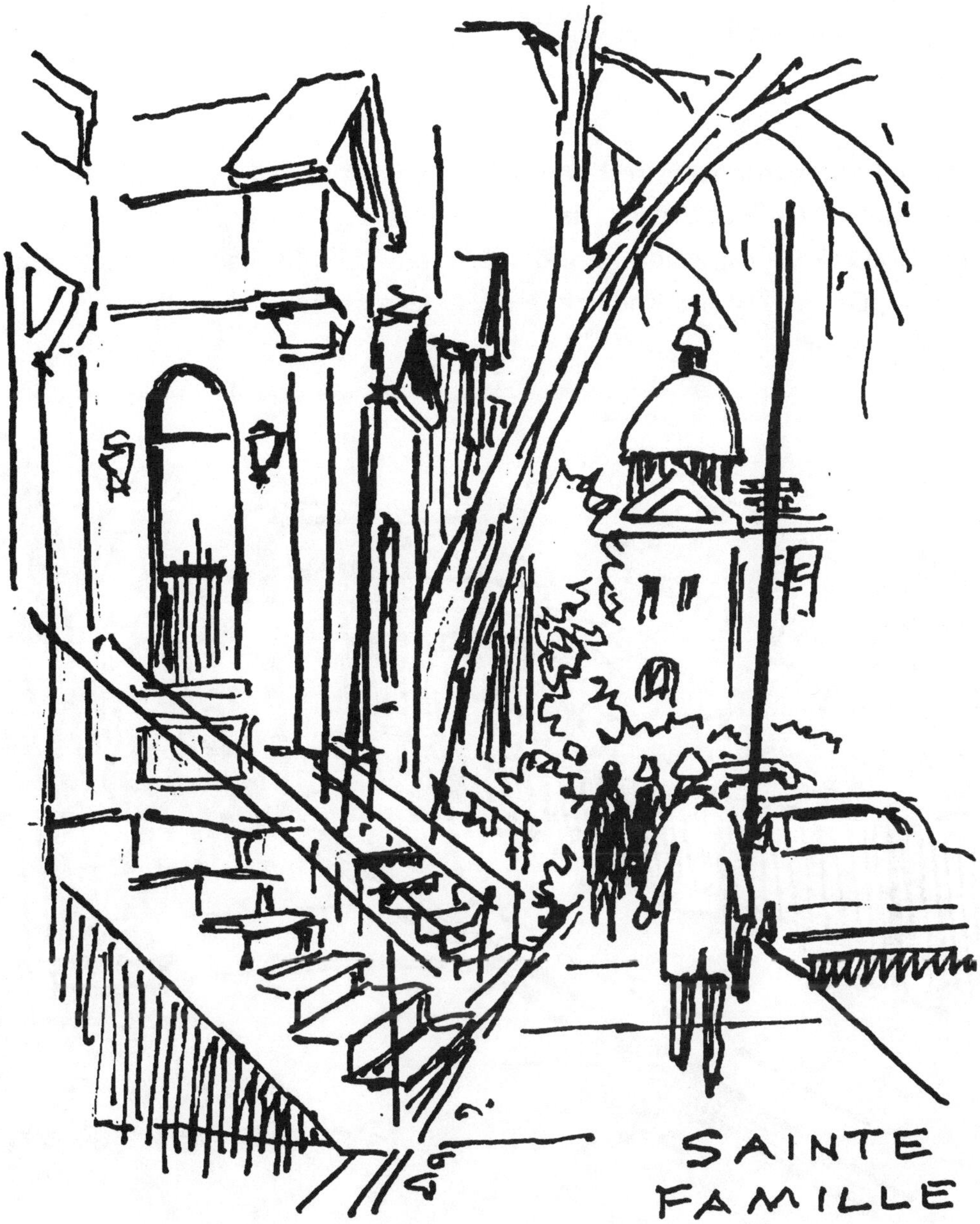
SAINTE
FAMILLE

Do you remember Sherbrooke Street with all its big old mansions and big old trees? At the head of McGill College Avenue is the entrance to the McGill University campus through the Roddick Gates, which were donated to McGill by Lady Roddick in memory of her husband, Dr. Sir Thomas Roddick, former Dean of the Medical Faculty.

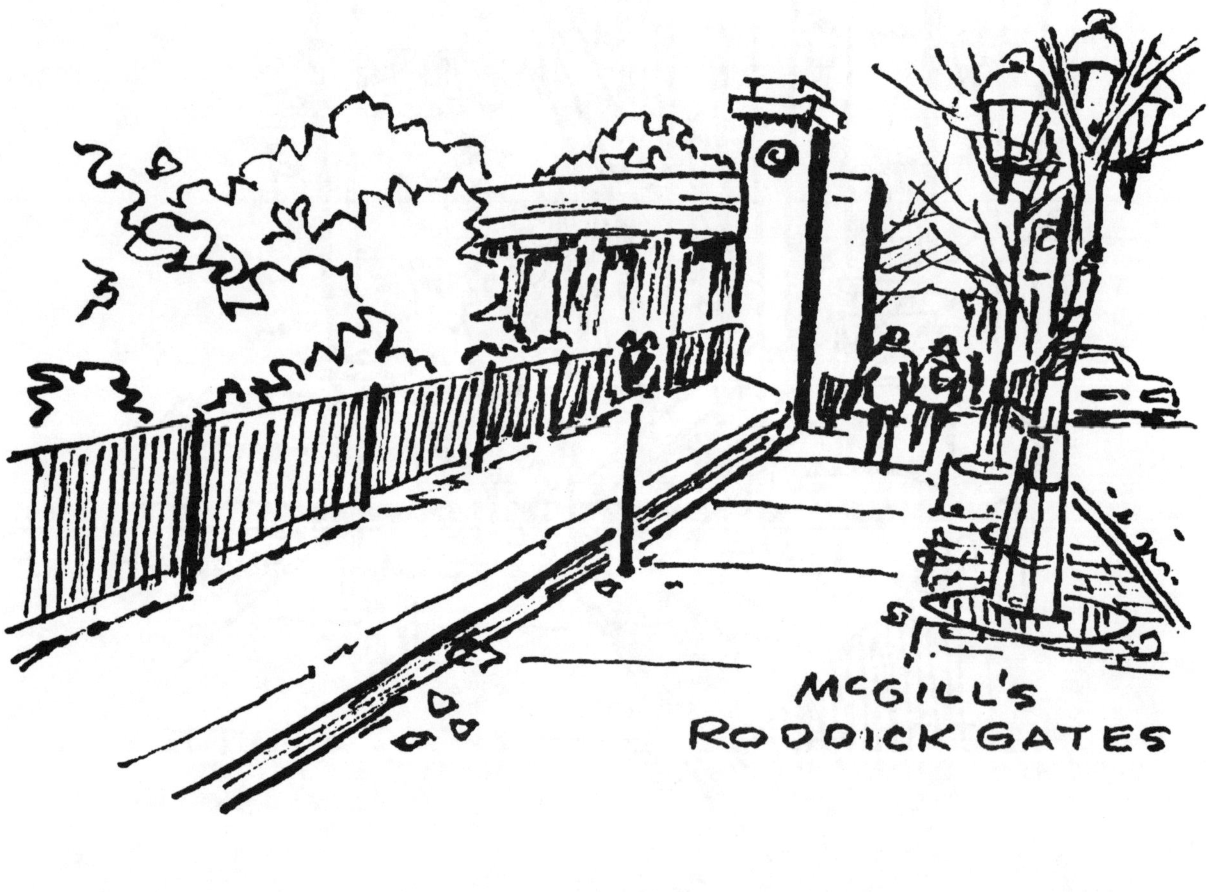

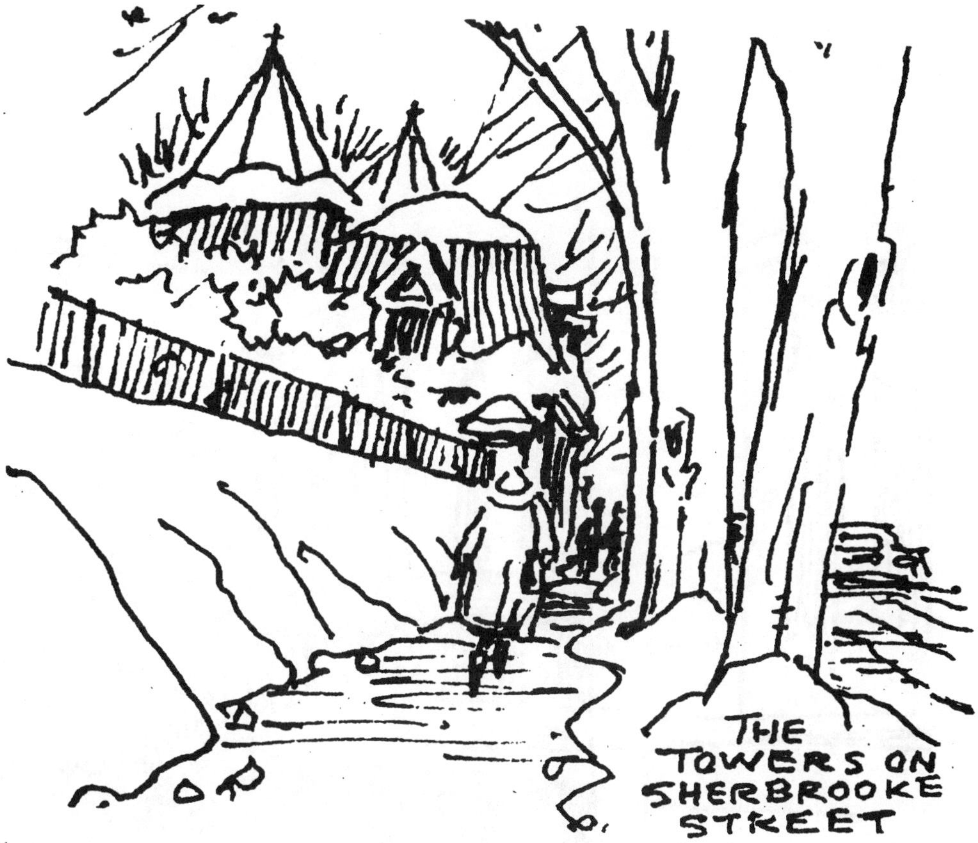
THE TOWERS ON SHERBROOKE STREET

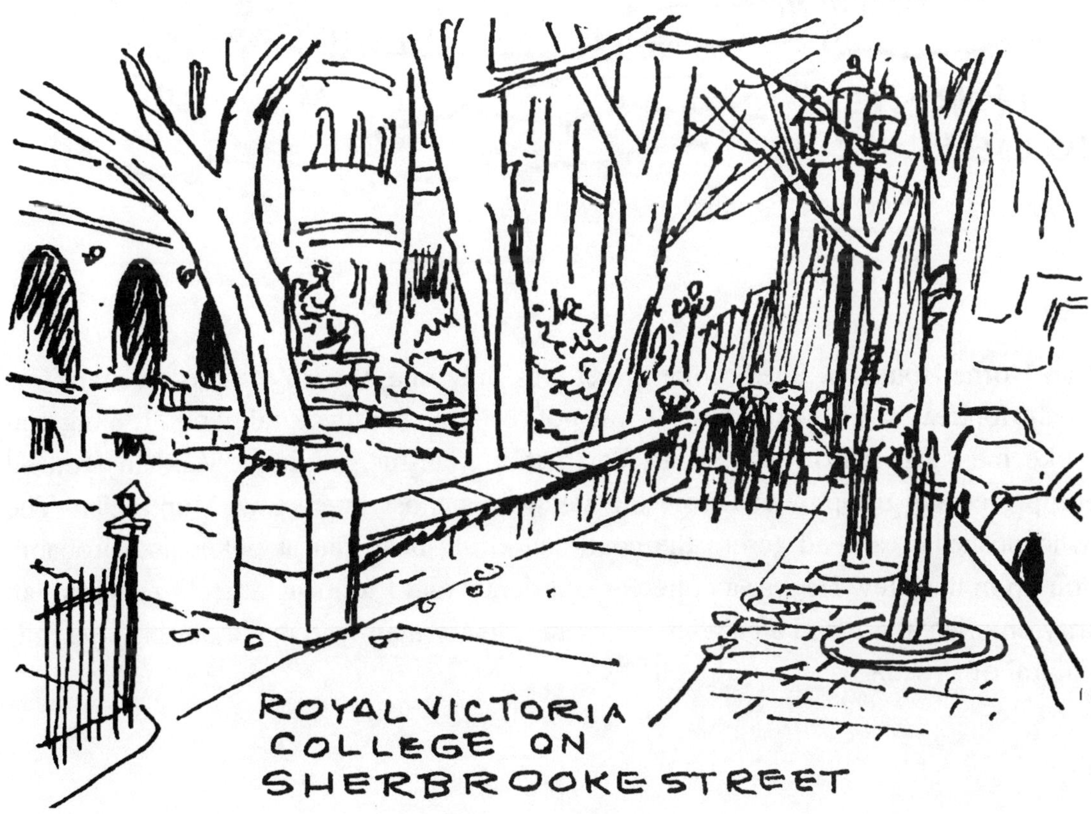
ROYAL VICTORIA COLLEGE ON SHERBROOKE STREET

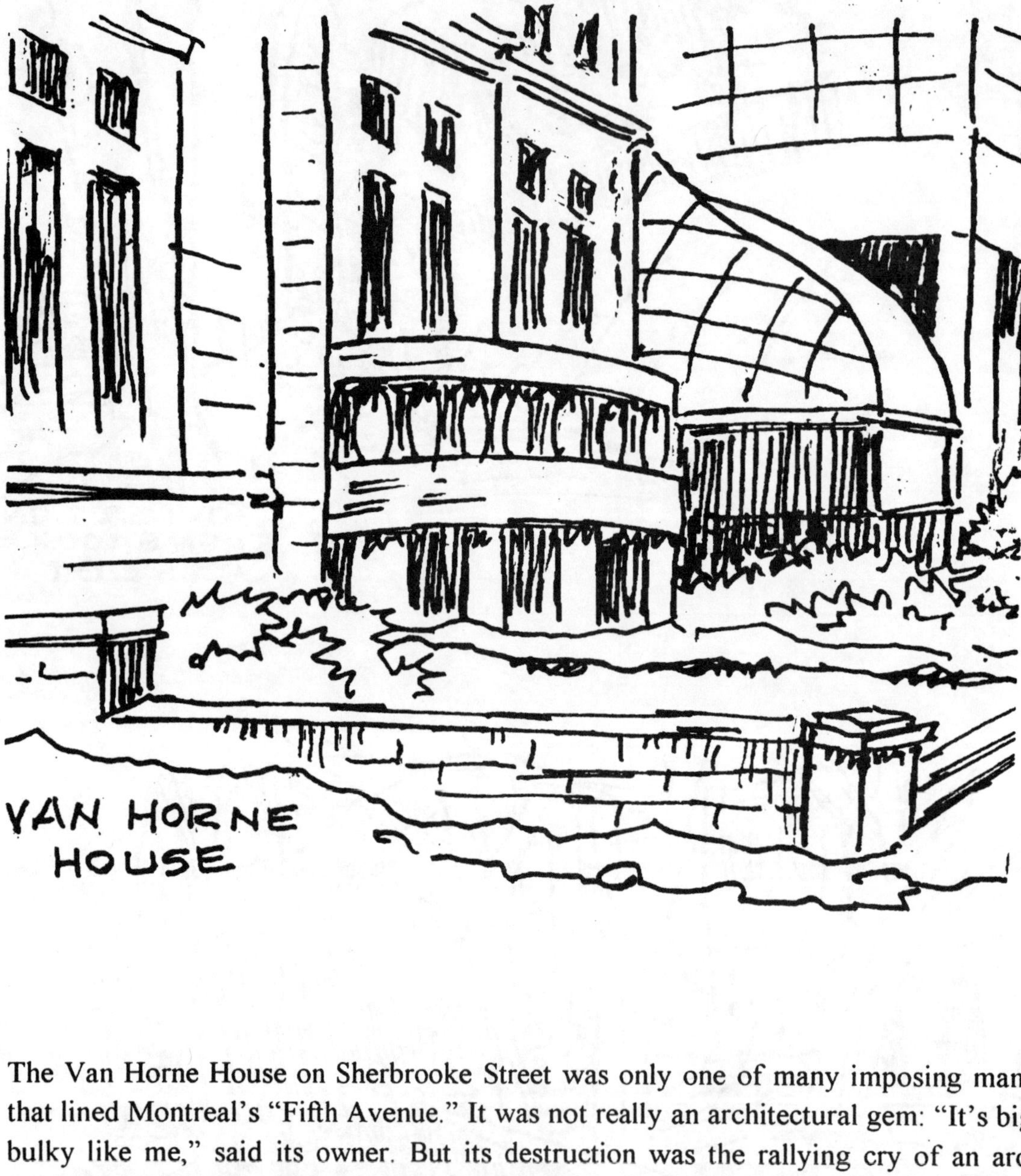


The Van Horne House on Sherbrooke Street was only one of many imposing mansions that lined Montreal's "Fifth Avenue." It was not really an architectural gem: "It's big and bulky like me," said its owner. But its destruction was the rallying cry of an aroused heritage protection group. Van Horne himself was a most interesting Montrealer. The man who pushed a railroad across the continent could beat you at poker and probably beat you up in the alley. He was a collector of oriental and European art (old masters), an authority on oriental art, and a painter - an extraordinary man who made our city the railroad capital of Canada.

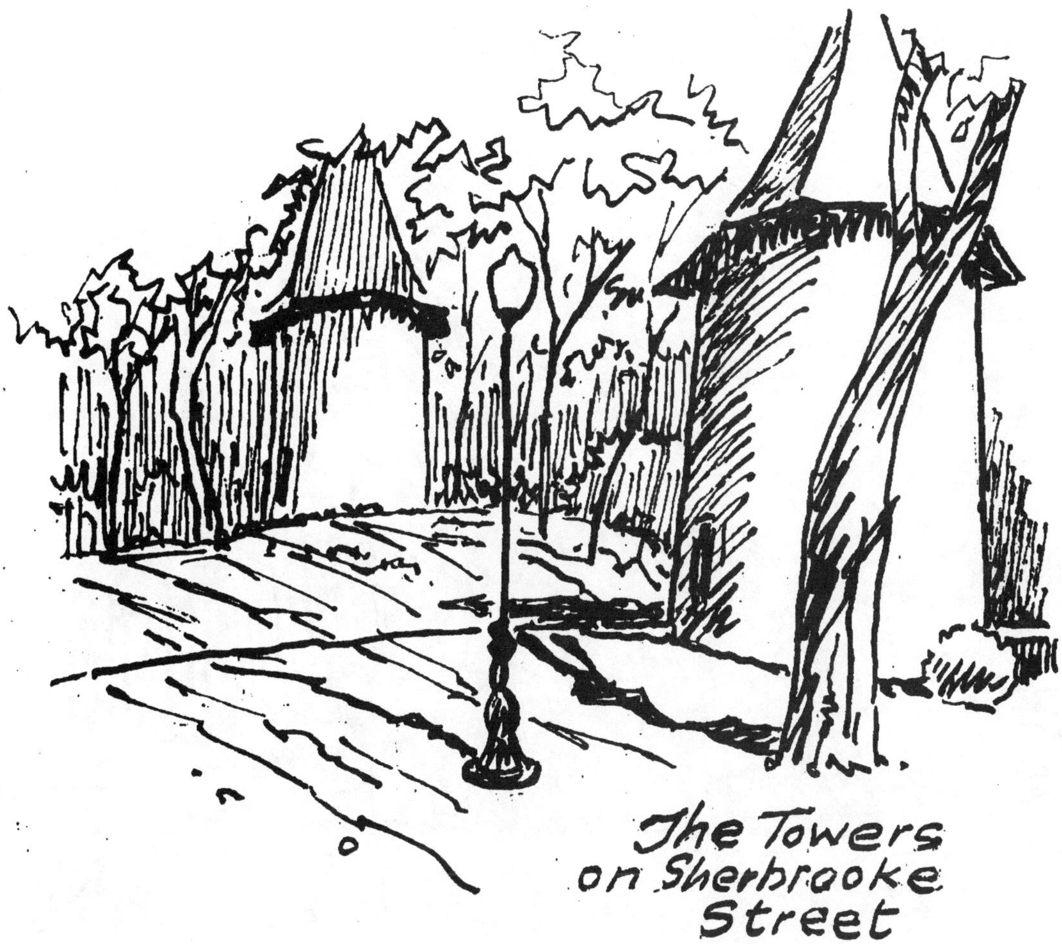


Montrealers have been looking at the towers on the Sherbrooke Street grounds of the Grand Seminaire well before the 20th Century. Those two towers have been standing on that spot since the earliest days of the city in the 17th Century.

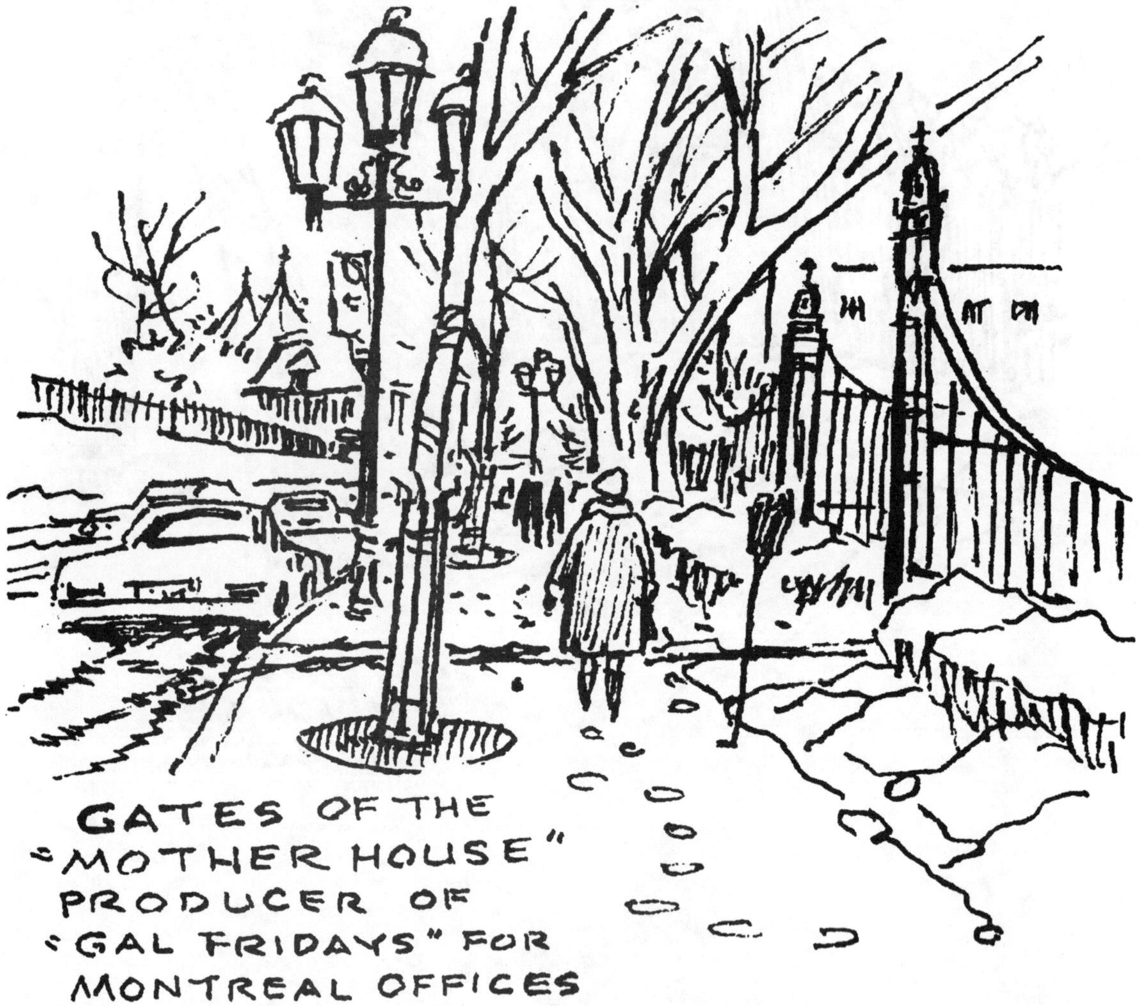
GATES OF THE
"MOTHER HOUSE"
PRODUCER OF
"GAL FRIDAYS" FOR
MONTREAL OFFICES

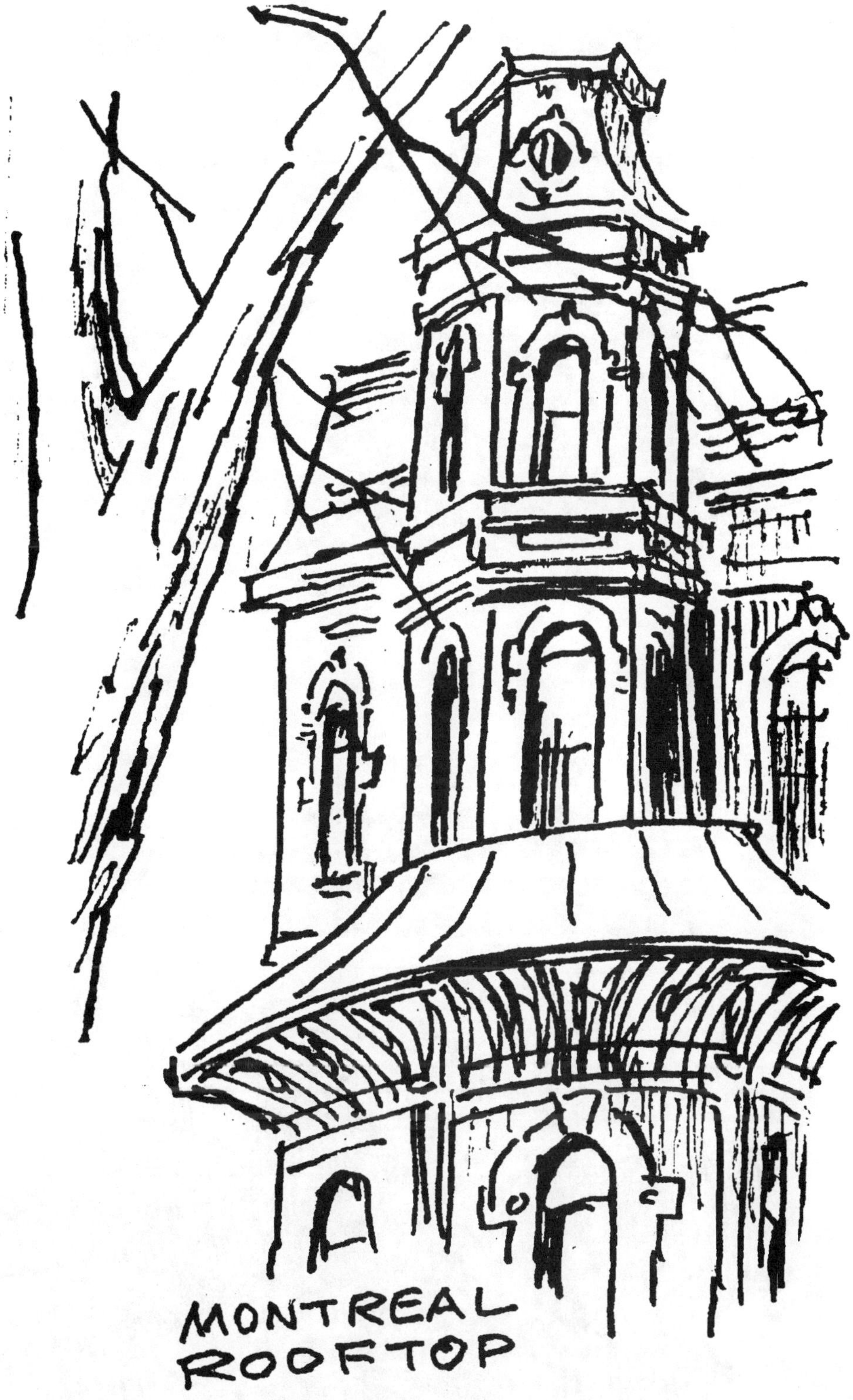


We miss a lot of the city's charm by looking down, not up. We notice the modern shop windows and restaurants without seeing the old buildings behind them. Look up at the roofs: there are towers, turrets and many touches of architectural whimsy.

THE STREET CAR DOMINATED LIFE FOR MONTREALERS IN THE FIRST HALF OF THE TWENTIETH CENTURY

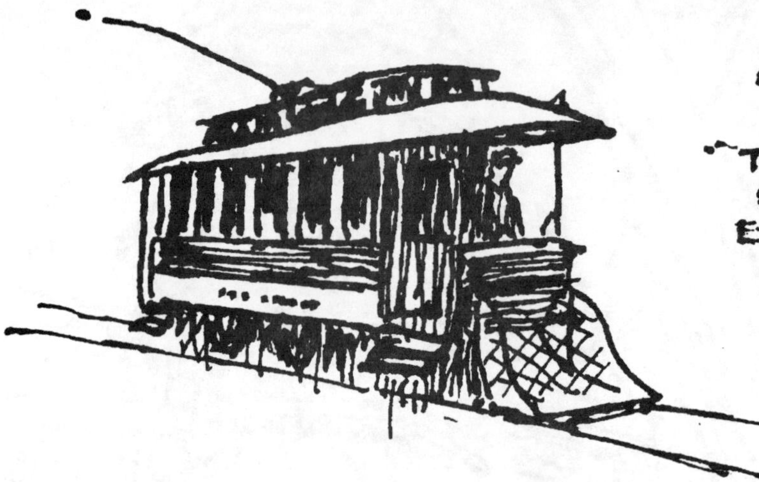

STARTING WITH "THE ROCKET" OUR FIRST ELECTRIFIED ONE

TO DAYS WHEN THEY HAD A RIGHT-OF-WAY FROM QUEEN MARY ROAD FOR THE OLD 83

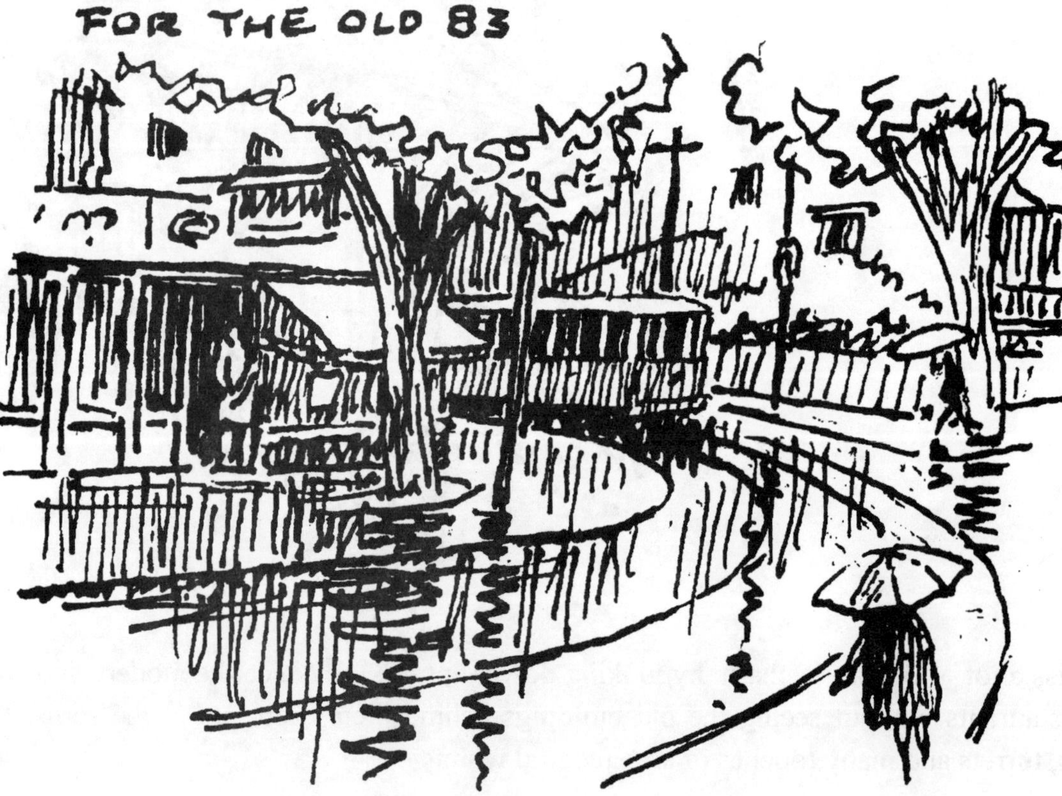

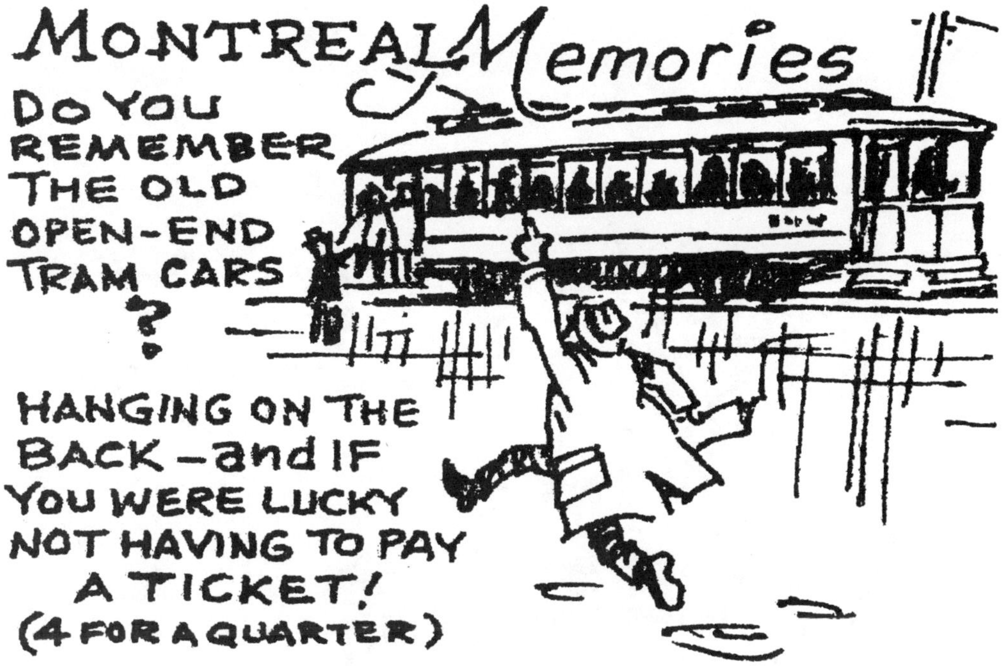


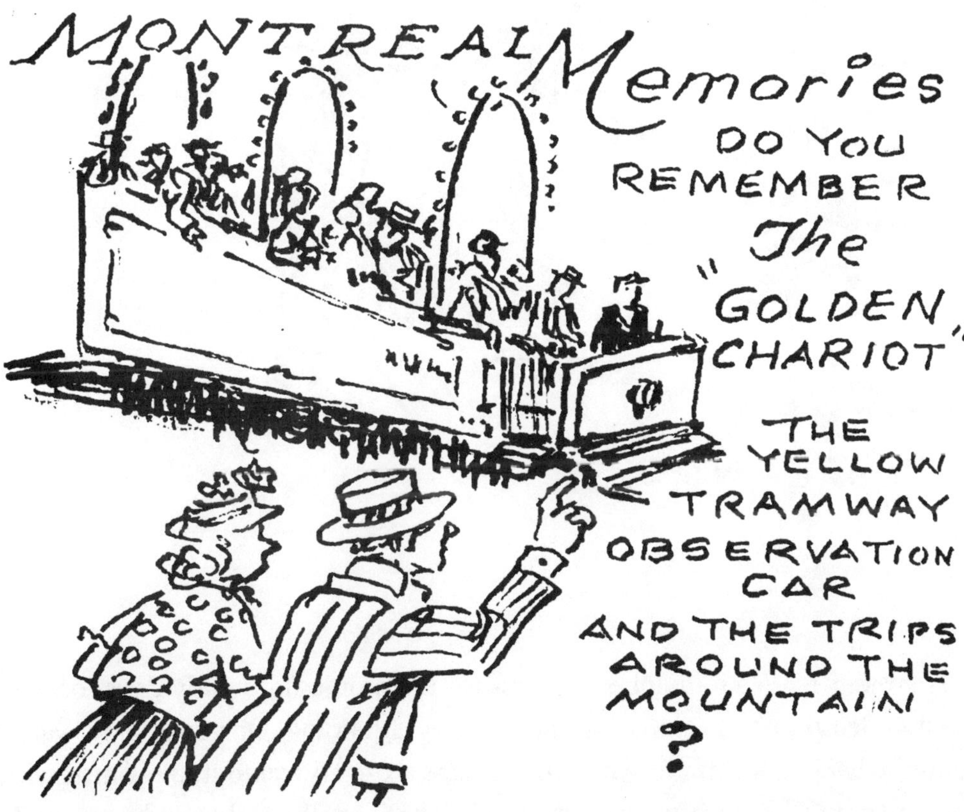


Electric streetcars came to Montreal in 1892 and operated in the city streets until 1959. Do you remember the motorman fishing for the switch or the conductor trying to re-attach the trolley after going through the switch? Easy to remember is the "Golden Chariot," the yellow open car that took tours around the Mountain in the summer. Before being replaced by buses, the old trams filled a big role in easing the city's transportation problems.

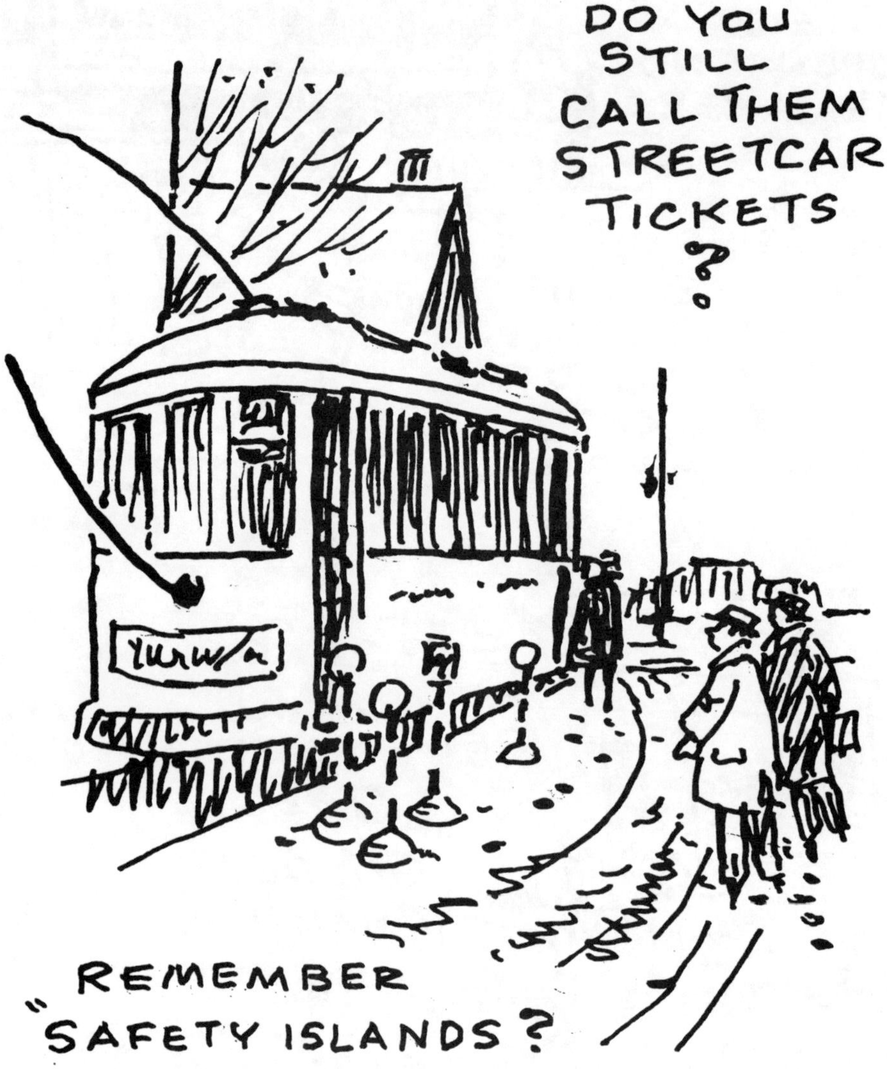


Most of us remember streetcars. We remember waiting for them on cold, windy days, or hanging onto the back of open-ended trams, or clutching those swinging straps. One spot, now vanished, was Snowdon Junction, where cars from downtown met cars from Outremont and Cartierville. In summer that Cartierville car was a dream trip for youngsters. Over the fields and past the farms we were taken to Belmont Park for rides, games and cotton candy. An earlier generation had gone to Dominion Park on Notre Dame Street, but for us the Cartierville car to Belmont Park was like a magic carpet.

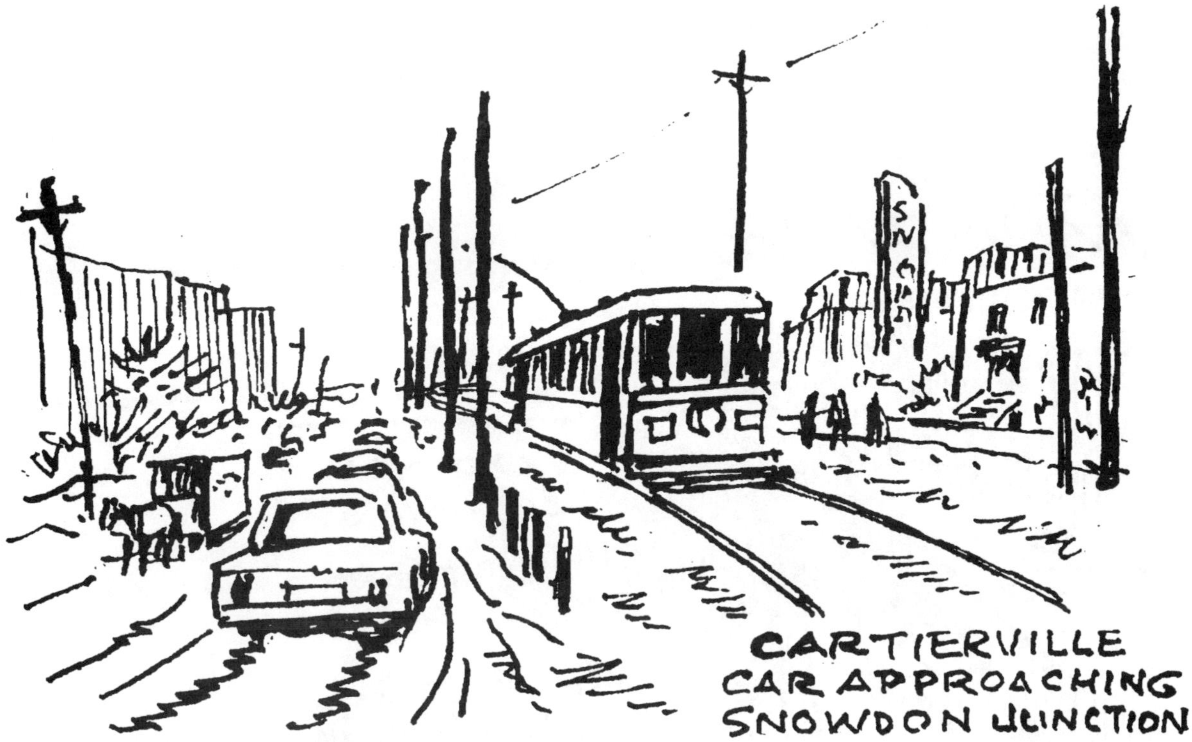
CARTIERVILLE
CAR APPROACHING
SNOWDON JUNCTION

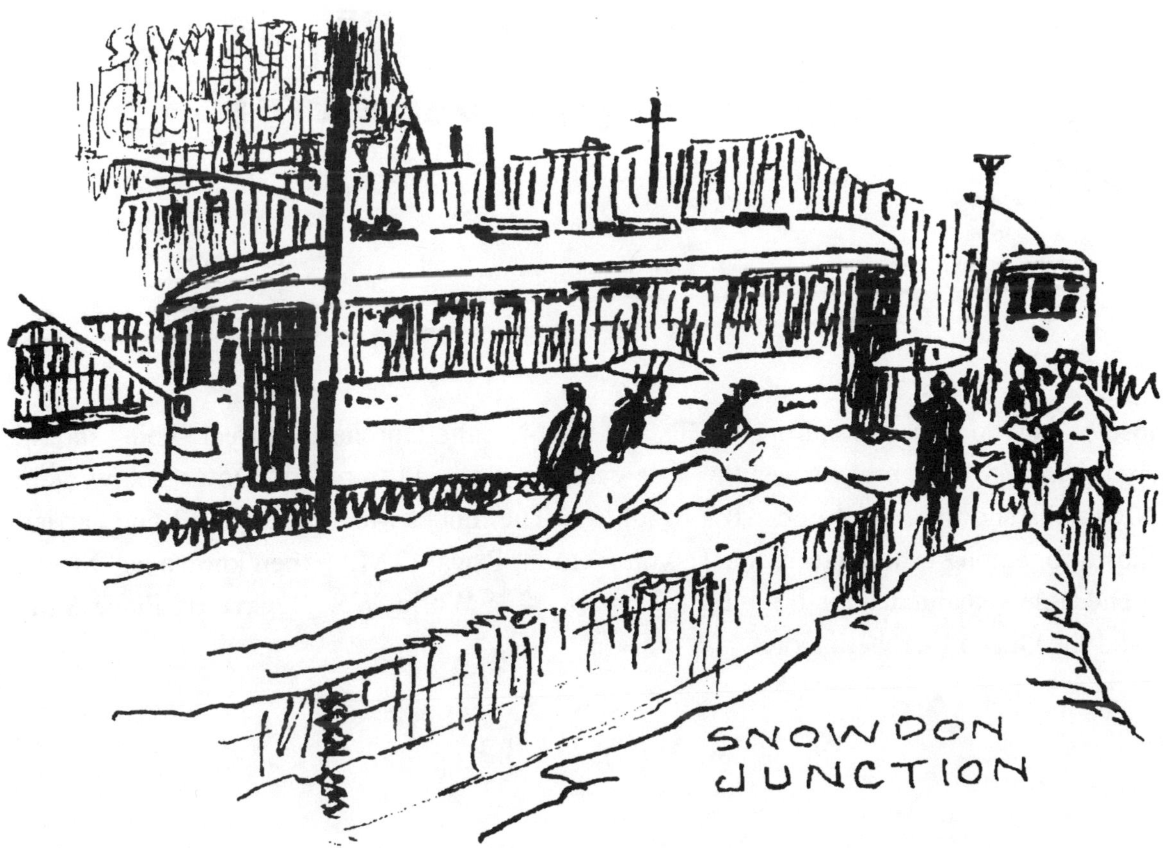
SNOWDON
JUNCTION

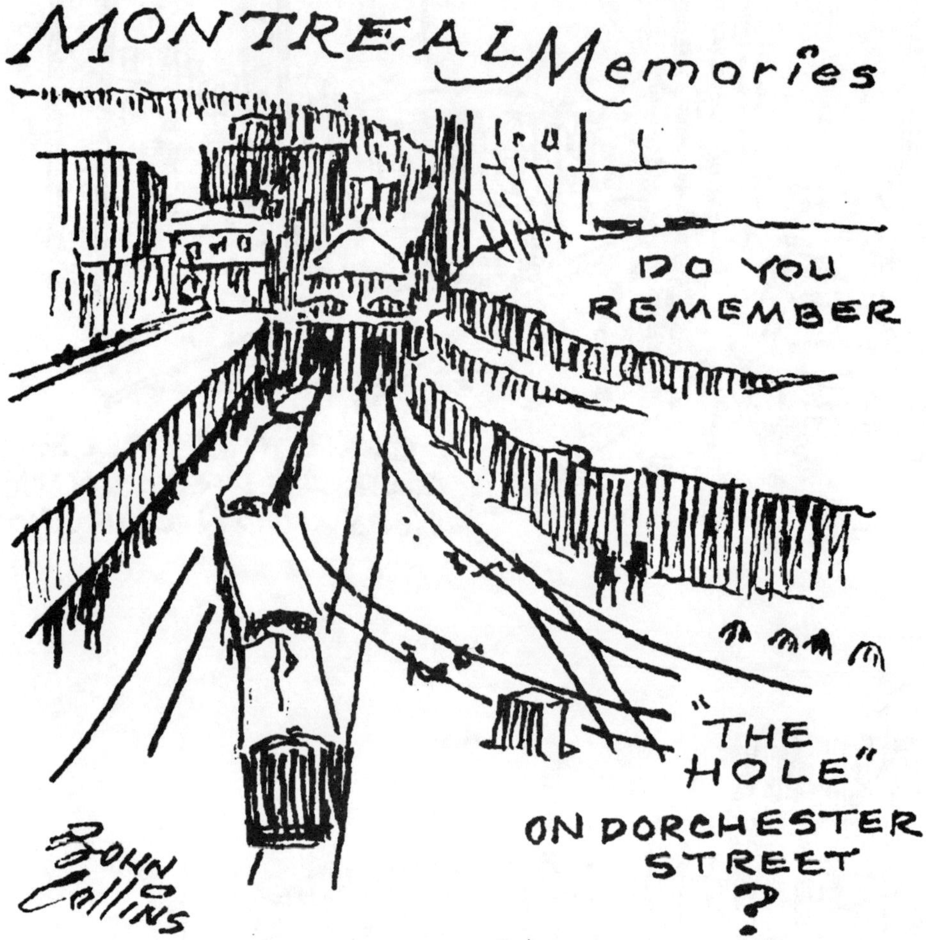


For those of us who were around in the '30s and the '40s, the Dorchester Street "hole" should be a vivid memory. The bridge over the hole carried autos and tramcars. Down below were the CNR tracks and the tunnel under the Mountain. The tunnel was built in 1913 and carried trains north to, among other places, the Town of Mount Royal (TMR), then known as "Model City." The hole remained until the building boom after World War II gave us Place Ville Marie and the Queen Elizabeth Hotel.

Thank goodness there is one part of Montreal that has largely escaped the improver and the developer. St. Louis Square, with its distinct architecture, still resembles a square of the last century, making it a favourite of artists and film-makers. But not all areas of our city have remained so unaltered. Consider the restaurants and bars we have lost. Remember the Mount Royal's Picadilly Lounge during the War, the Windsor's Embassy Room, or even Slitkin and Slotkin's, the hangout of the sports writers? All just memories of days and places long gone.

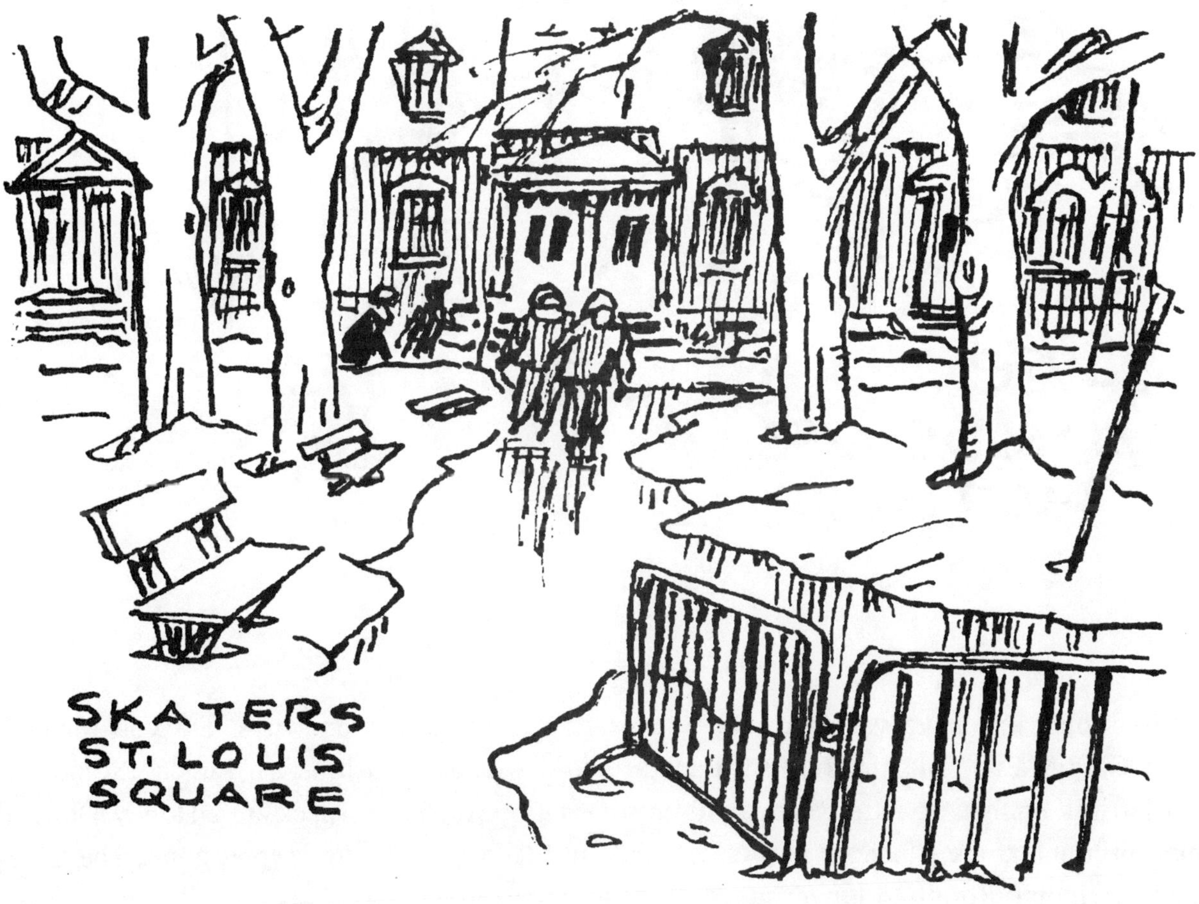

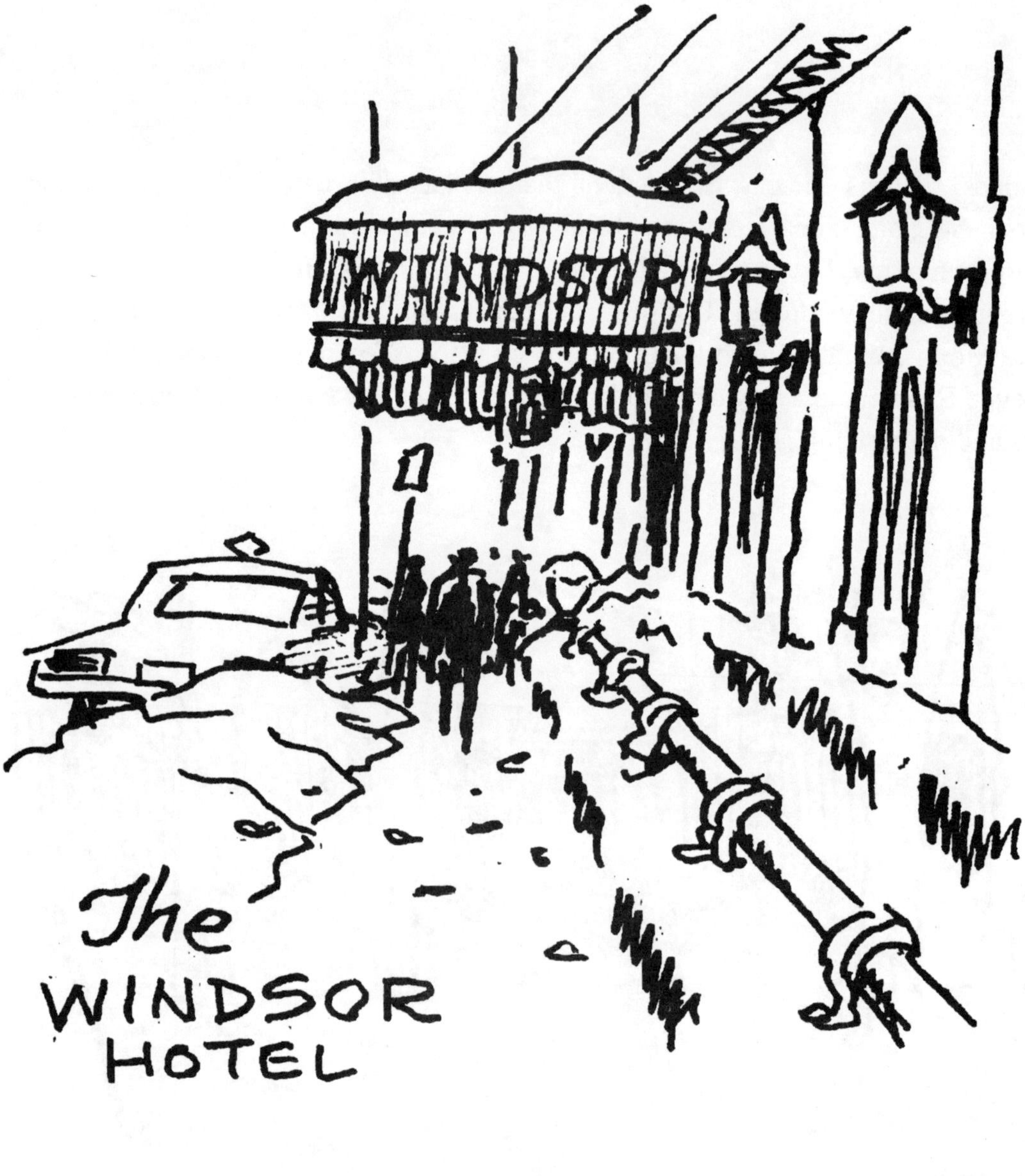


Among the things that have vanished over the years are restaurants and bars. Do you remember Drury's or Café Martin? Maybe you had lunch at Child's or the Northeastern Lunch? Some ate at Mother Martin's or the Alouette Room in Windsor Station, or had a snack in a Honey Dew. The three-martini lunch at the Bluenose or the Stampede in Place Ville Marie is long gone. The Chic-n-Coop and the Indian Room no longer grace Ste. Catherine Street. Nor does Scotts's, where people from high school or frat dances often ended up late at night.

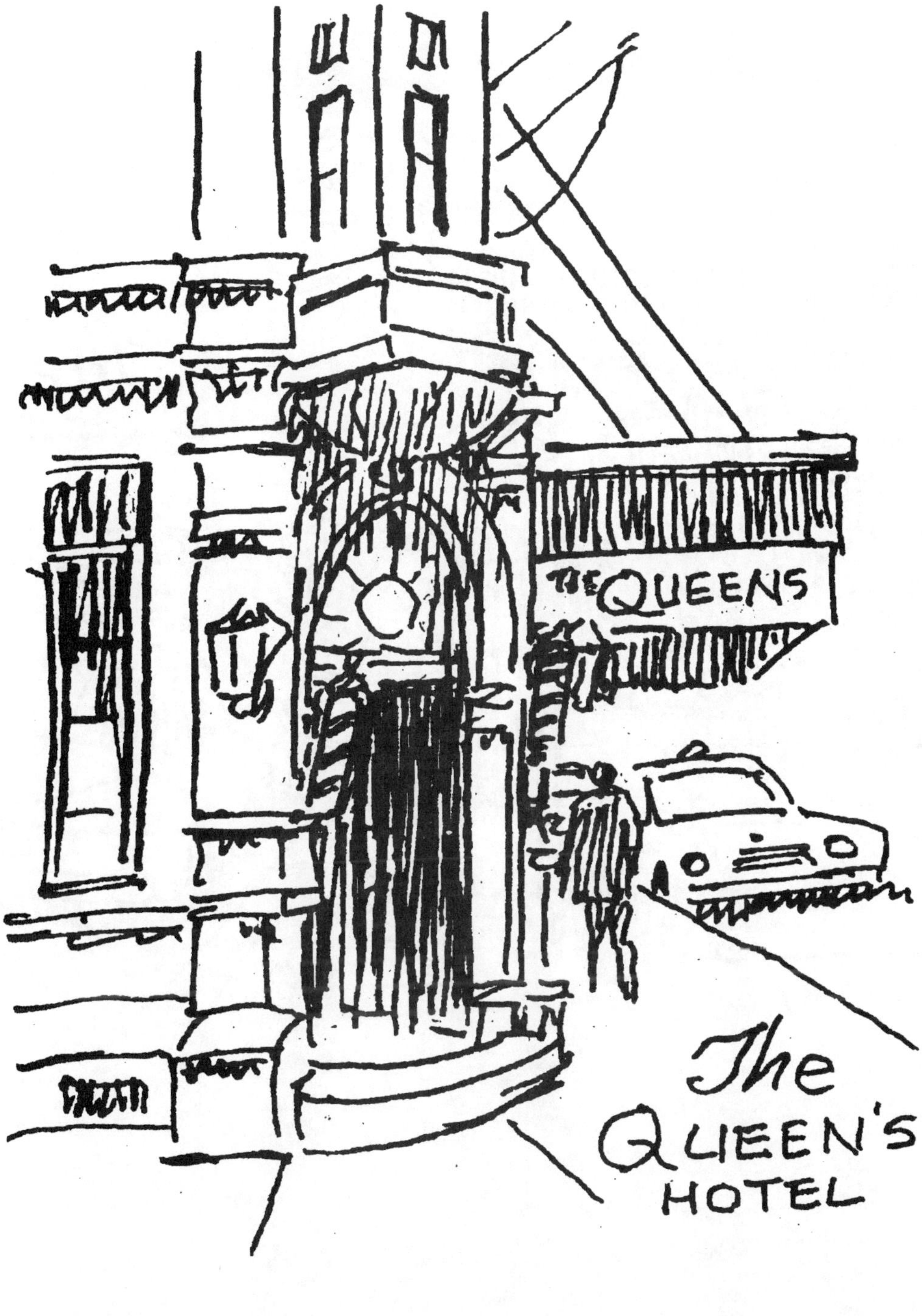
THE QUEENS
The
QUEEN'S
HOTEL

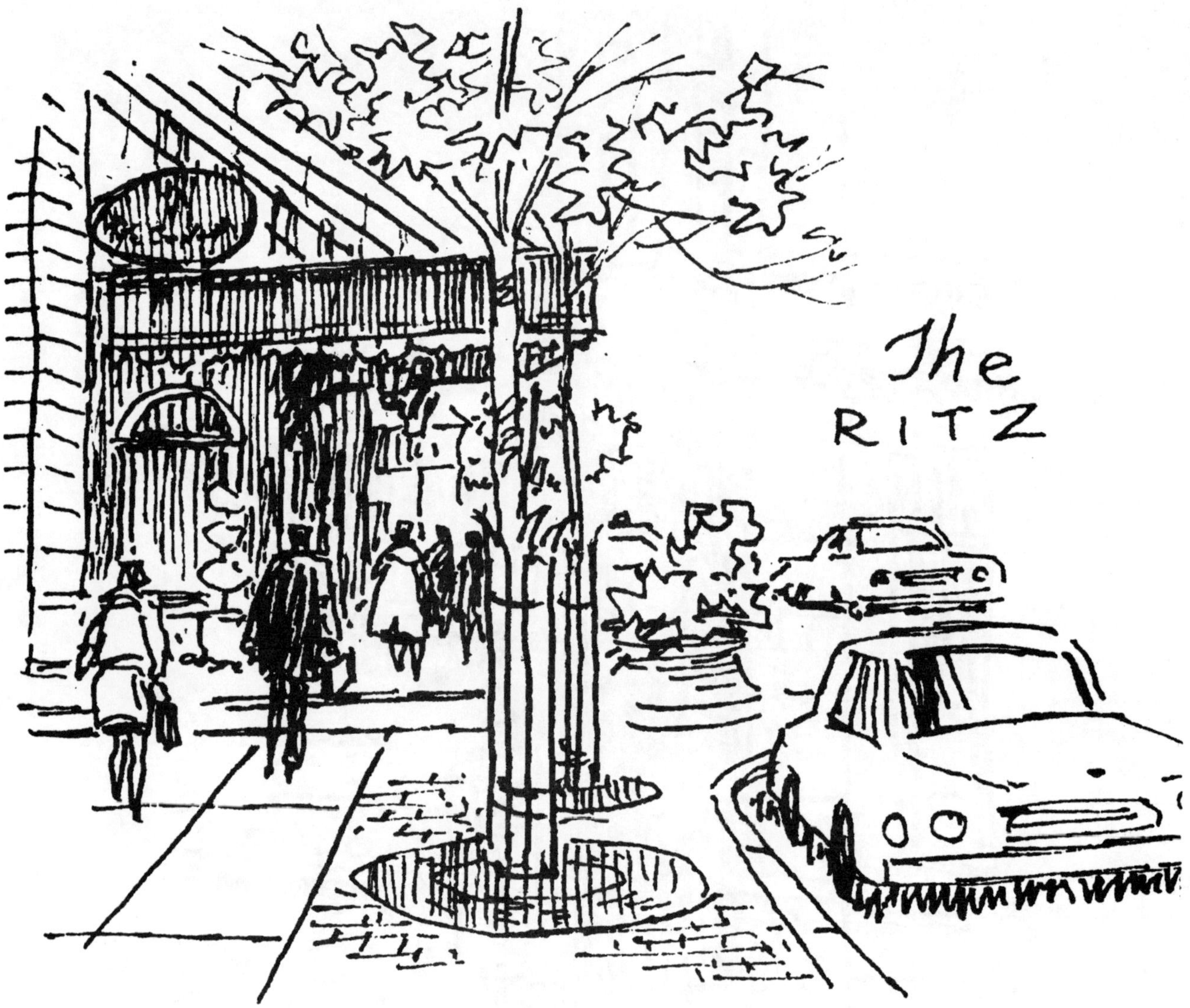
The
RITZ

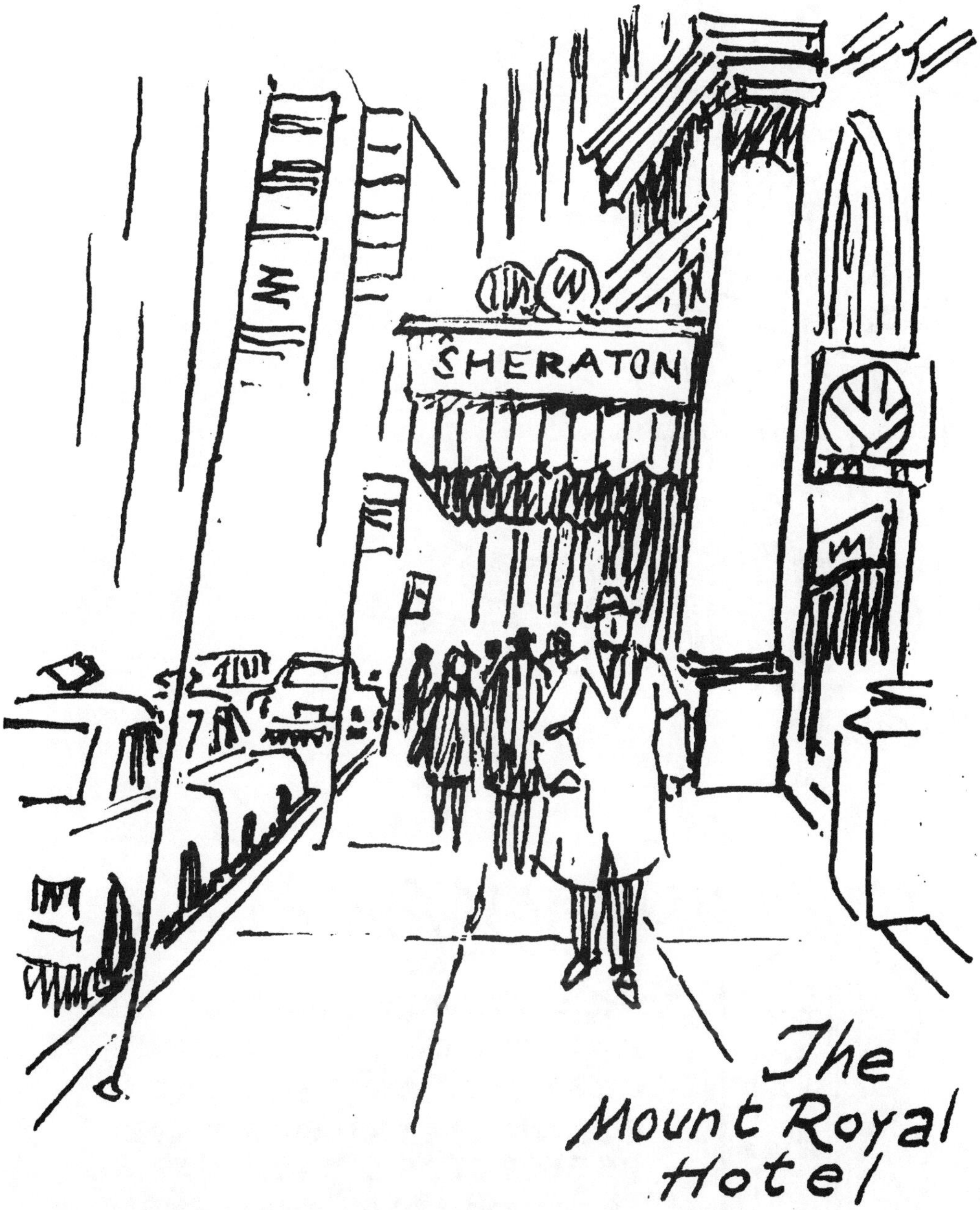


# The Mount Royal Hotel

WHEN IT OPENED IN 1922 THE MOUNT ROYAL WAS THE LARGEST HOTEL IN THE BRITISH EMPIRE. WHEN IT CLOSED IN 1984 IT LEFT MEMORIES FOR MANY MONTREALERS OF THE KON TIKI AND THE NORMANDIE ROOF

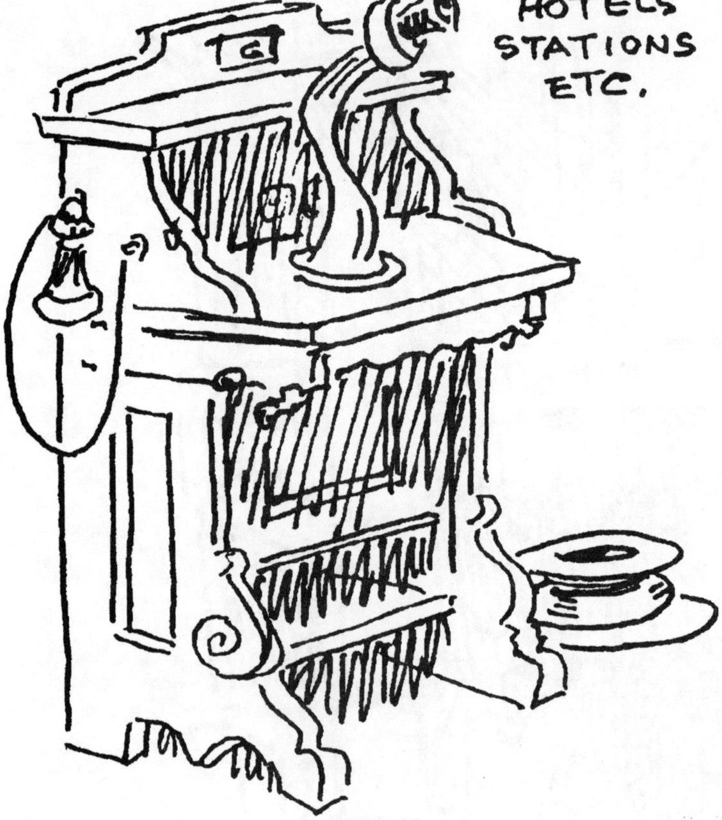

EARLY PAY PHONE IN HOTELS STATIONS ETC.

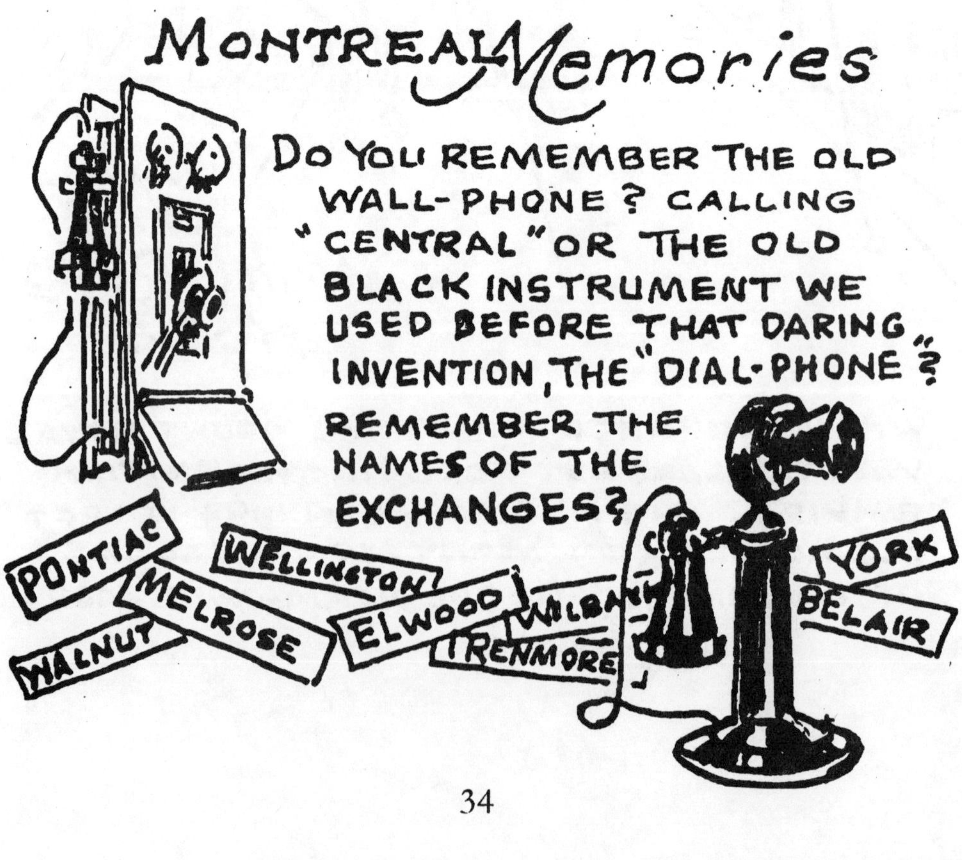

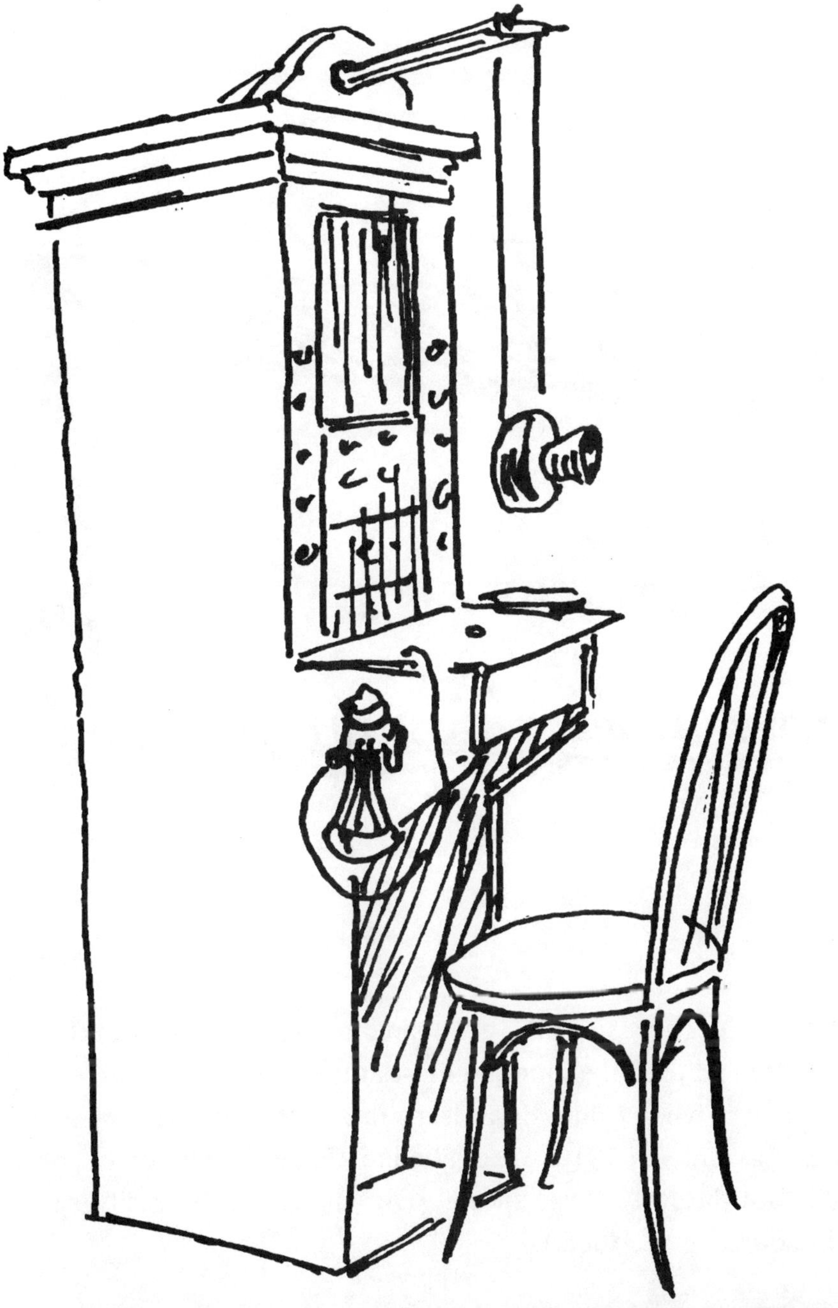

EARLY SWITCHBOARD
MADE BY NORTHERN ELECTRIC

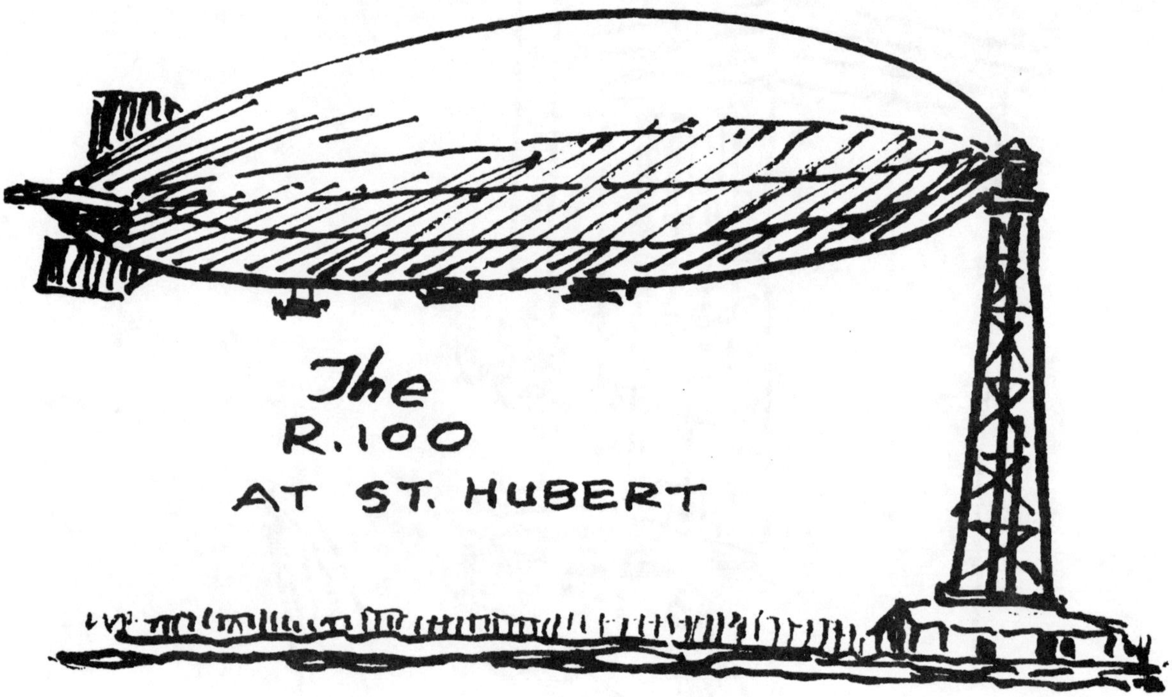


Do you remember the R-100? The visit of the giant airship was a big event in the Montreal of the '30s. It sailed over the city and used the mooring mast at the St. Hubert airfield. We had had earlier tastes of aviation activity when Count de Lesseps in a Bleriot monoplane gave a demonstration at an air show at Lakeside in 1910. Later, Italian General Italo Balbo flew his seaplane squadron to Montreal. But the R-100 was special. Big enough to be easily seen in the sky, it drew crowds to see it moored at St. Hubert.

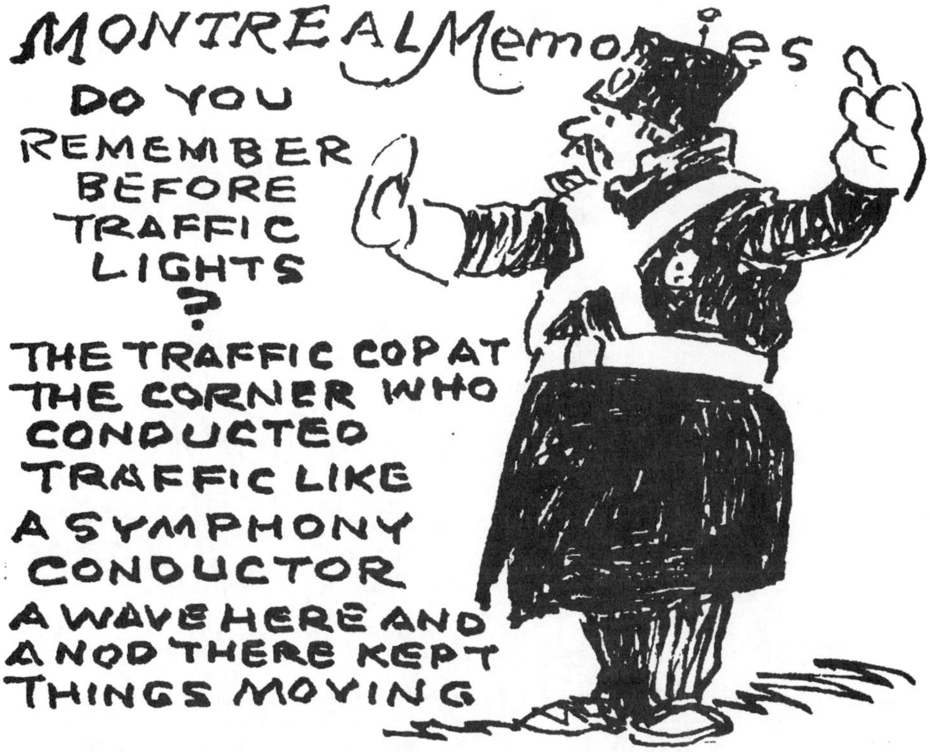
MONTREAL Memories
DO YOU REMEMBER BEFORE TRAFFIC LIGHTS ?
THE TRAFFIC COP AT THE CORNER WHO CONDUCTED TRAFFIC LIKE A SYMPHONY CONDUCTOR
A WAVE HERE AND A NOD THERE KEPT THINGS MOVING

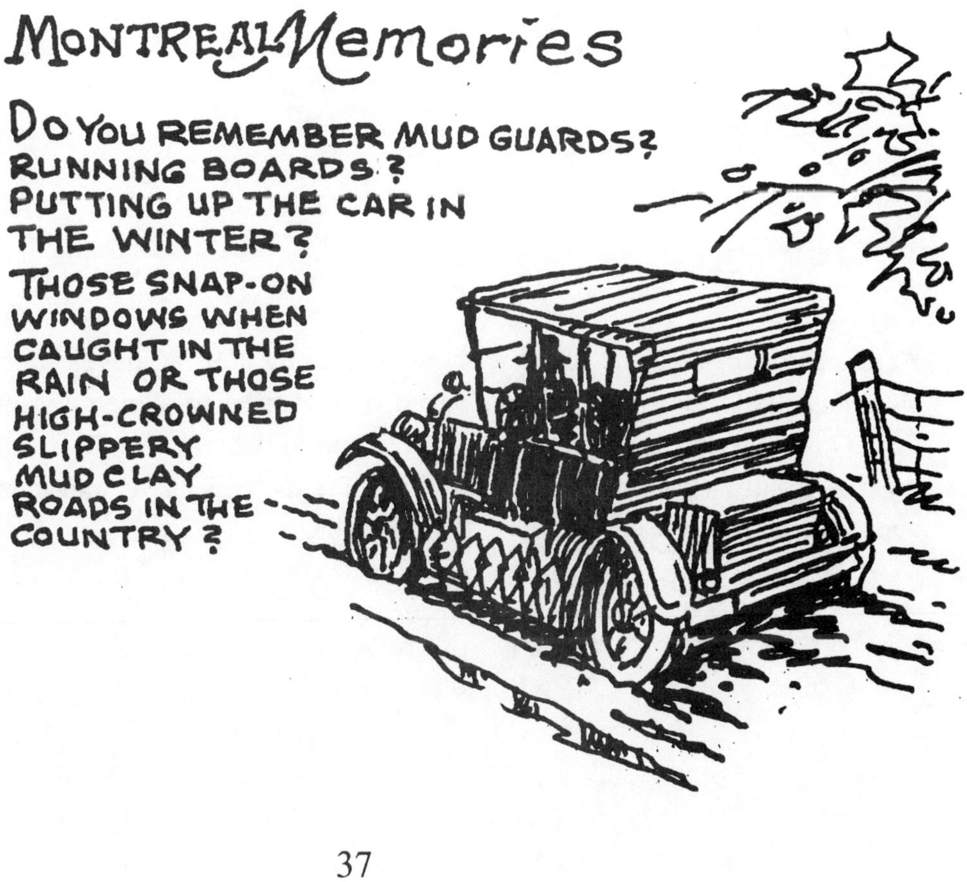
MONTREAL Memories
DO YOU REMEMBER MUD GUARDS?
RUNNING BOARDS?
PUTTING UP THE CAR IN THE WINTER?
THOSE SNAP-ON WINDOWS WHEN CAUGHT IN THE RAIN OR THOSE HIGH-CROWNED SLIPPERY MUD CLAY ROADS IN THE COUNTRY?

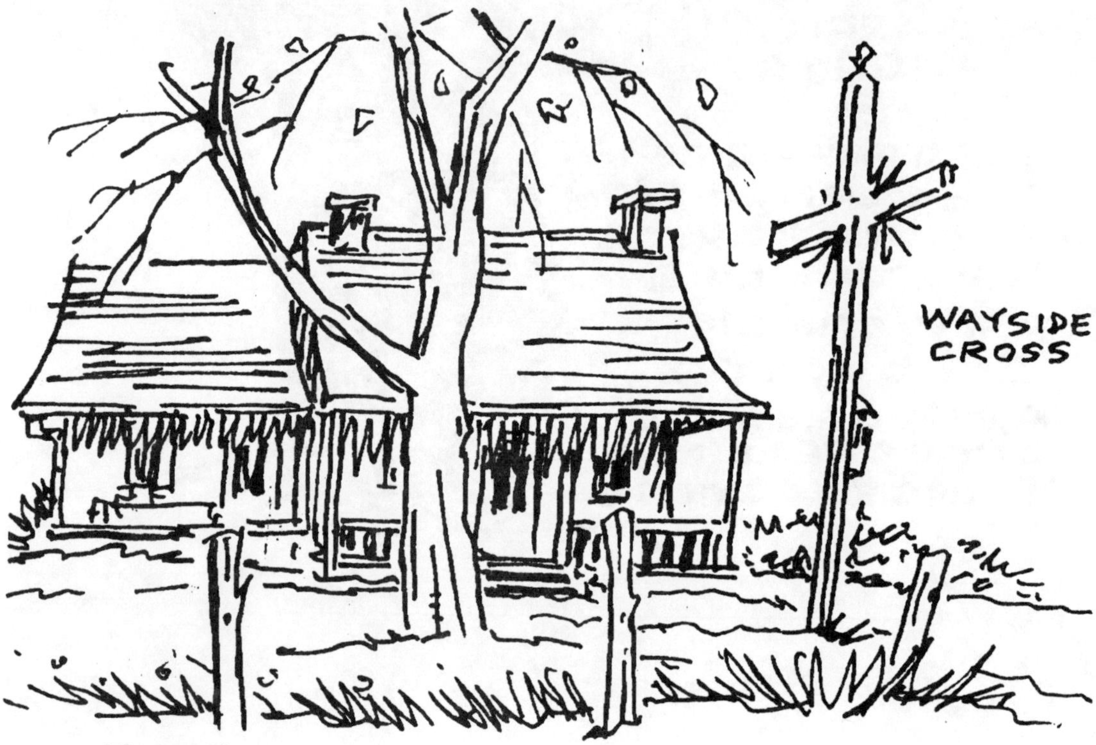


OLD FARM HOUSE
ON ST. CHARLES ROAD

As the city expanded, farmland was gobbled up by housing developments, industry and shopping malls. Before it was all paved over, I tried to sketch and paint some of the farms in the West Island. Sources, St. Jean and St. Charles Boulevards were once country roads with attractive houses and barns. Fields, cow barns and apple orchards have been replaced with used-car lots and strip malls.

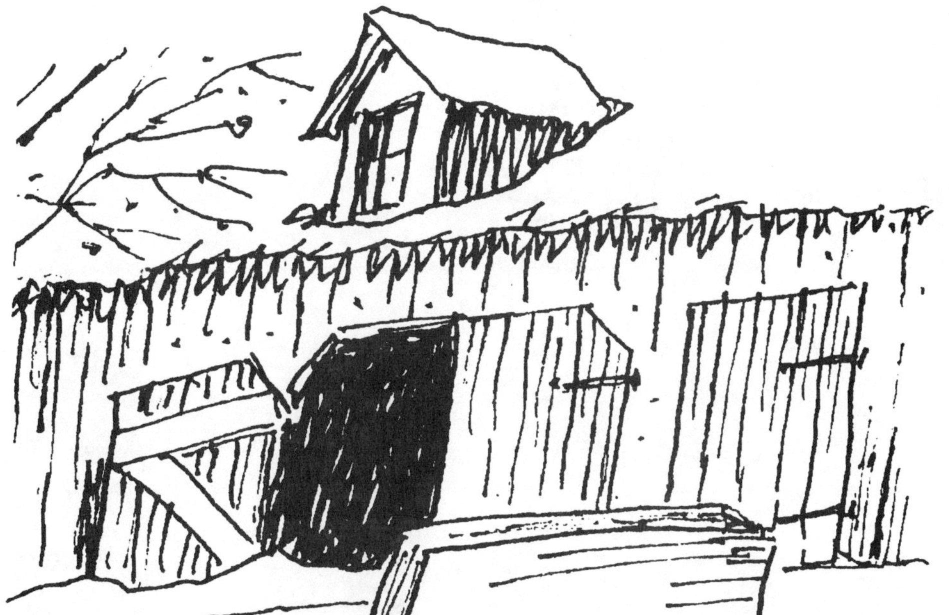

OLD SLEIGH AND AN OLD BARN IN BEACONSFIELD

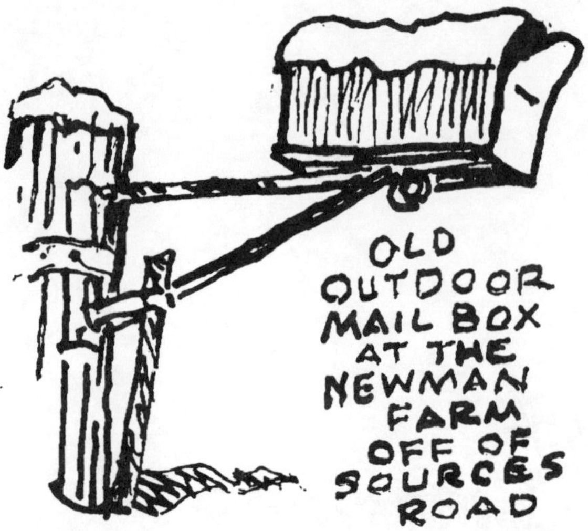

OLD OUTDOOR MAIL BOX AT THE NEWMAN FARM OFF OF SOURCES ROAD

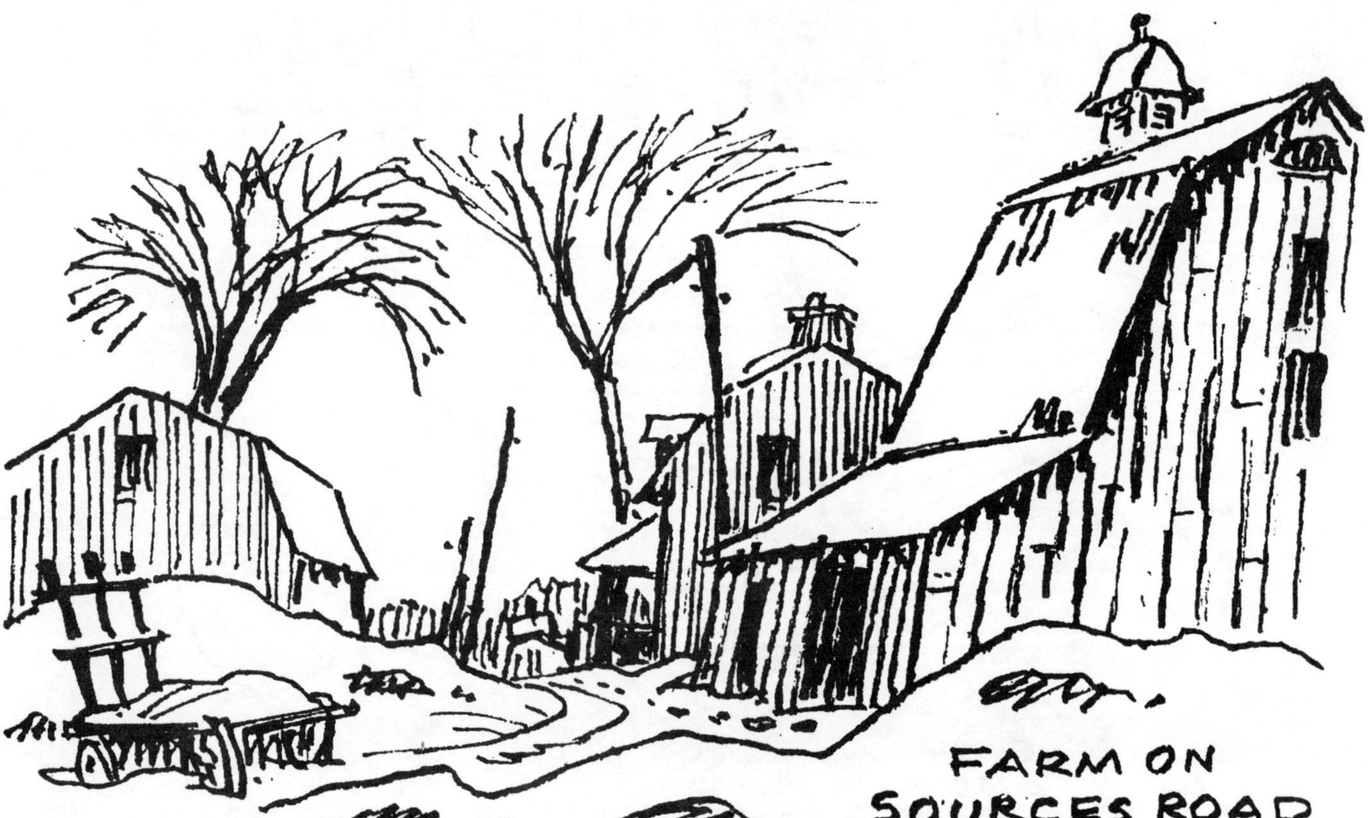

FARM ON SOURCES ROAD

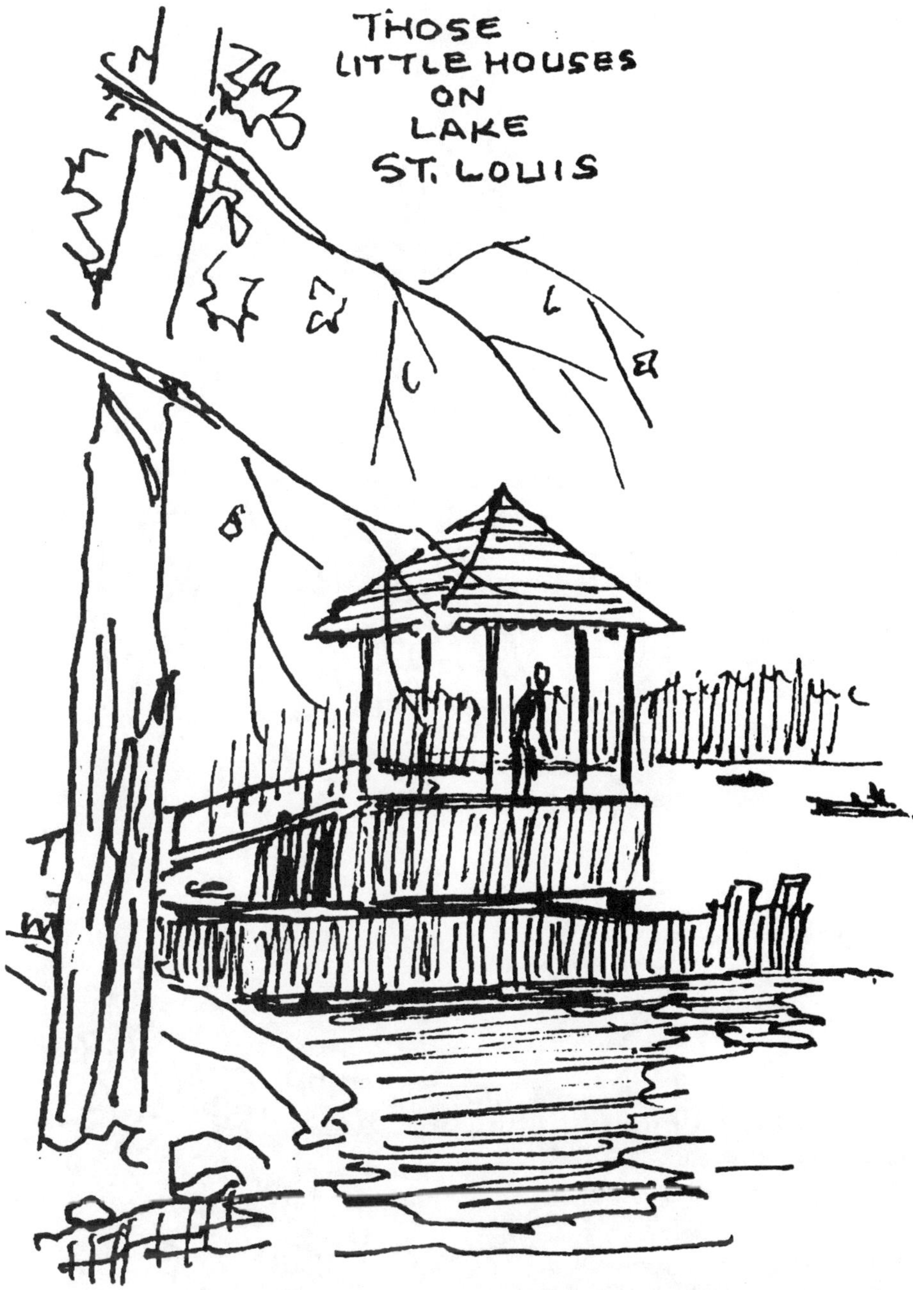


Do you still call it the "Lakeshore," not the "West Island"? Then you are enough of an old timer to remember the little piers jutting out on Lake St. Louis all along the old Lakeshore Road. Families could keep their canoes and rowboats underneath and sit on the deck above to admire the view. We would see lots of these piers on our Sunday drive, but none was quite so large and spectacular as that of the Valois Boat Club on Valois Bay. It was a community country club where movies were shown, and dances, boating and swimming events were held. Of course you must remember the waterside porch of the Edgewater Hotel, where on a summer day you would have to fish the shad flies out of your drinks.

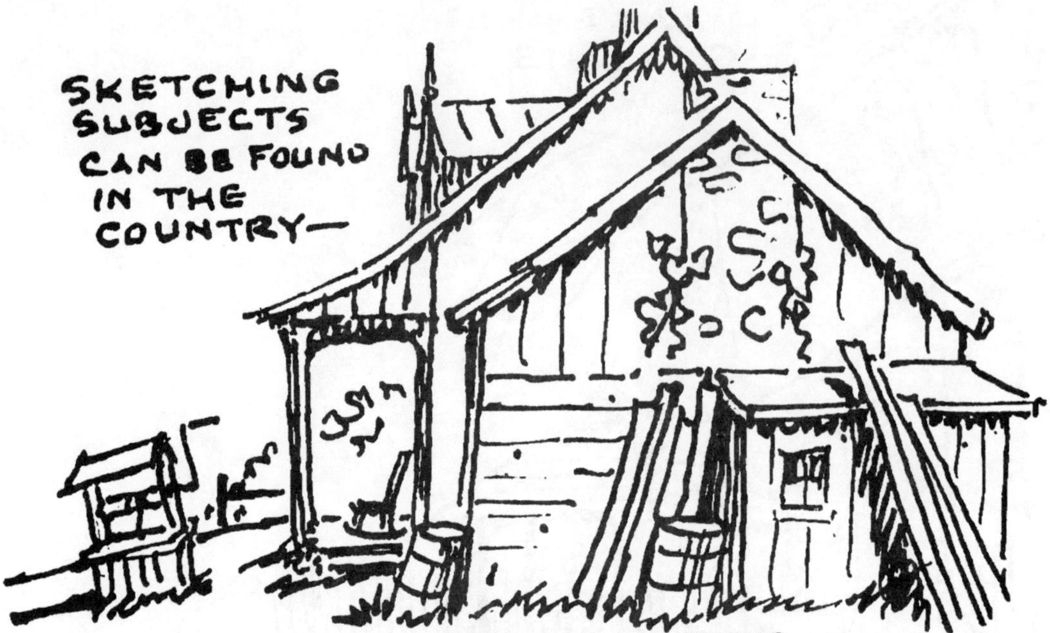


OLD FARMHOUSE WITH A WELL

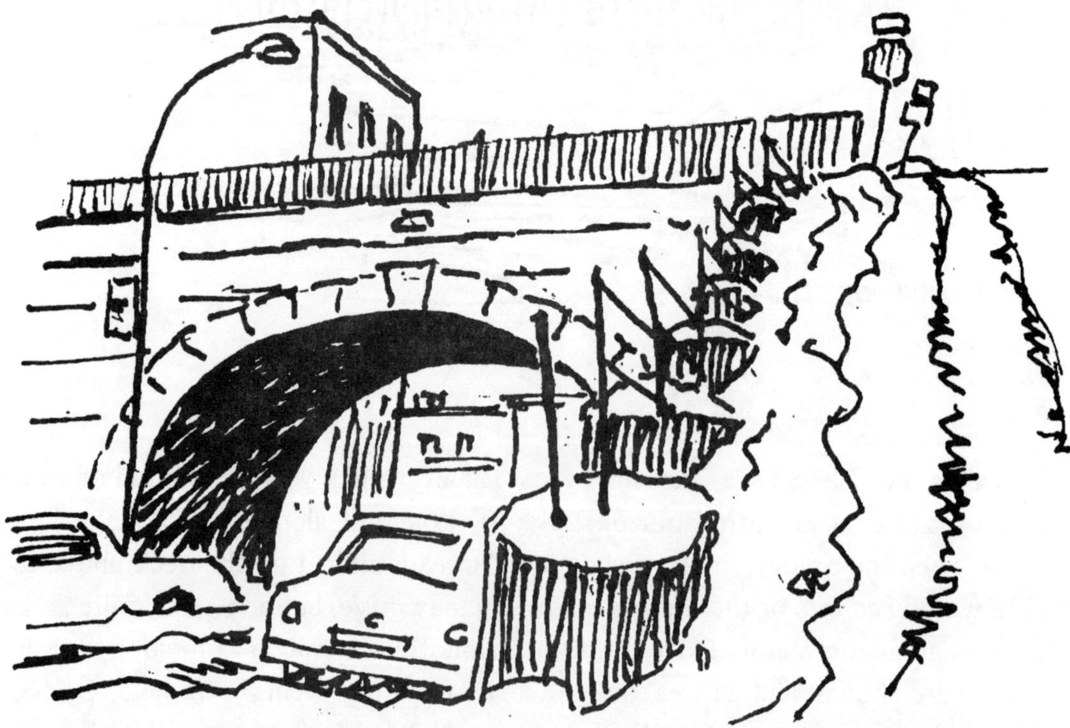

—OR IN THE CITY— BERRI STREET

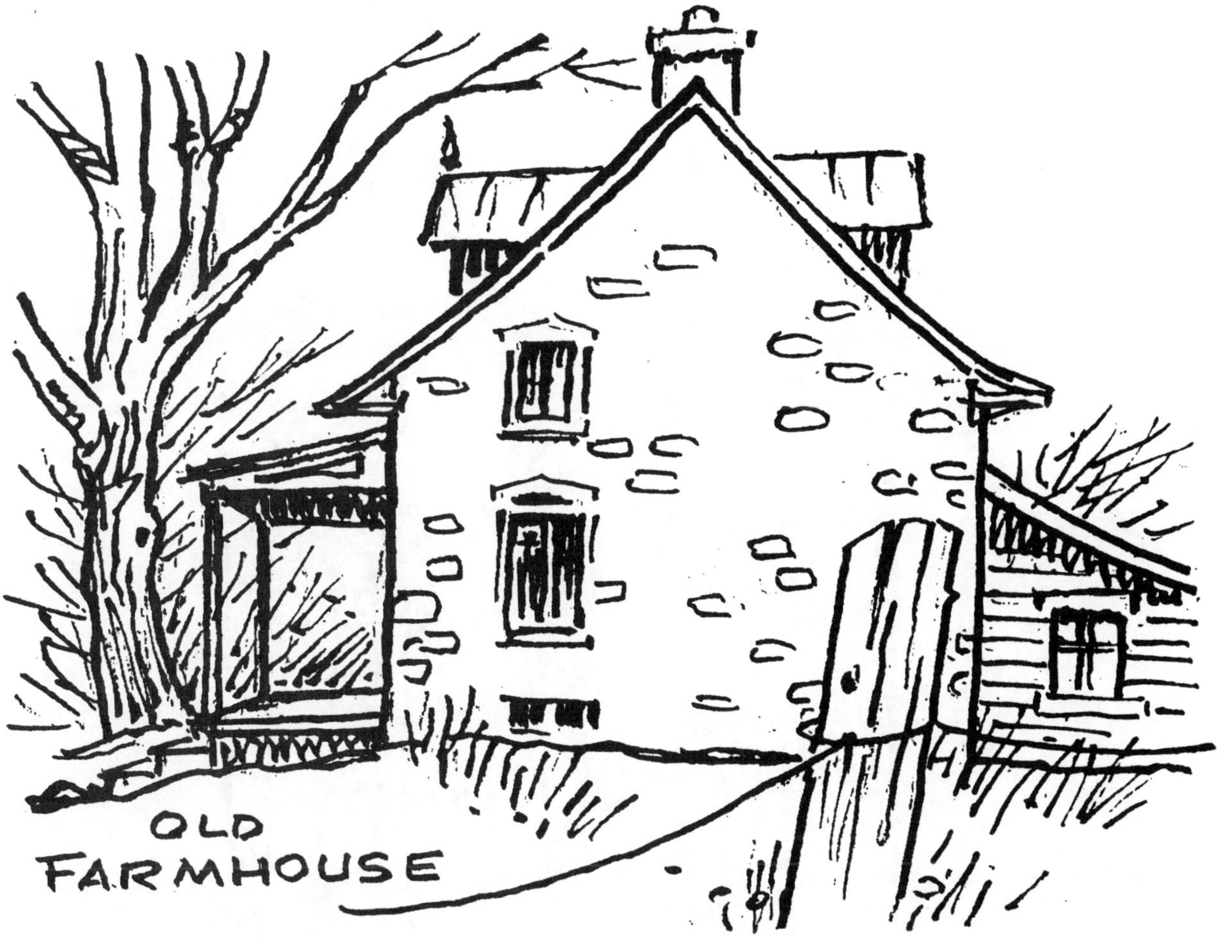


People living in Côte St. Luc apartments or condos might be surprised to learn that Côte St. Luc Road was once a winding dirt road through a countryside of fields, barns, farmhouses, and outbuildings. I remember sketching country scenes, noting that even Harry Ship's barbotte gambling layout hardly disturbed the rural outlook.

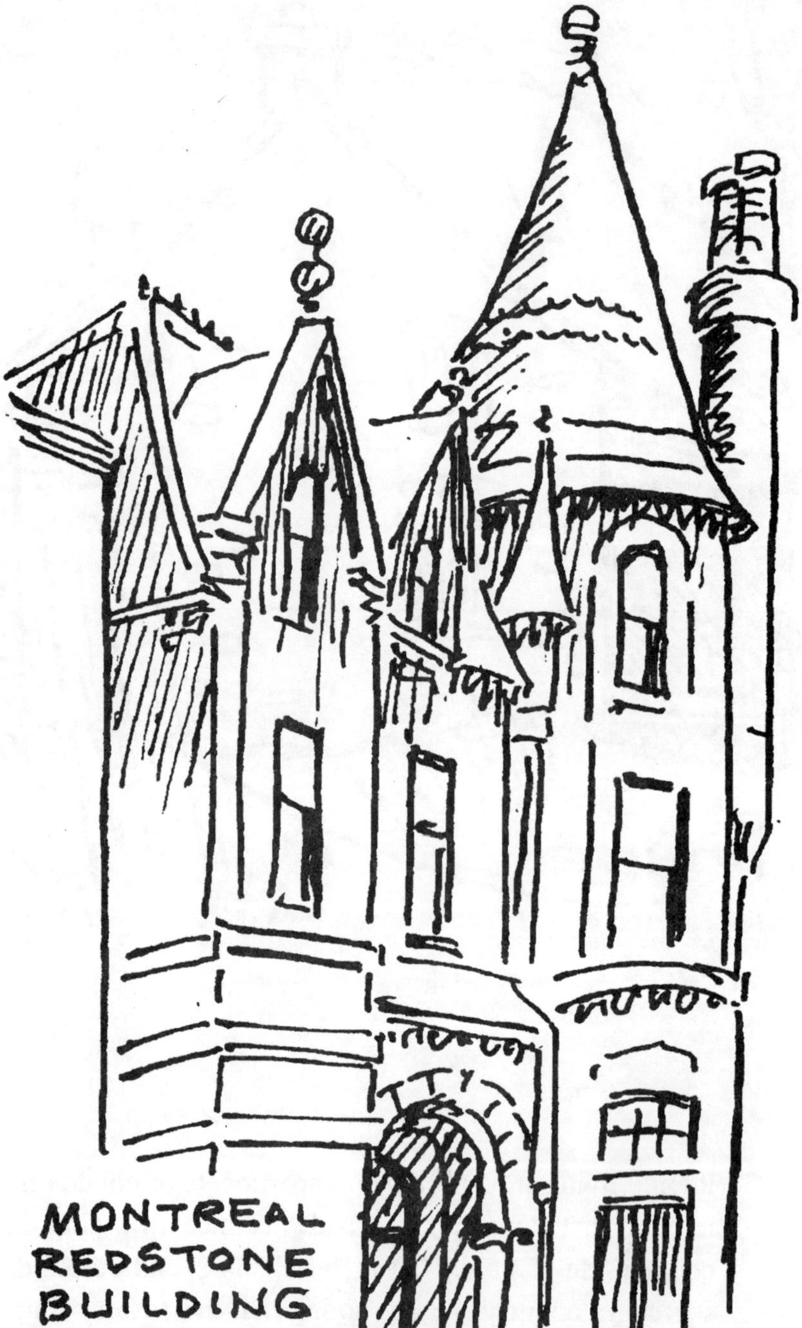
MONTREAL
REDSTONE
BUILDING

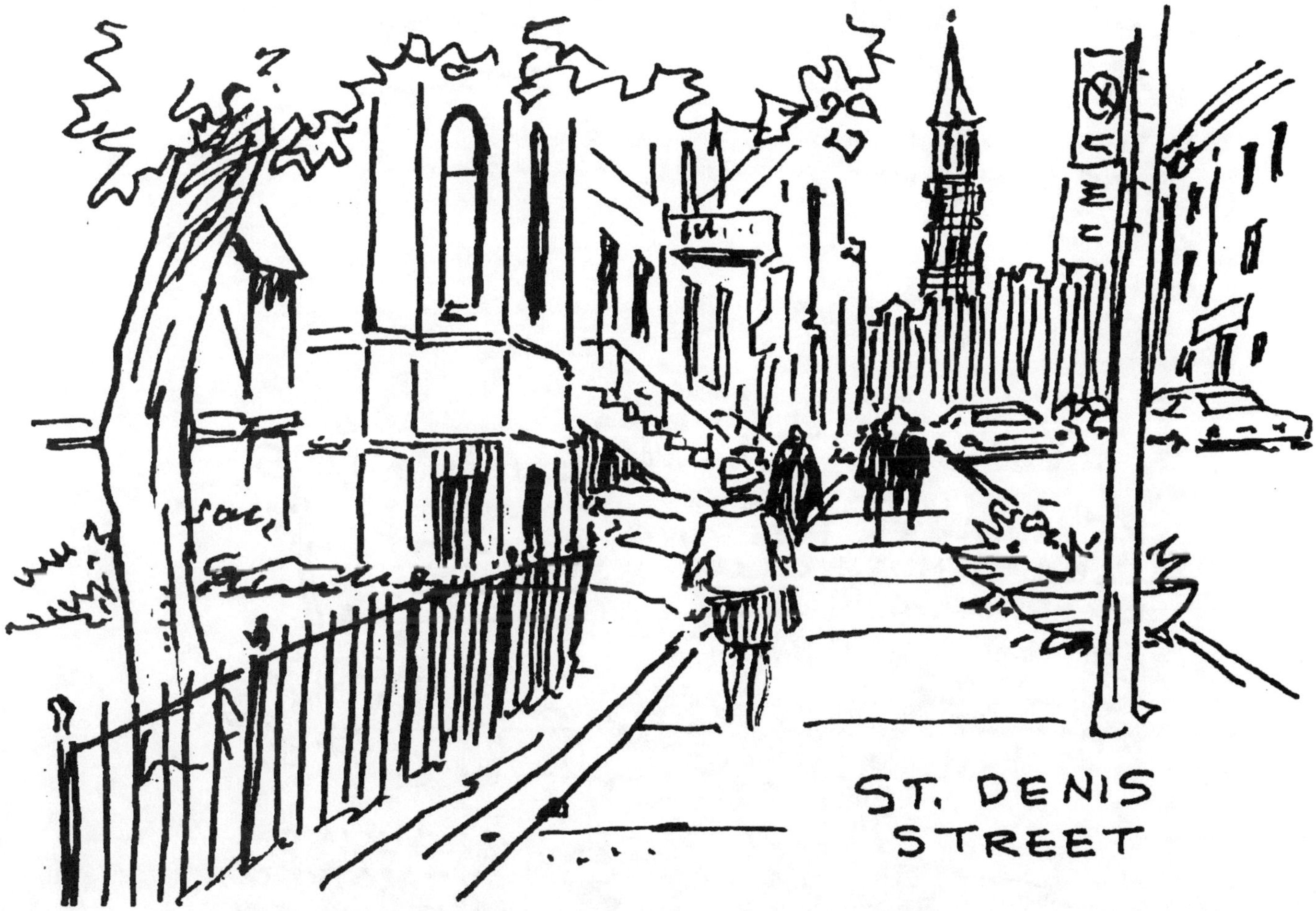
ST. DENIS
STREET

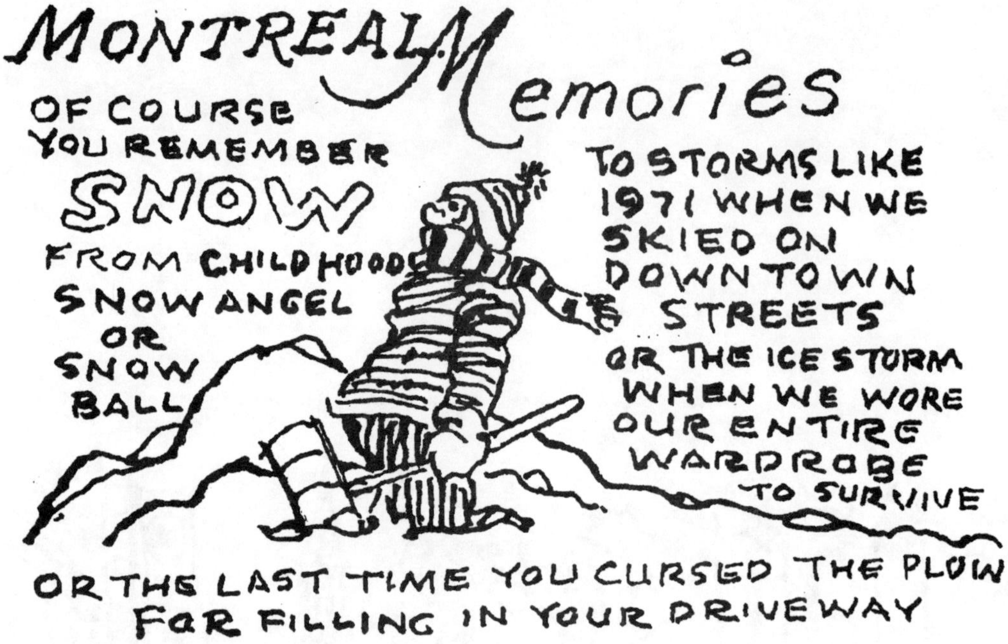
MONTREAL Memories
OF COURSE YOU REMEMBER SNOW
FROM CHILDHOOD SNOW ANGEL OR SNOW BALL
TO STORMS LIKE 1971 WHEN WE SKIED ON DOWNTOWN STREETS
OR THE ICE STORM WHEN WE WORE OUR ENTIRE WARDROBE TO SURVIVE
OR THE LAST TIME YOU CURSED THE PLOW FOR FILLING IN YOUR DRIVEWAY

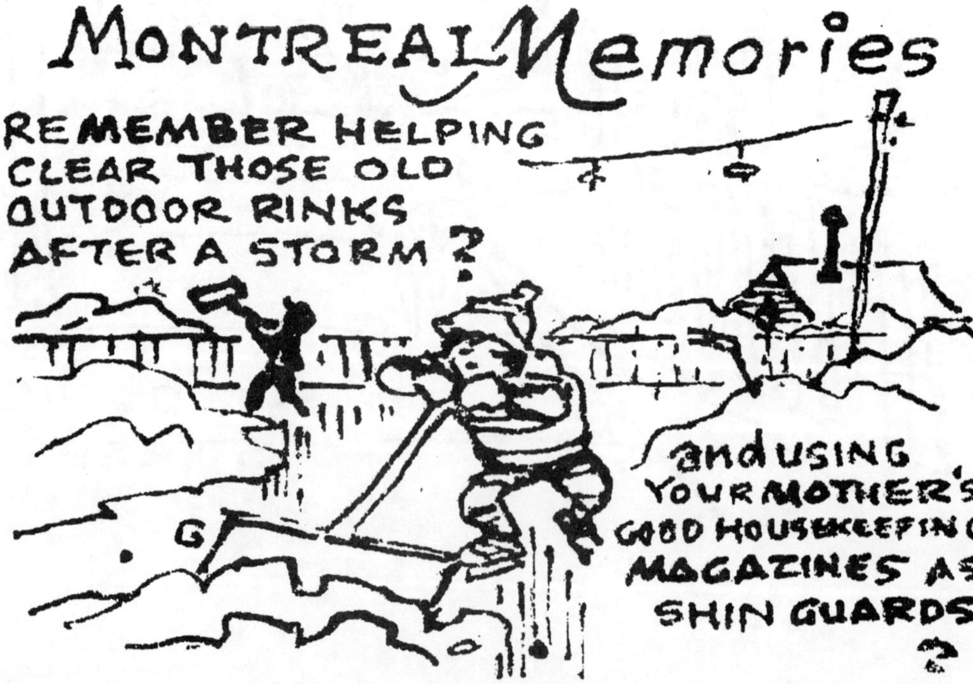
MONTREAL Memories
REMEMBER HELPING CLEAR THOSE OLD OUTDOOR RINKS AFTER A STORM?
and USING YOUR MOTHER'S GOOD HOUSEKEEPING MAGAZINES AS SHIN GUARDS?

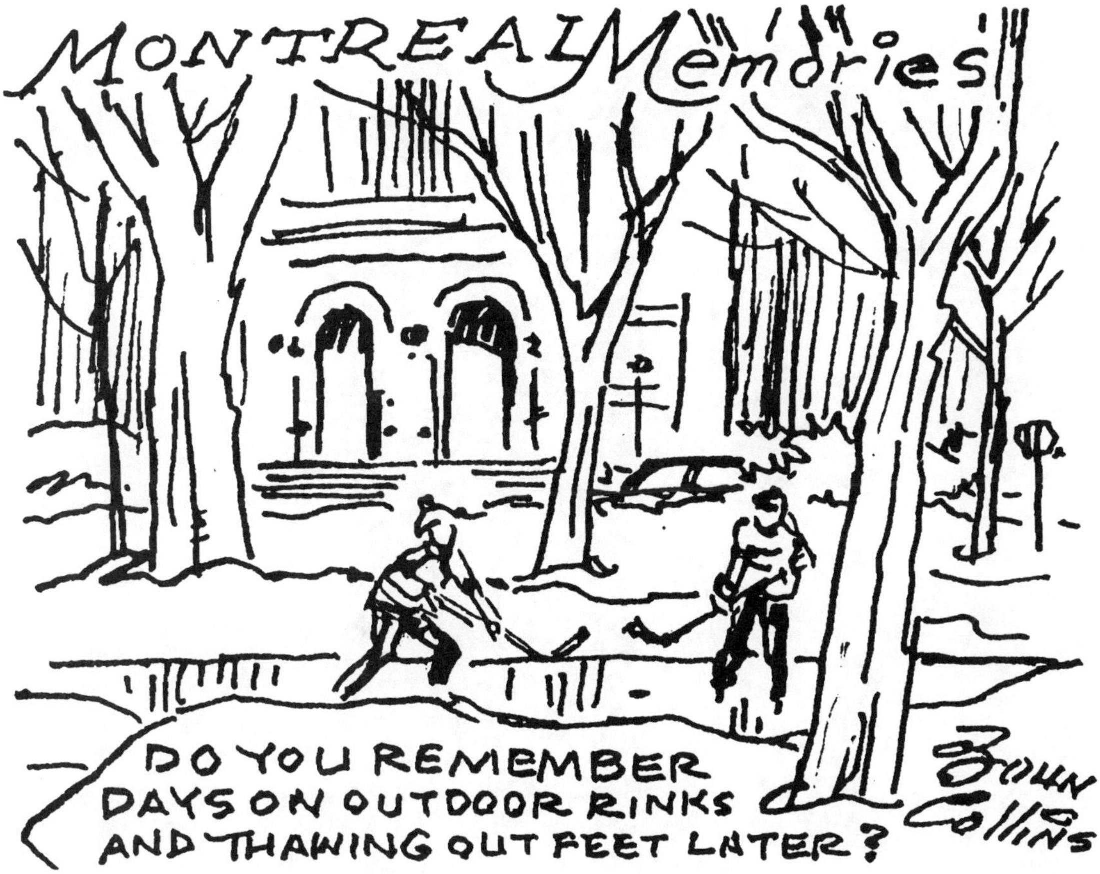


Unlike today, most skating rinks of the '20s and '30s were outdoor ones. Little hockey players usually wore rag-tag uniforms, and their shin pads were magazines stuffed into overstockings. Skates were quite often outgrown ones bought from older chums. Sometimes the clearing of a rink wasn't as fast as we wanted so we helped in this cleanup job. Most rinks had a shack of some kind for changing. Do you remember the pain in your feet when you took off your skates and those frozen toes started to thaw?

Did your skating career start with "cheesecutters" and a pillow shock-absorber stuffed in the seat of your pullovers? Cheesecutters - double-bladed skates you strapped over your winter boots - were good only for shuffling around the ice. The early skates had flat blades as on figure skates, but in the '20s we bought "tube skates," which were a big thrill and supposed to give us greater speed.

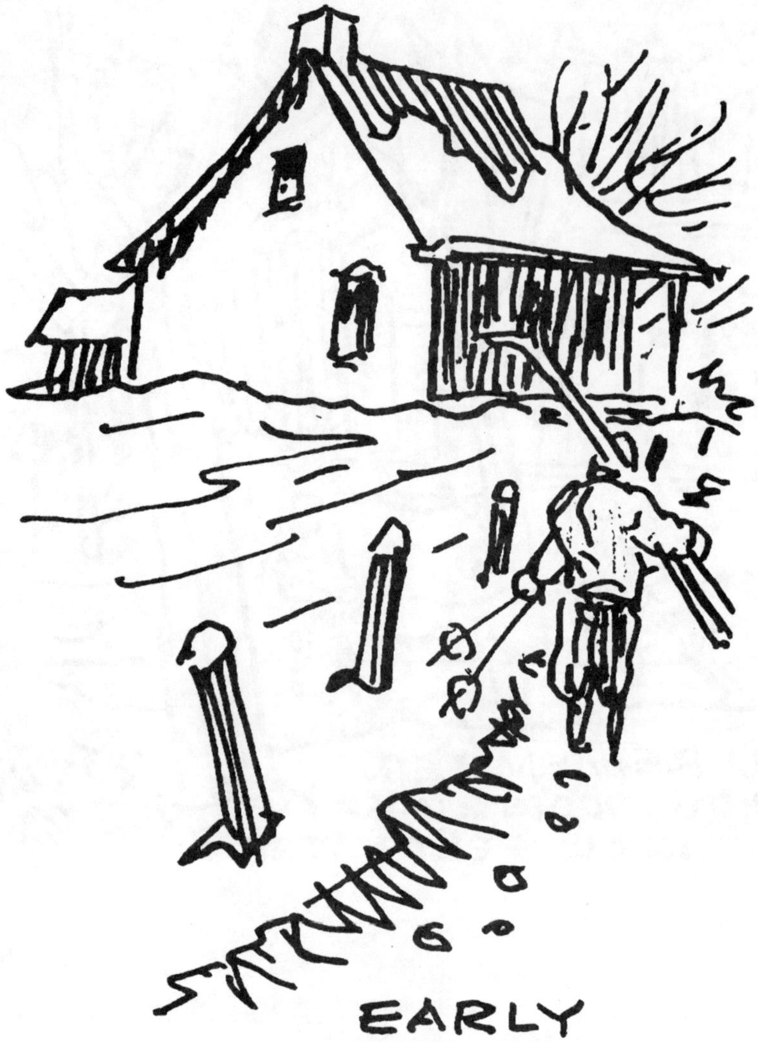

# EARLY SKIING DAYS IN THE LAURENTIANS

Winter sports have always been important in Montreal. We always skated and played hockey on outdoor rinks. The beginning of the last century belonged to the snowshoers, but then skiing took over. Begun experimentally on Mount Royal, skiing was taken north to the Laurentians, inspired by "Jackrabbit" Johannsen's cross-country exploits and Ryan's developing of Lac Tremblant. Do you remember the ski trains to the Laurentians? Did you go to Côte des Neiges Road to watch the ski jumping?

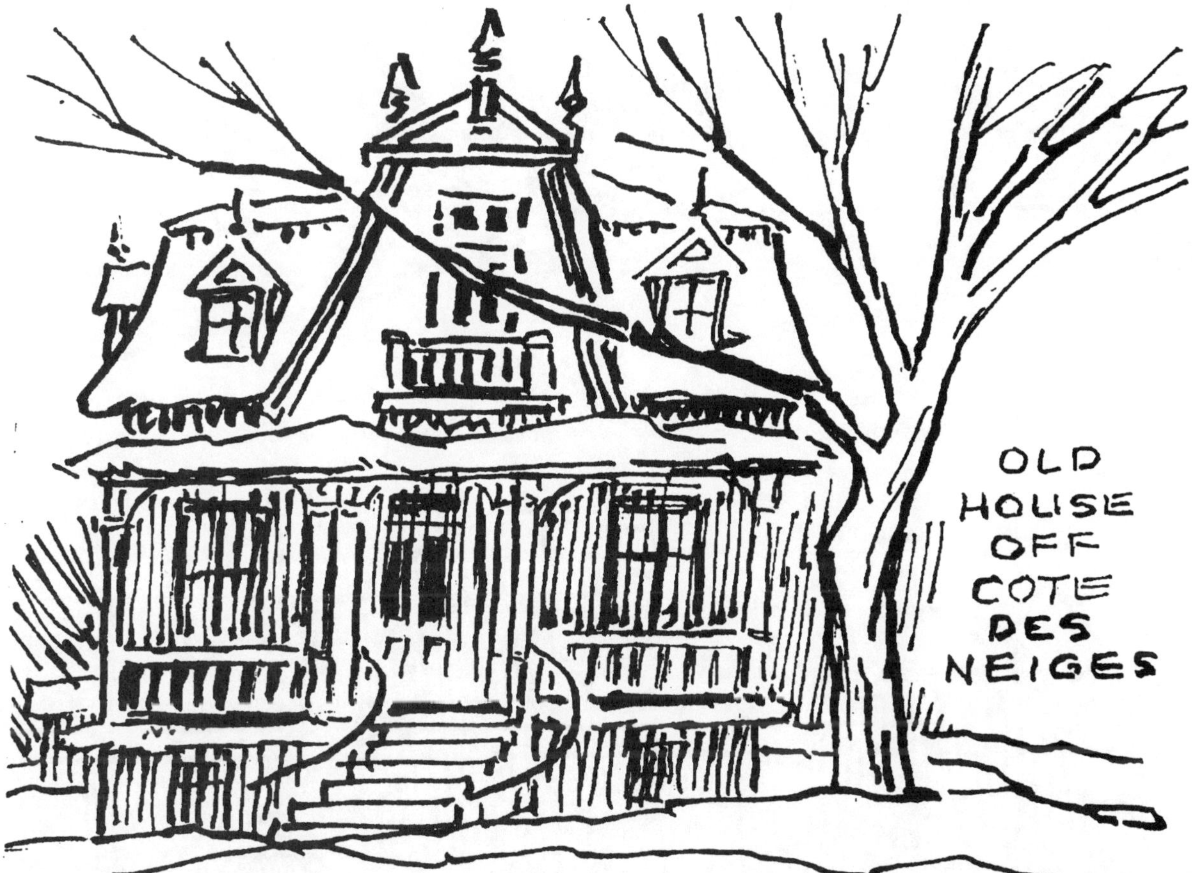
OLD
HOUSE
OFF
COTE
DES
NEIGES

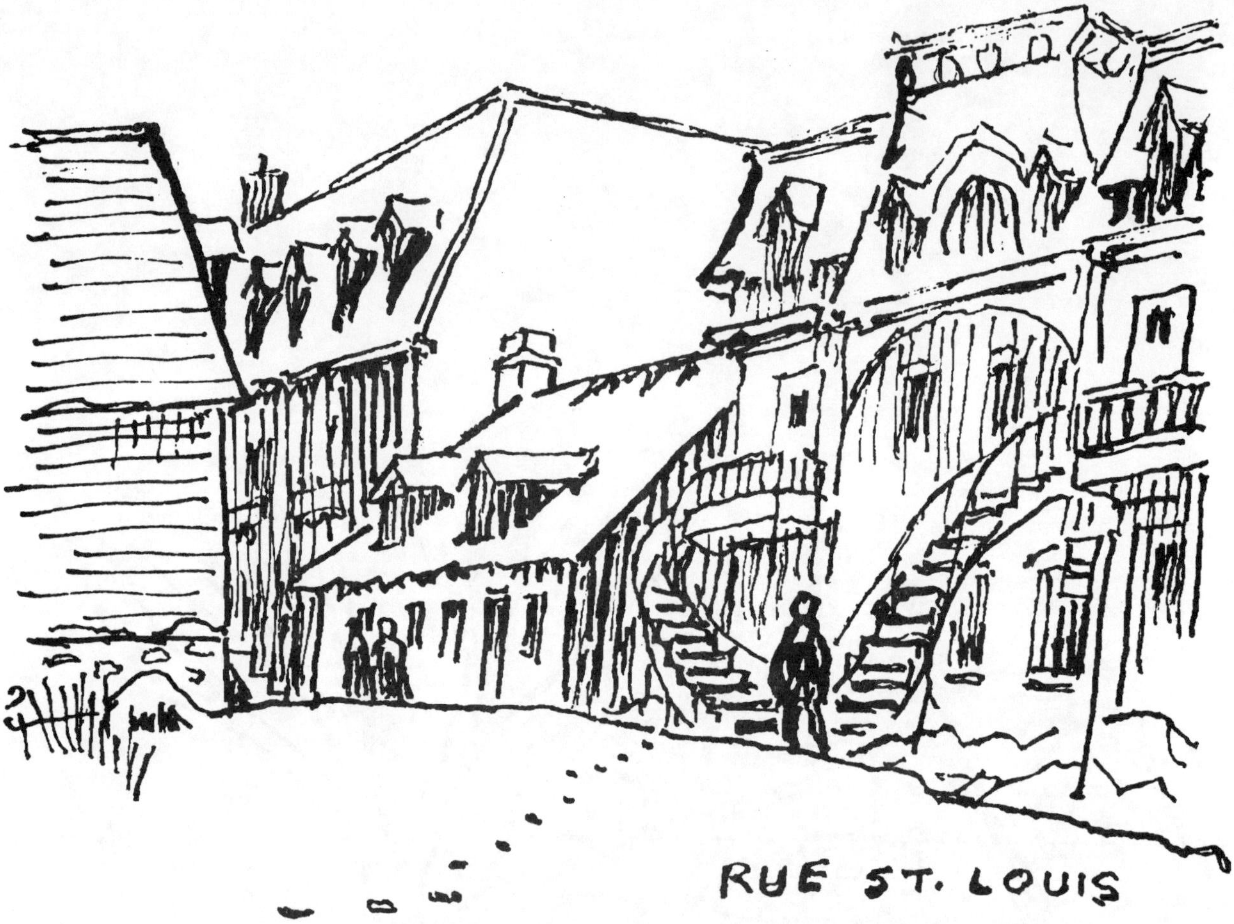

RUE ST. LOUIS

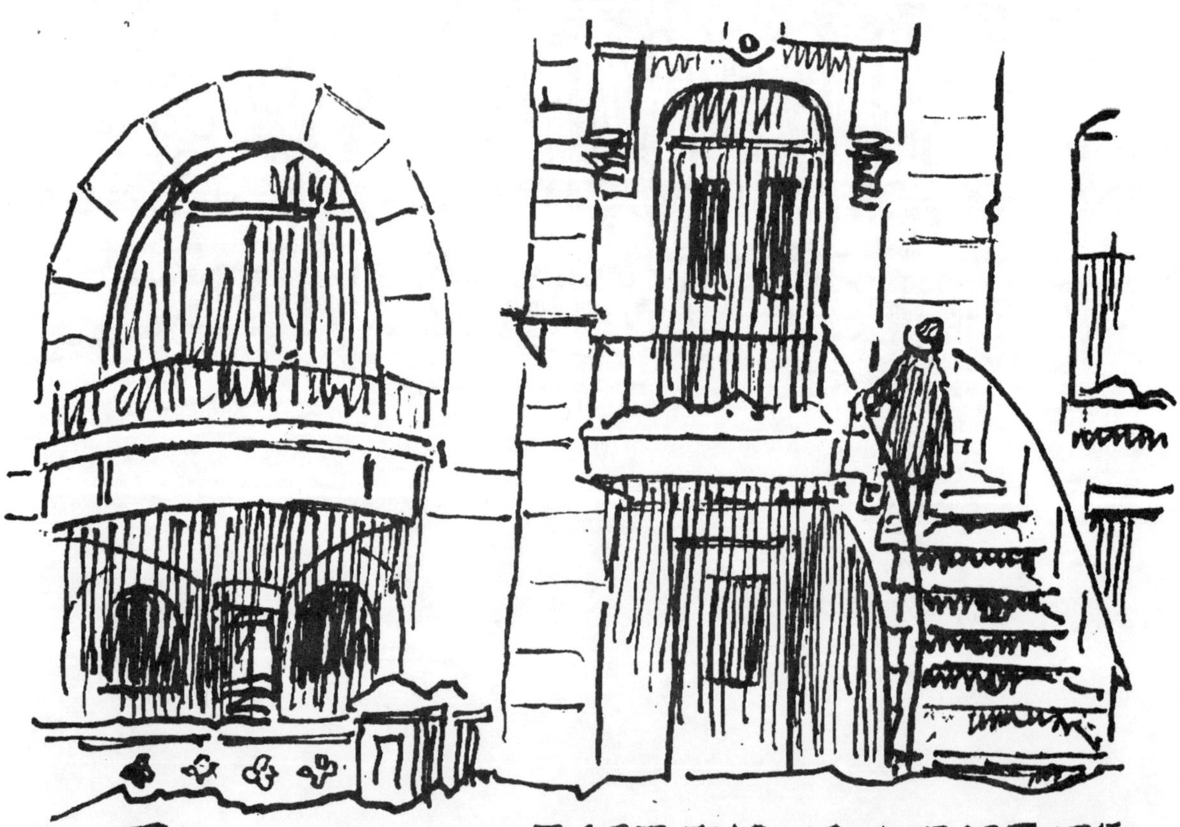

EAST END ARCHITECTURE

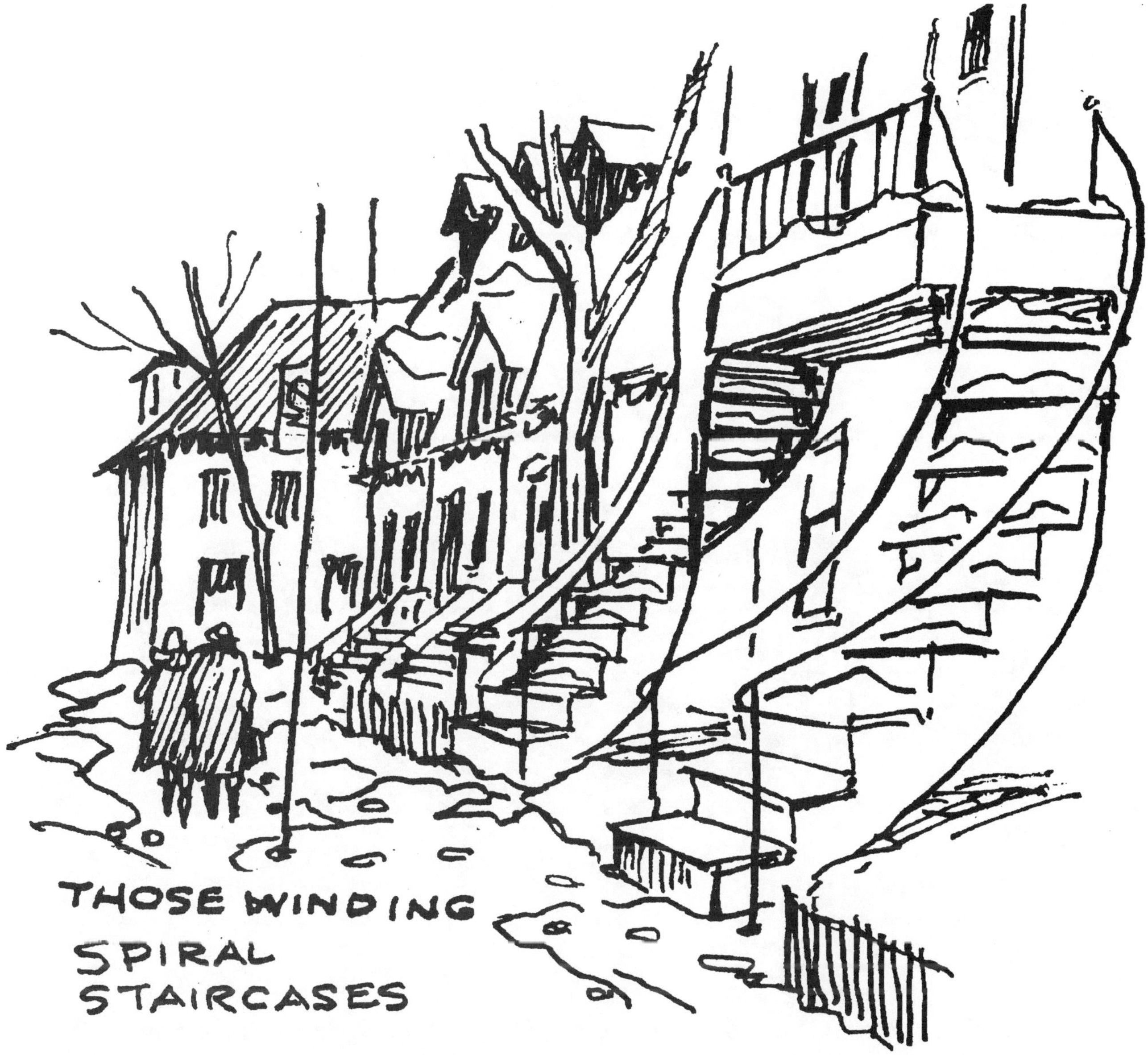


The winding outdoor stairs are as much a part of Montreal as the Cross on the Mountain or Potholes in the spring. You can easily spot a newcomer to the city by observing how they climb the stairs: while natives go up and down with the ease of mountain goats, visitors clutch the railings, and gingerly, slowly, proceed one hesitant step at a time.

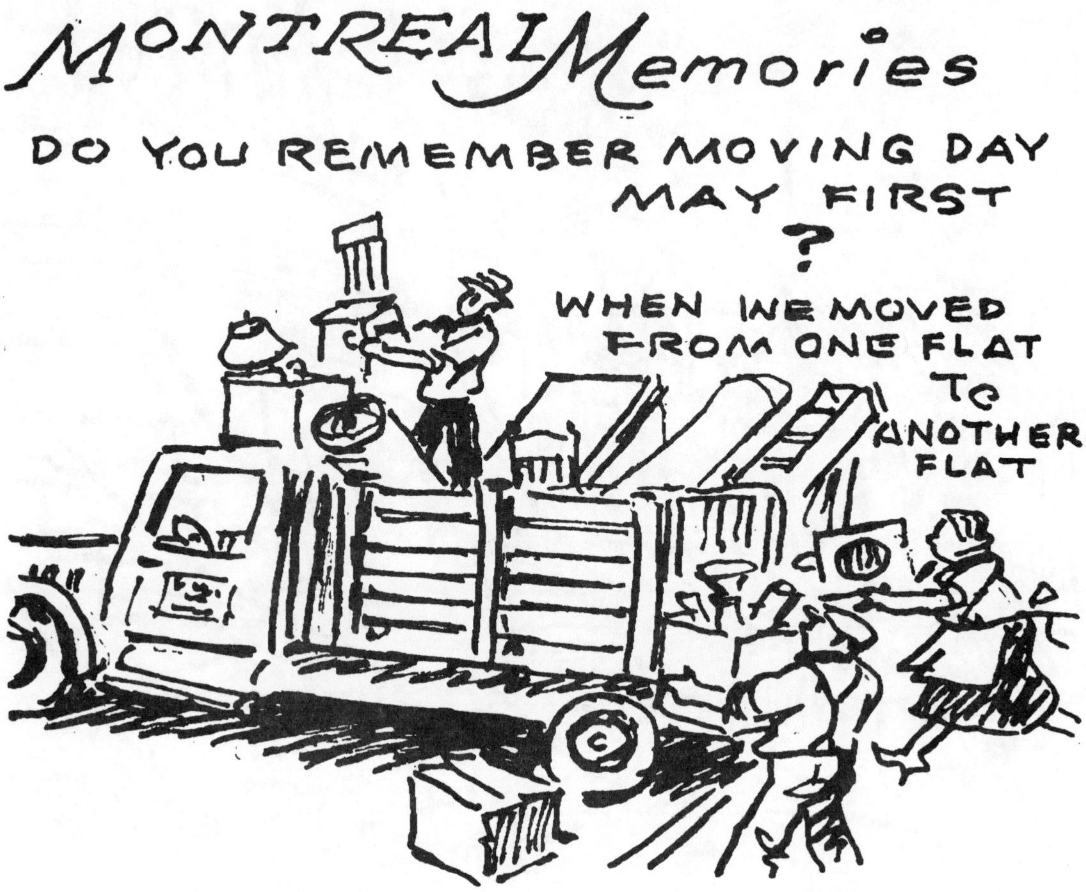


For most of this century, May First was Moving Day, apartment leases customarily ending on the last day of April. In a city of renters, almost everybody was on the move in a wide variety of vehicles: horse-drawn carts, borrowed trucks and moving vans, all loaded with household goods, beds, mattresses, pots and pans. The tenants would leave one rented flat for another, always hoping the new quarters would be just what they wanted - only to go through the whole business again the next year.

Today, when we want a little more heat in our homes, we just turn up the thermostat. However, fifty years ago, it was coal, not oil, that was burned in furnaces to heat most houses and flats. Do you remember "Welsh Anthracite," taking out the ashes, or a "clinker"? Some flats, however, had "Quebec Heaters," with pipes throughout the rooms. A big job each spring was cleaning the pipes. Newspapers were spread on the floor to catch the soot, and the pipes were lowered from the ceiling and taken apart. After the soot was shaken out, the pipes were stored in the shed until next winter.

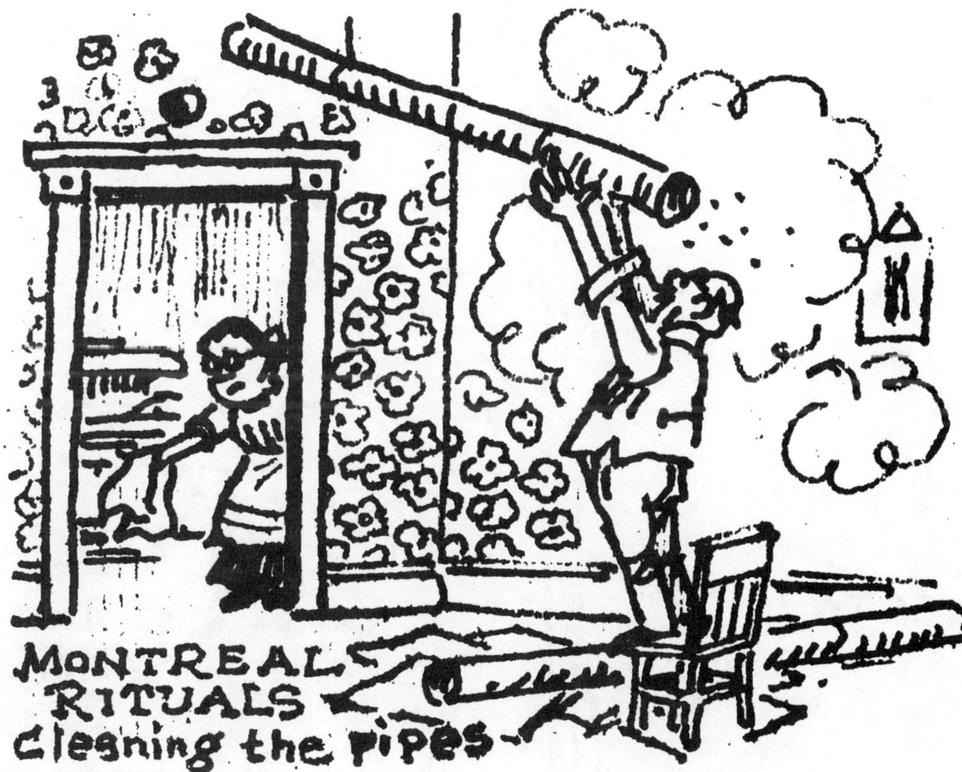

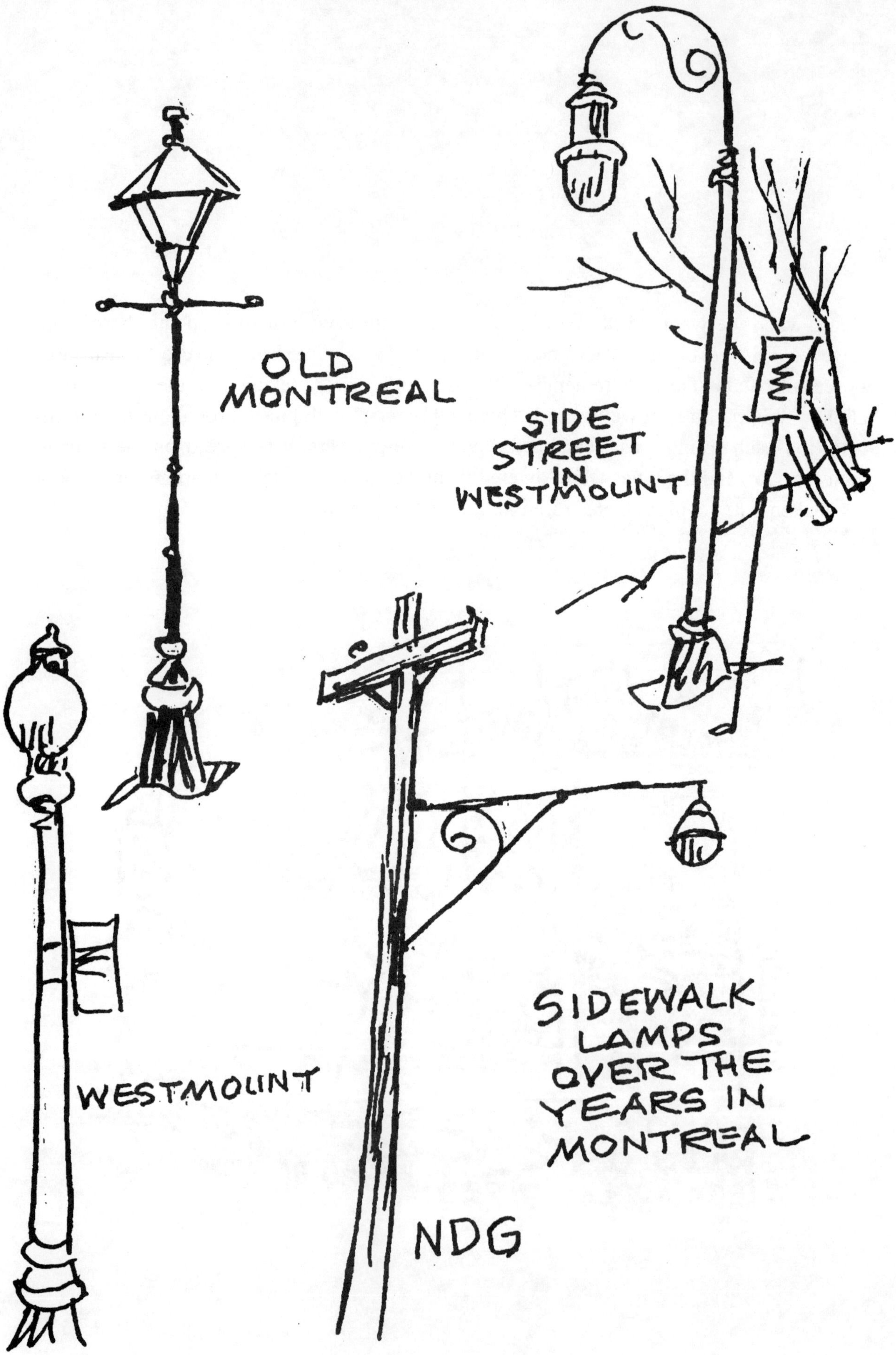
OLD MONTREAL
SIDE STREET IN WESTMOUNT
WESTMOUNT
SIDEWALK LAMPS OVER THE YEARS IN MONTREAL
NDG

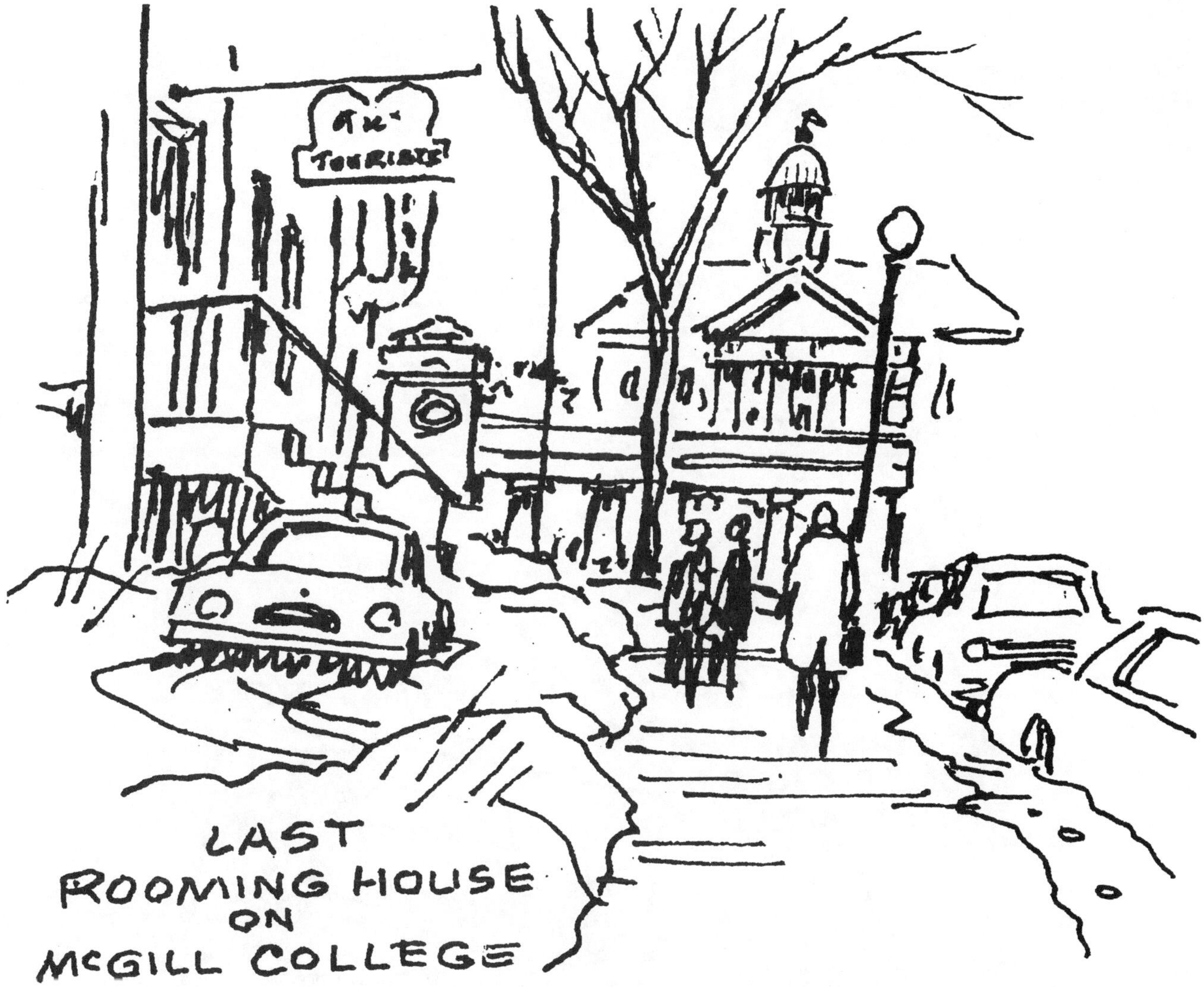


The city has had many forms of street lighting over the years, from the early solitary poles and their dim lights, to the scientific lighting with its odd oranges and greens, and finally to the stylish poles in Old Montreal and on Sherbrooke and Ste. Catherine Streets. I remember in the '20s, watching a man come along in a cart to a lamppost, let down the globe from the post with a rope, replace the cartridge in the globe, then hoist the globe back up. The used-up cartridge left in the gutter was much prized by little boys, who are natural junk collectors.

The old telephone poles used to be the centres of childhood activity. Long before playgrounds, the street was our play area. The poles served as home base for games of hide-and-seek, and a place to meet and plan youthful activities.

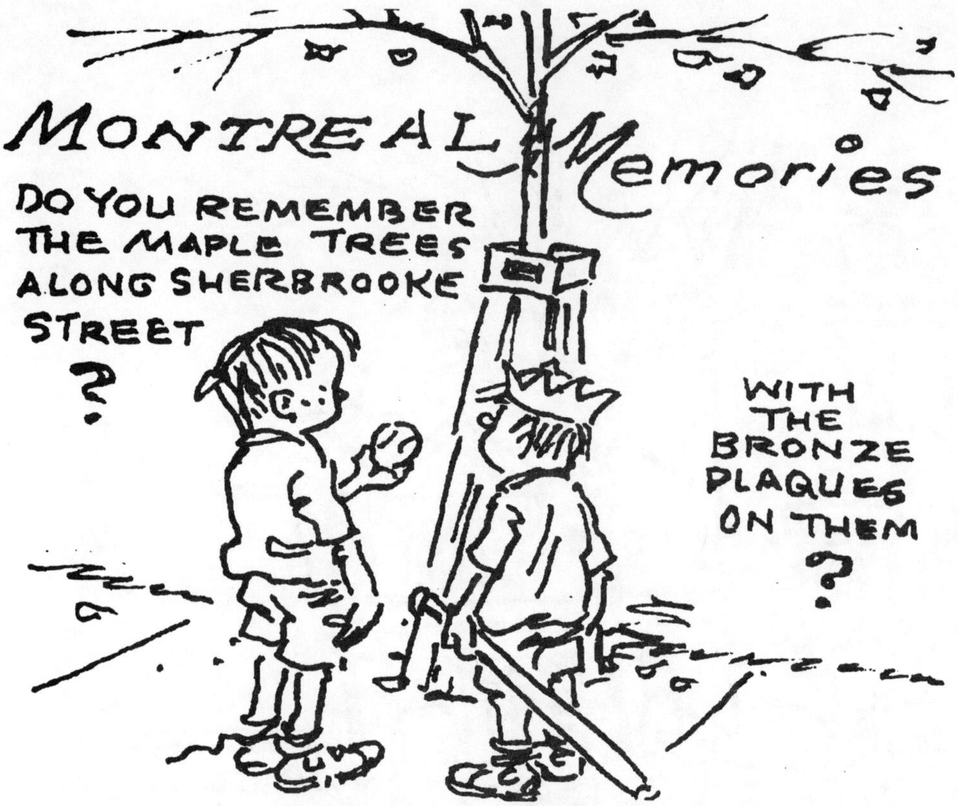


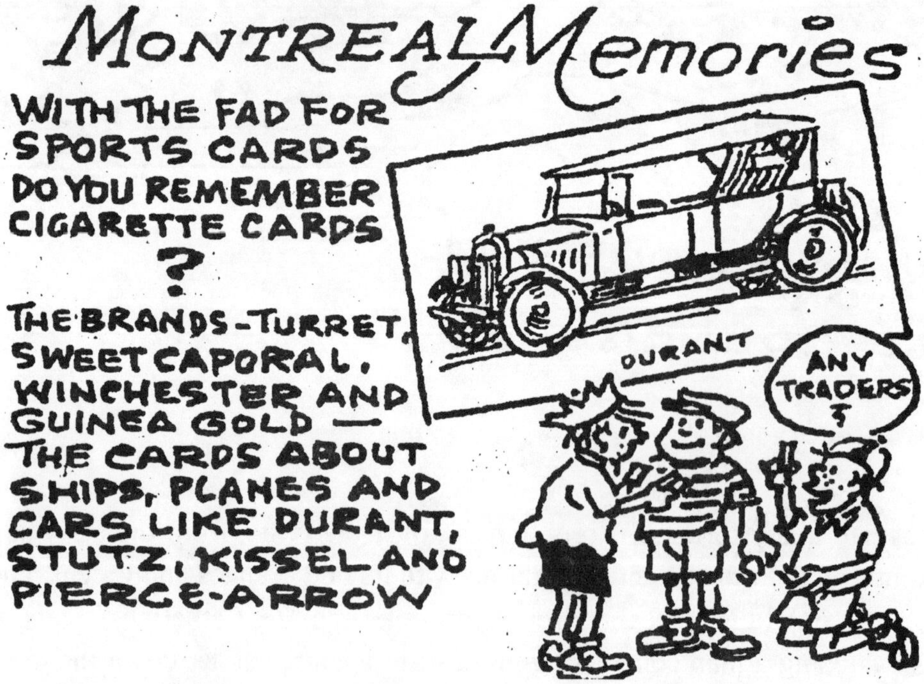


If you remember the maple trees planted along Sherbrooke Street in honour of the dead of World War I, you should recall youngsters wandering along looking for a ball game Outside of baseball there were many activities during a long school-free summer. Do you remember the Yo-Yo, Bolo-Bat, Hula Hoop, or Frisbee? Could you "walk the dog" or get your Yo-Yo to go "round the world"? Little girls, in addition to playing with dolls, had skipping ropes twirling everywhere and designs for hopscotch chalked on driveways and sidewalks.

By the end of the century, two changes evident in Montreal were the greater variation in population and a loss of Britishness. Early in the century, children saw school maps with large red-toned areas marking the British Empire. We studied English history and literature. At Christmas, girls received dolls and books such as *Winnie the Pooh* and *Paddington Bear*. Boys received Meccano sets - where you always kept losing vital pieces, and model kits of balsa wood airplanes - which you usually crashed into walls or door frames. But they also received copies of *Chums* or *Boys' Own Annual*, full of stories of English lads in schools, playing games unknown to us. The books also filled our minds with images of heroic youth defending the Honour of the Empire or the Indian frontier. No mention in our Christmas reading of hockey, lacrosse or baseball.

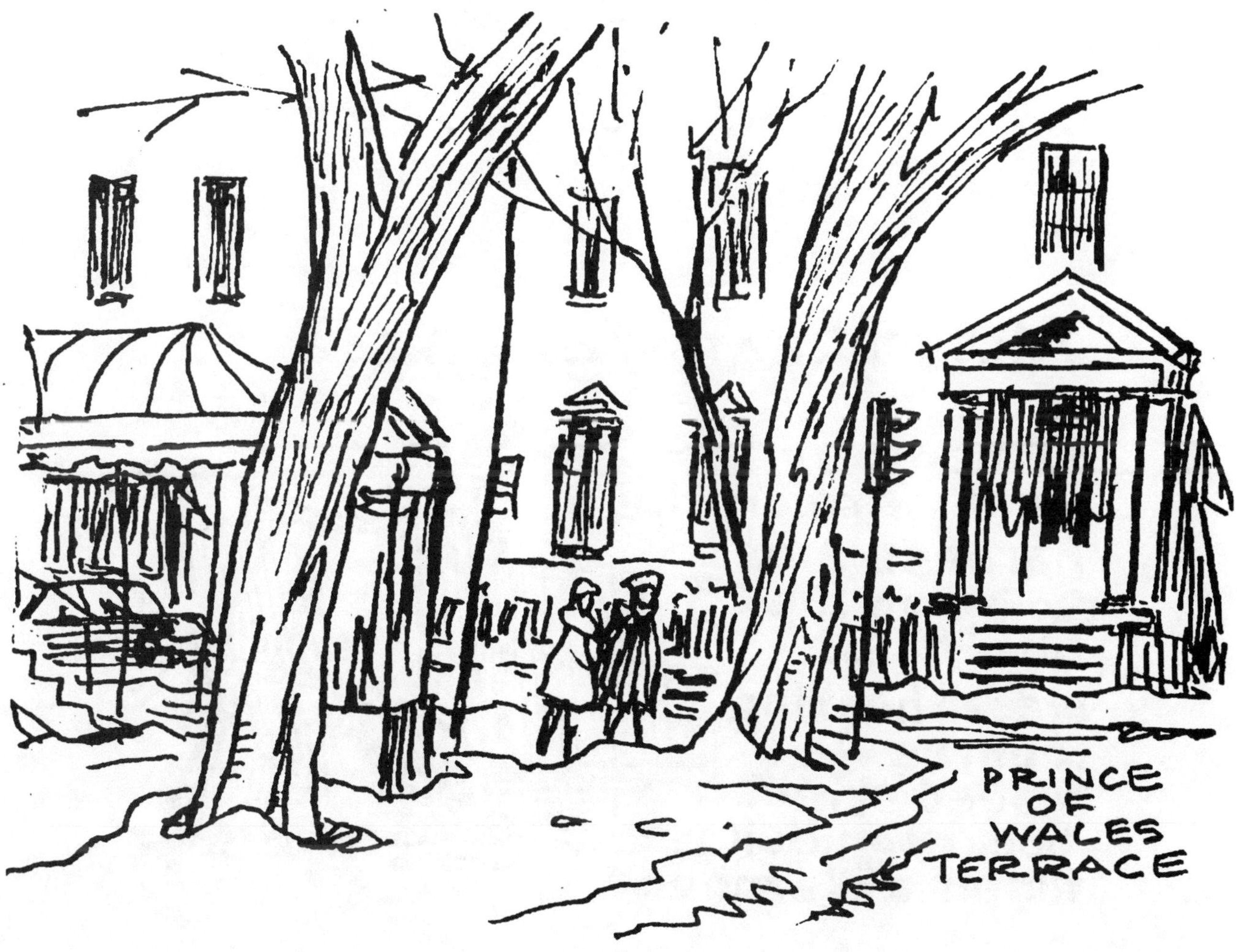

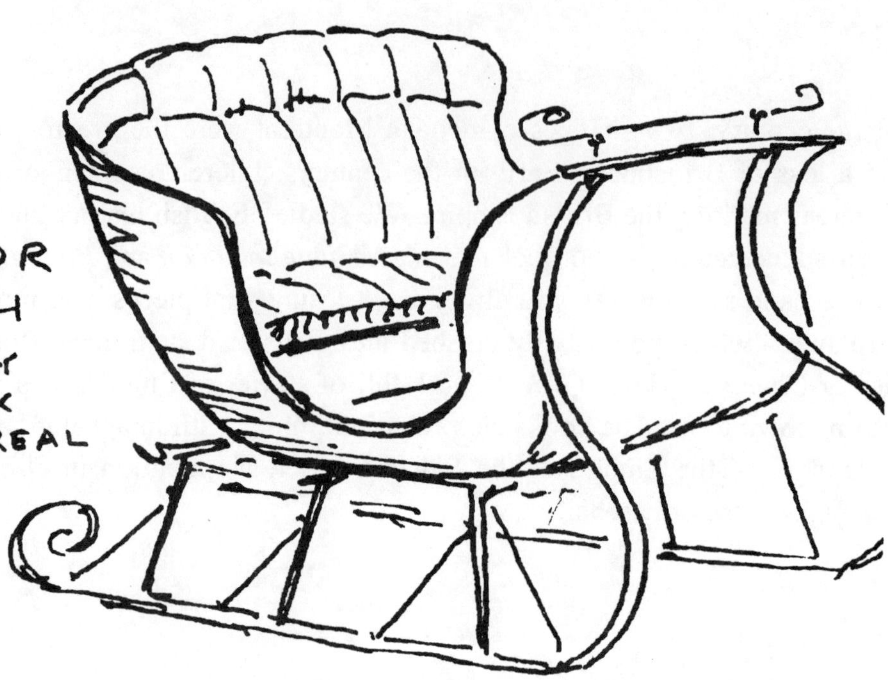

WINDSOR SLEIGH
BUILT BY LEDOUX OF MONTREAL

## MONTREAL Memories

Remember Sleigh-Bells? Some were on the harness and some on the shafts _ I recall hearing them as we played street hockey on dull winter afternoons.

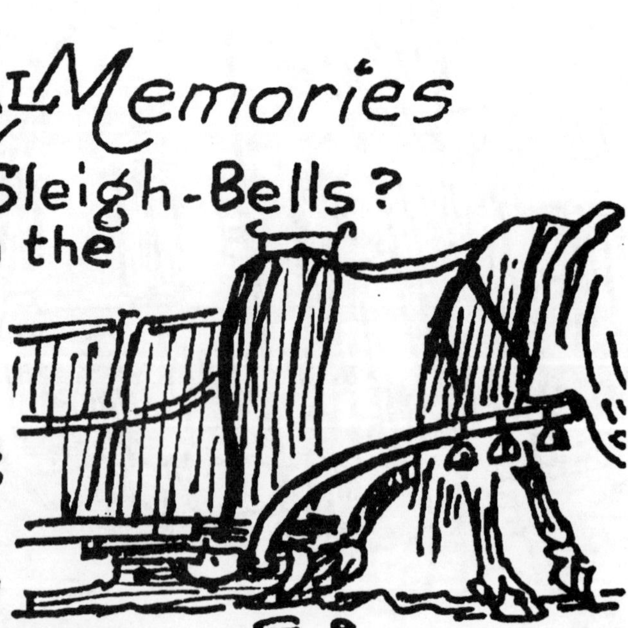

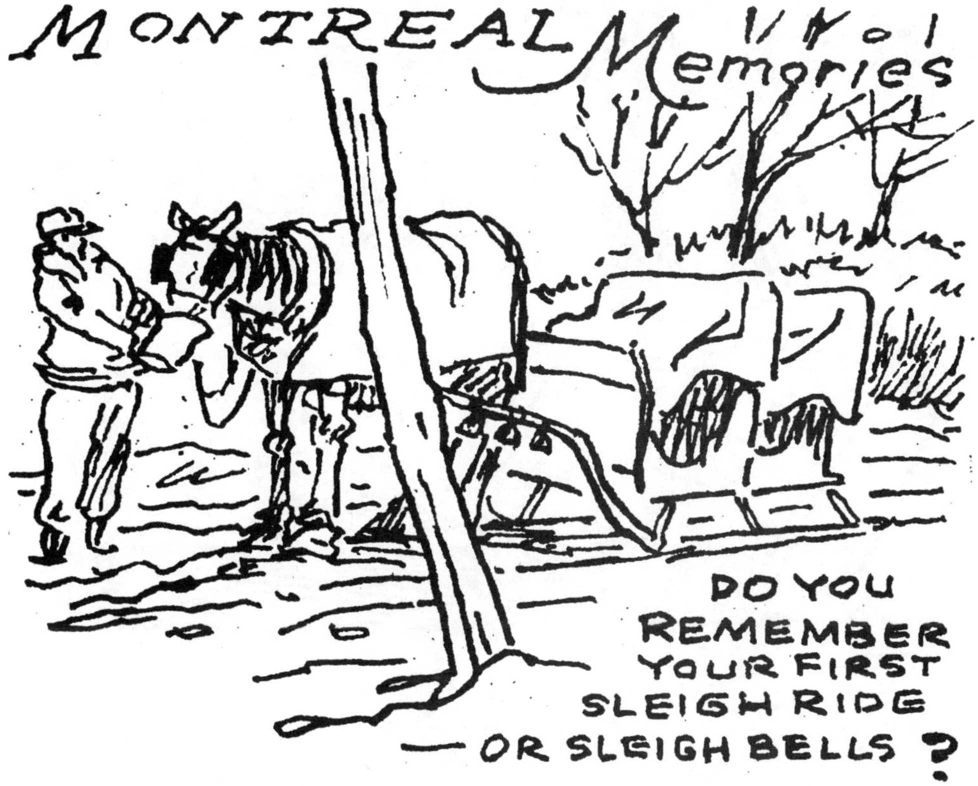
MONTREAL Memories
DO YOU REMEMBER YOUR FIRST SLEIGH RIDE — OR SLEIGH BELLS ?

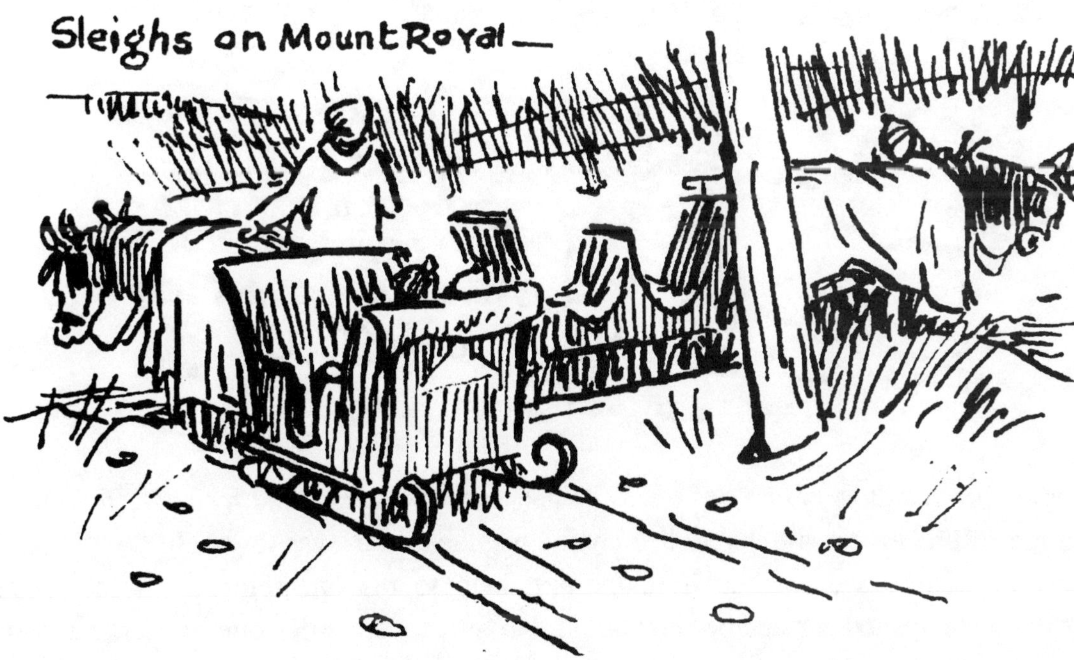
Sleighs on Mount Royal—

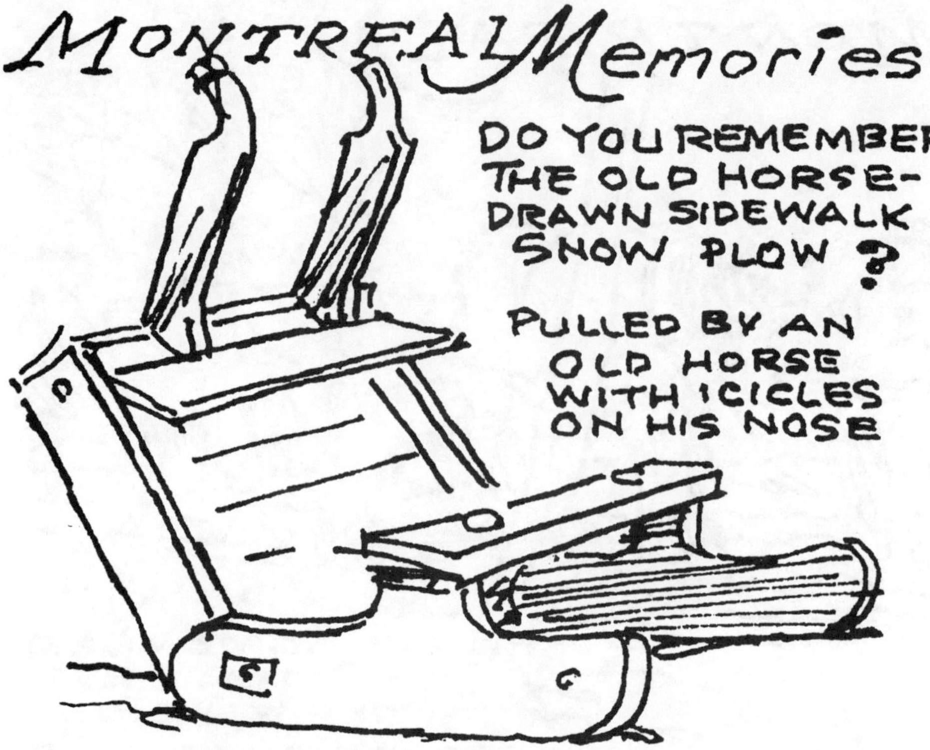


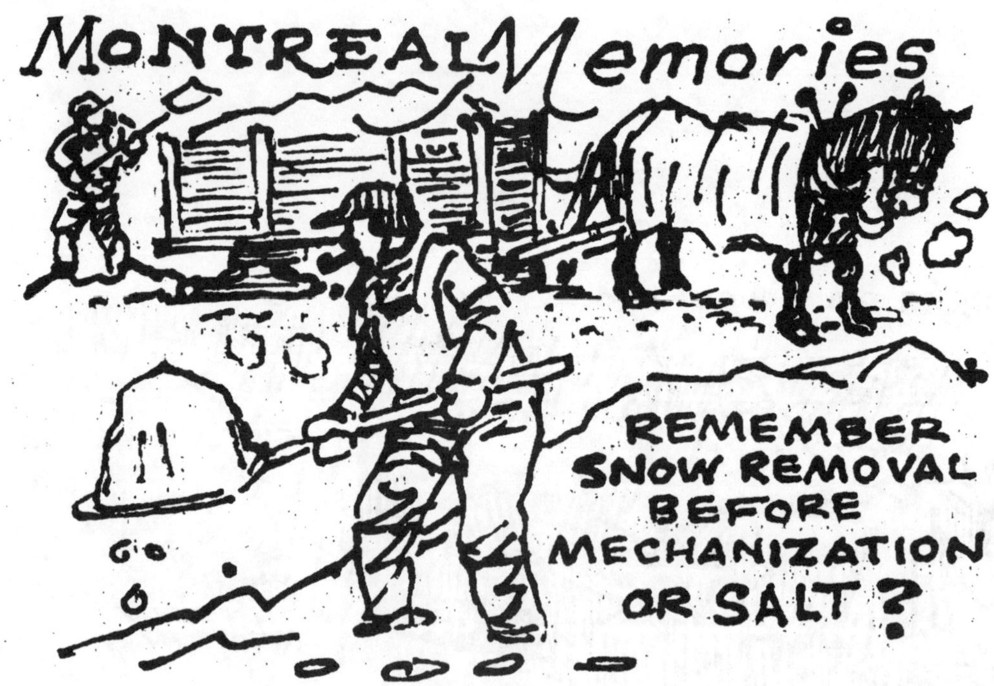


Do you remember the days before road salt? When snow was removed by horse-drawn plows, and the sound of broken cross-links on tire chains was heard all over town? In the "Dirty Thirties," snow-shovel jobs were a big, if temporary, help to the unemployed. Streets were not cleared down to the paved surface because most deliveries were still done by horse and sleigh. No doubt you remember putting the family car up, either on blocks or in a garage, for the winter, and then the ruts in spring, or how the sight of a bit of pavement on a residential street had children begging to go without rubbers or overshoes.

## The GROCERY DELIVERY SLEIGH

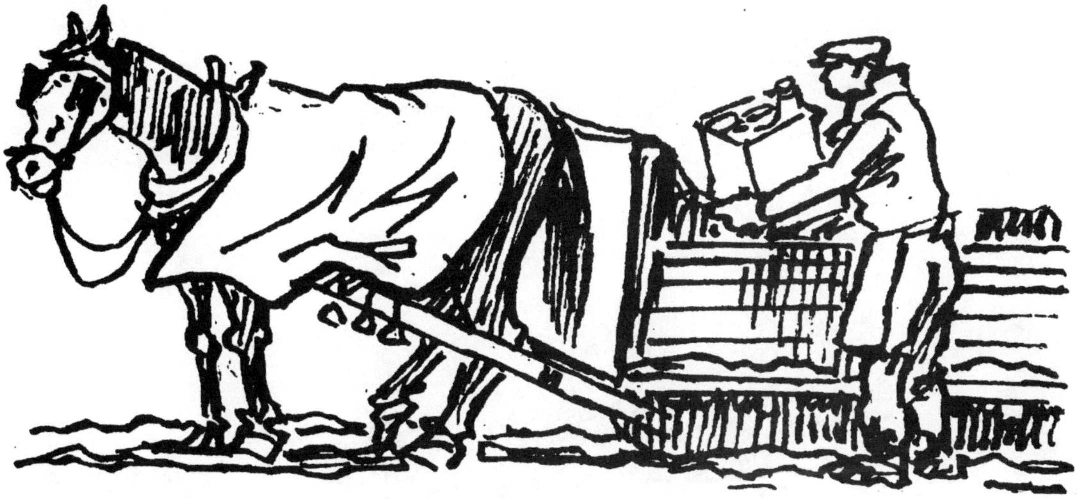

## MONTREAL Memories

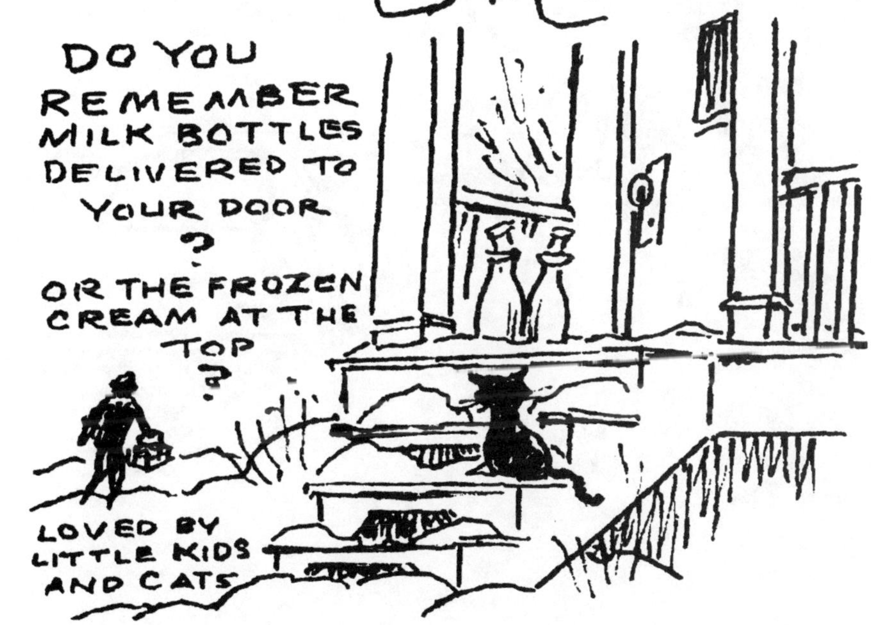


Citizens of a more mature age should remember horse-drawn deliveries. Do you remember the milkman, bread man, or the delivery sleigh from the corner store? The city left a covering of snow on the streets so sleighs could operate and little boys could play street hockey. Before trucks, all companies used horses. There were big ones to pull beer wagons and smaller ones for home delivery. The pets of school children, those horses knew the routes as well as the deliverymen.

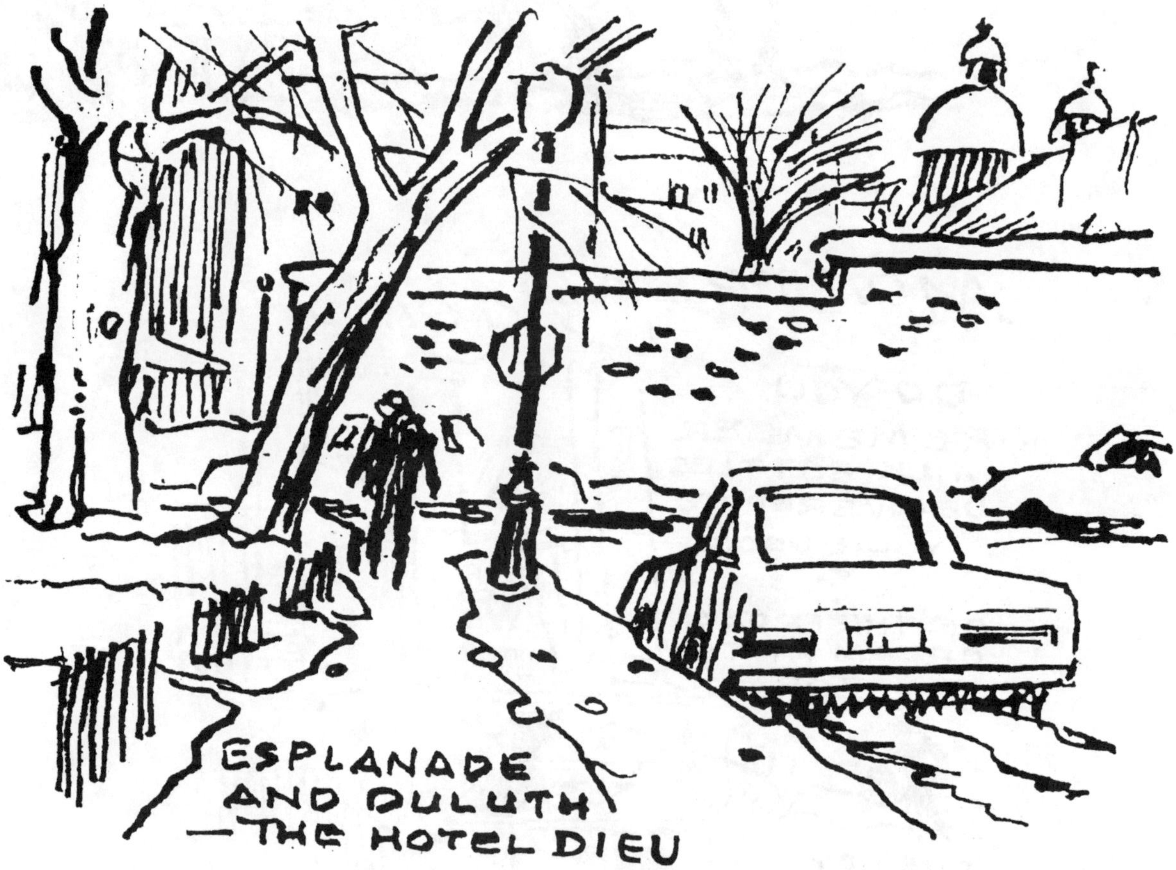
ESPLANADE
AND DULUTH
— THE HOTEL DIEU

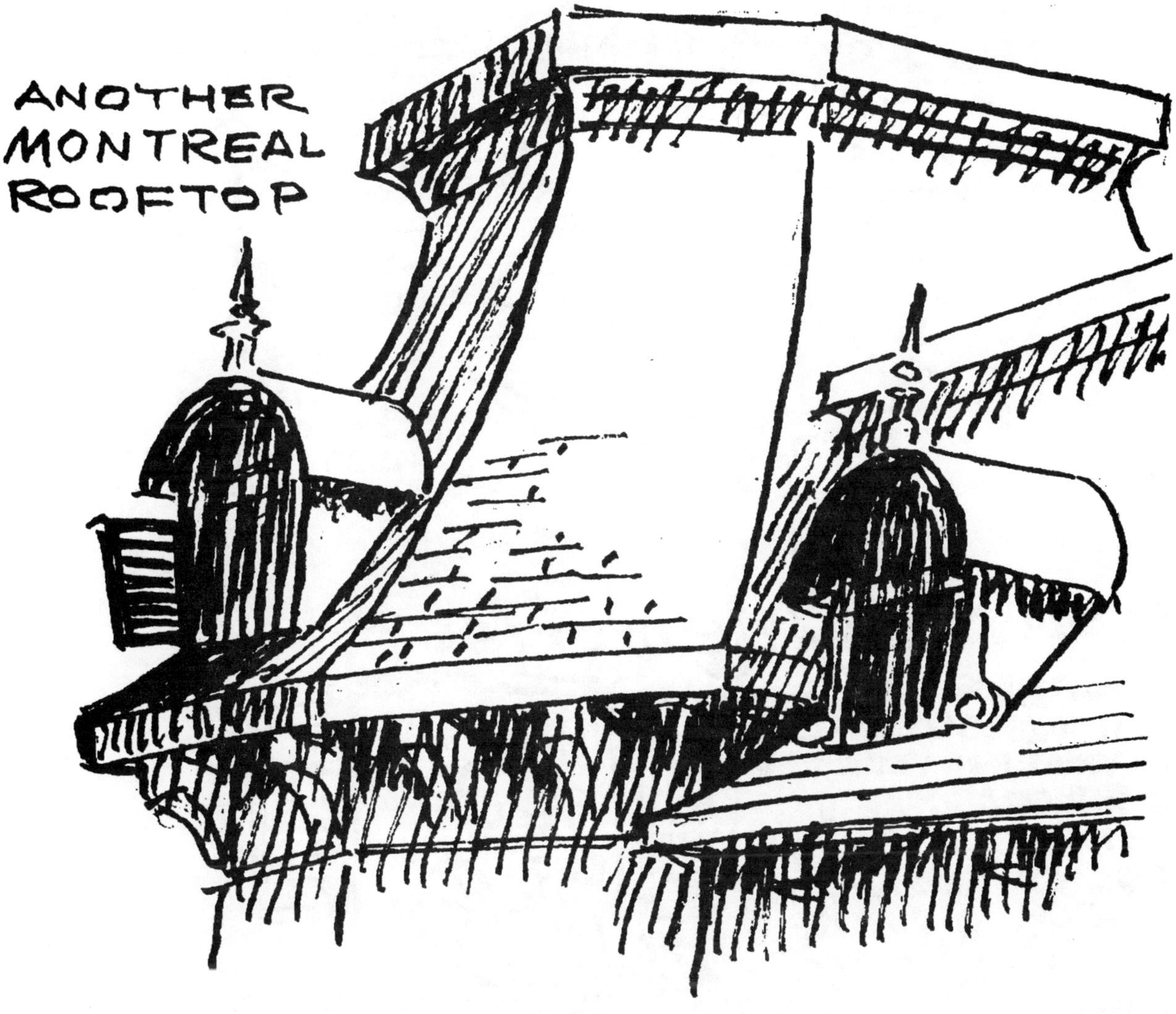


Montreal boasts a wide selection of architectural styles. Builders have used gray limestone, red Scottish sandstone, brick, wood, and now glass walls. Roofs are peaked, mansard or flat - all great snow catchers and icicle producers. Do you have any memories of shoveling snow off a rooftop?

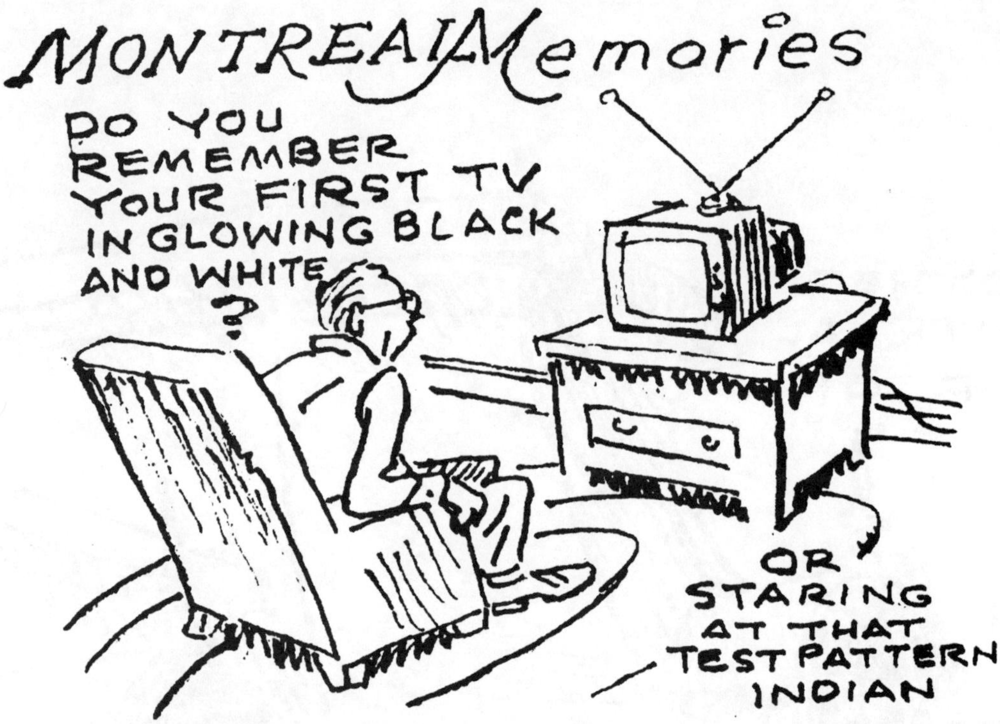


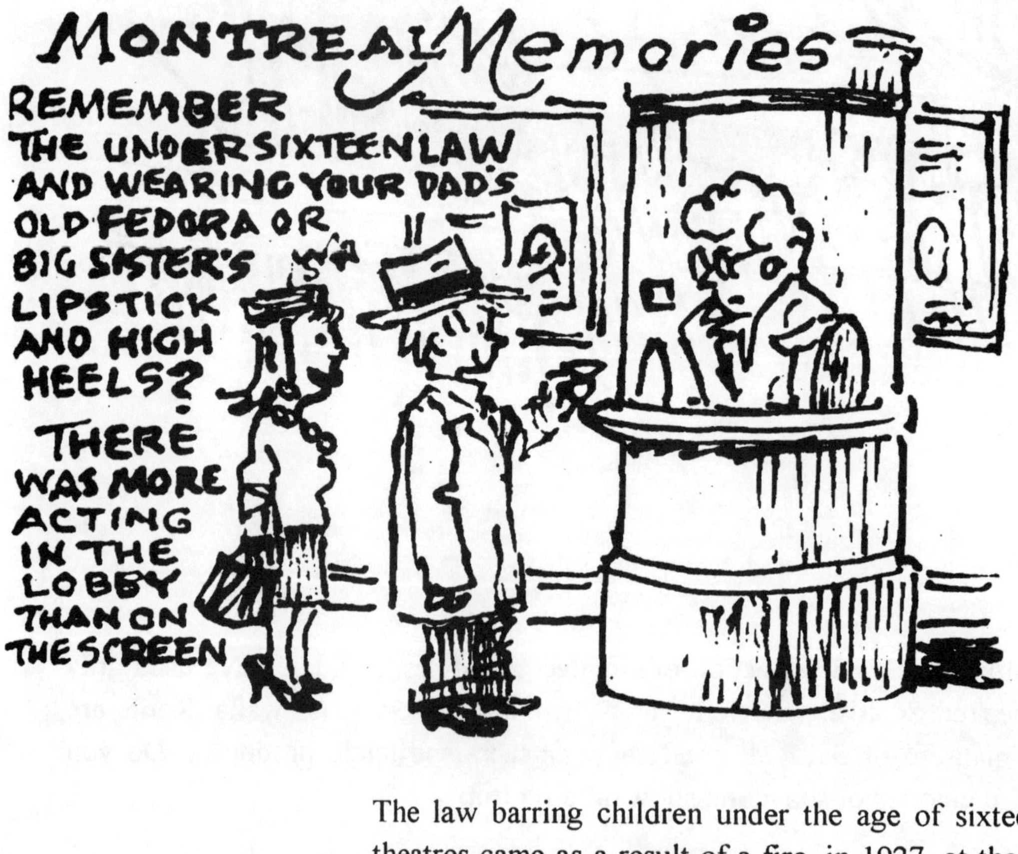


The law barring children under the age of sixteen from movie theatres came as a result of a fire, in 1927, at the Laurier Palace Theatre, which cost the lives of 78 children

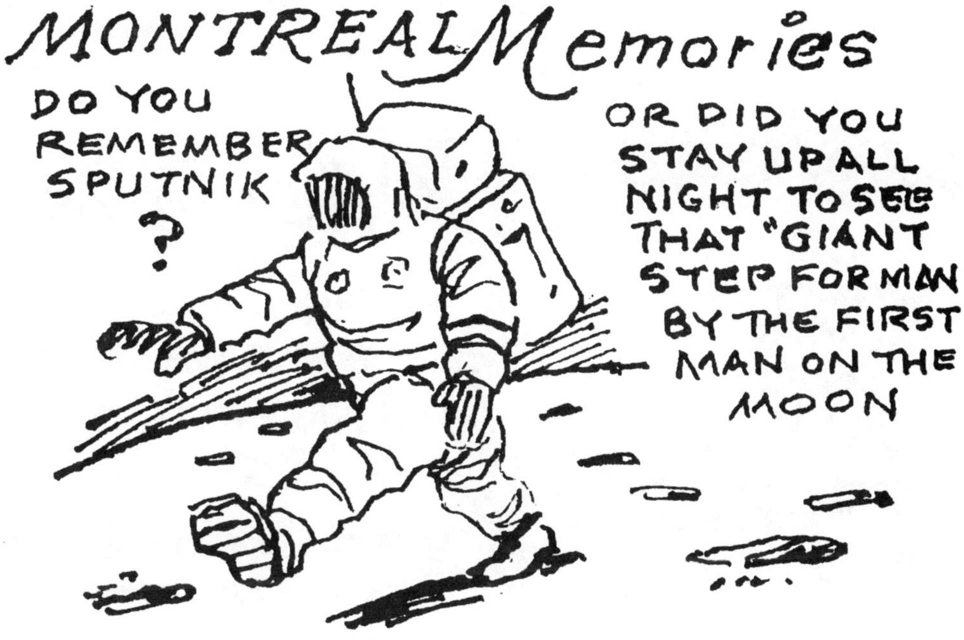
MONTREAL Memories
DO YOU REMEMBER SPUTNIK ?
OR DID YOU STAY UP ALL NIGHT TO SEE THAT "GIANT STEP FOR MAN" BY THE FIRST MAN ON THE MOON

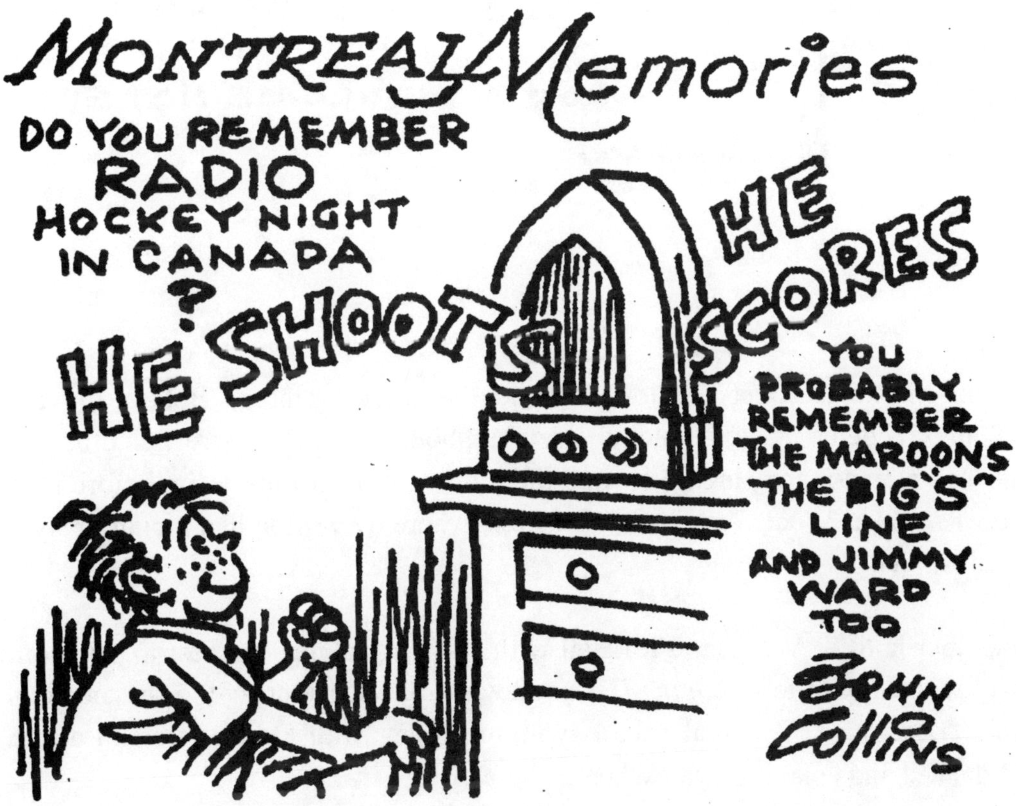
MONTREAL Memories
DO YOU REMEMBER RADIO HOCKEY NIGHT IN CANADA ?
HE SHOOTS
HE SCORES
YOU PROBABLY REMEMBER THE MAROONS "THE BIG 'S'" LINE AND JIMMY WARD TOO
JOHN Collins

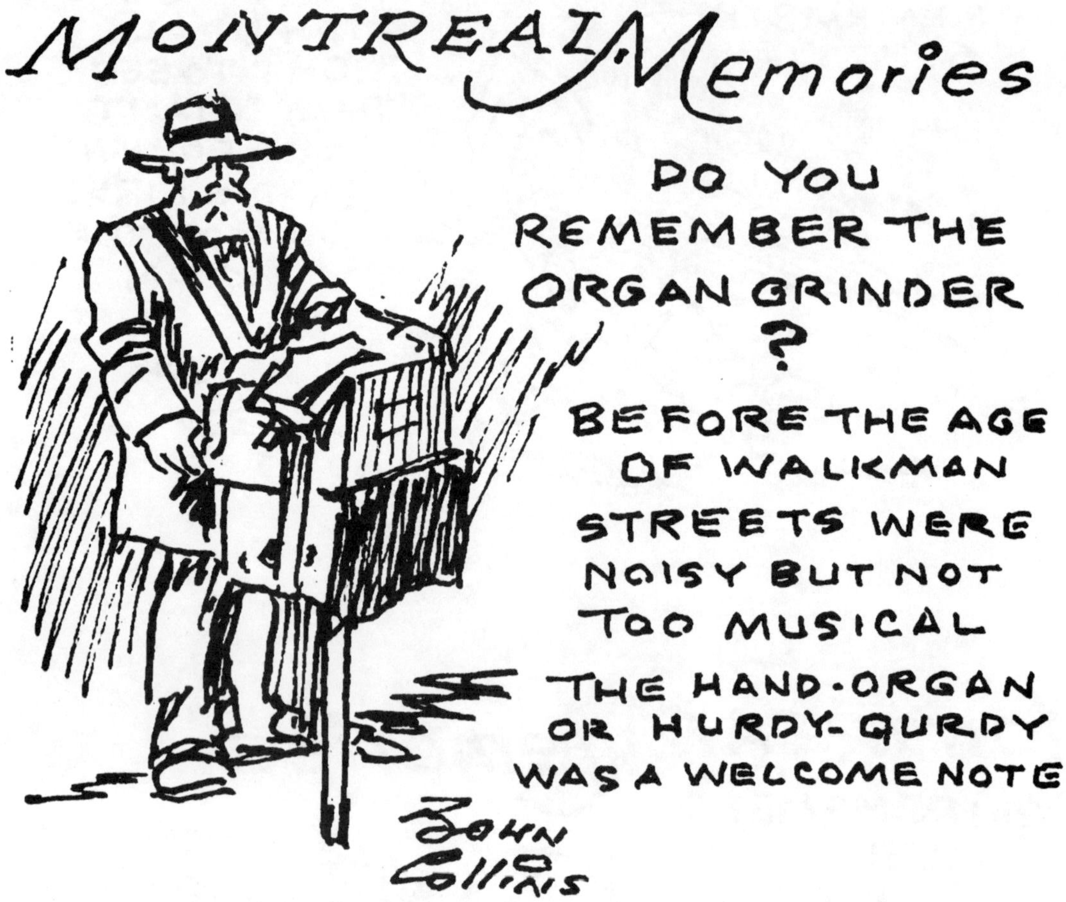


Someone from Montreal streets of long ago is the organ grinder. Before the age of the "Walkman," he provided a musical touch to our neighbourhoods. But there was other music, too. Many homes had a piano, and singing around the piano provided family fun before radio or TV. Sheet music was sold at Woolworth's and Kresge's, where they often had a piano player demonstrating the latest hits.

Do you remember hops at Victoria (Vic) Hall with Johnny Holmes' orchestra? Did some of you sedate elderly women used to jitterbug? Did you swoon at Sinatra or jive to the music of the Big Band sound? Those days, Montreal was a swinging town, with Oscar Peterson at the Alberta Lounge and dance bands playing everywhere.

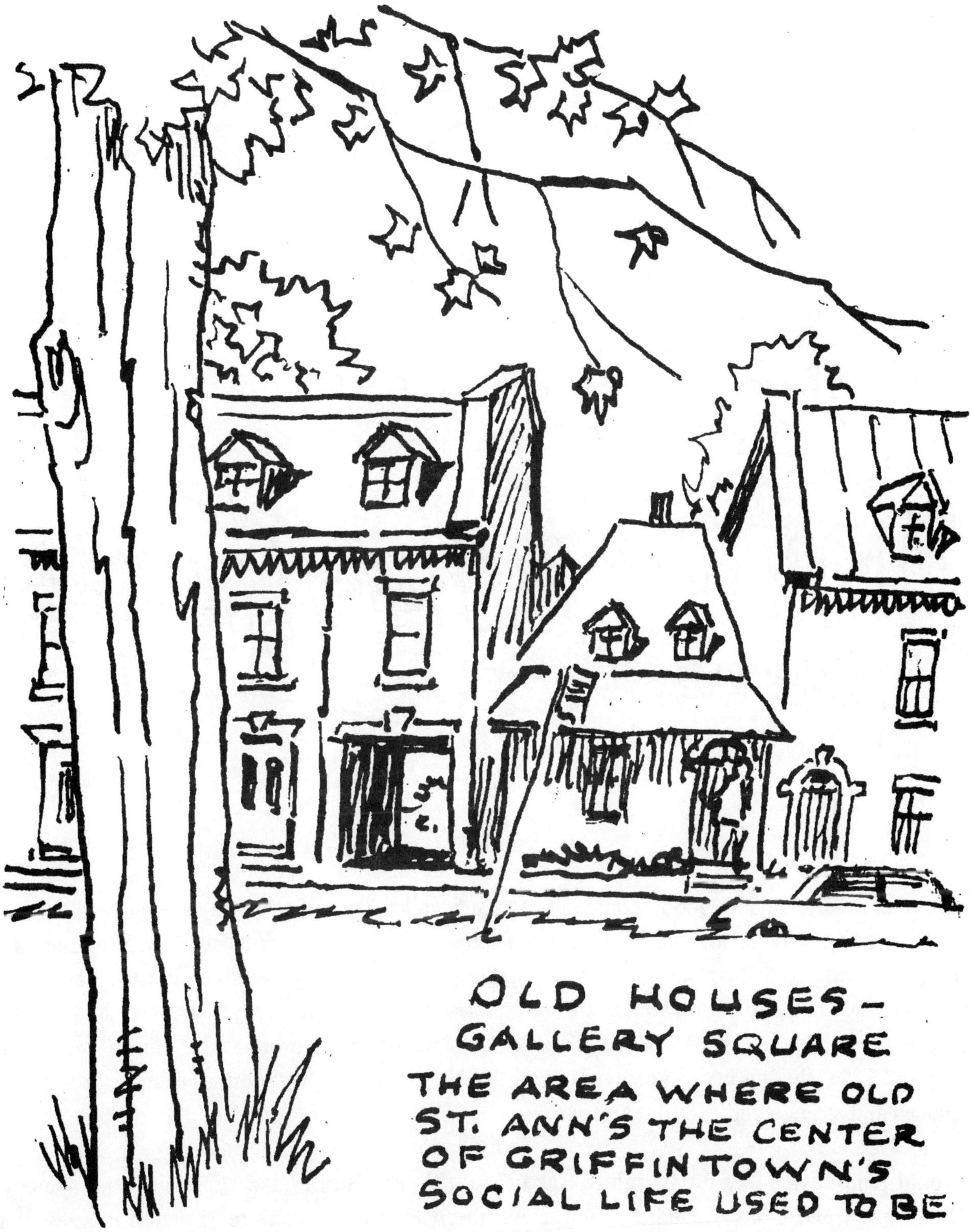
17
OLD HOUSES -
GALLERY SQUARE
THE AREA WHERE OLD
ST. ANN'S THE CENTER
OF GRIFFINTOWN'S
SOCIAL LIFE USED TO BE

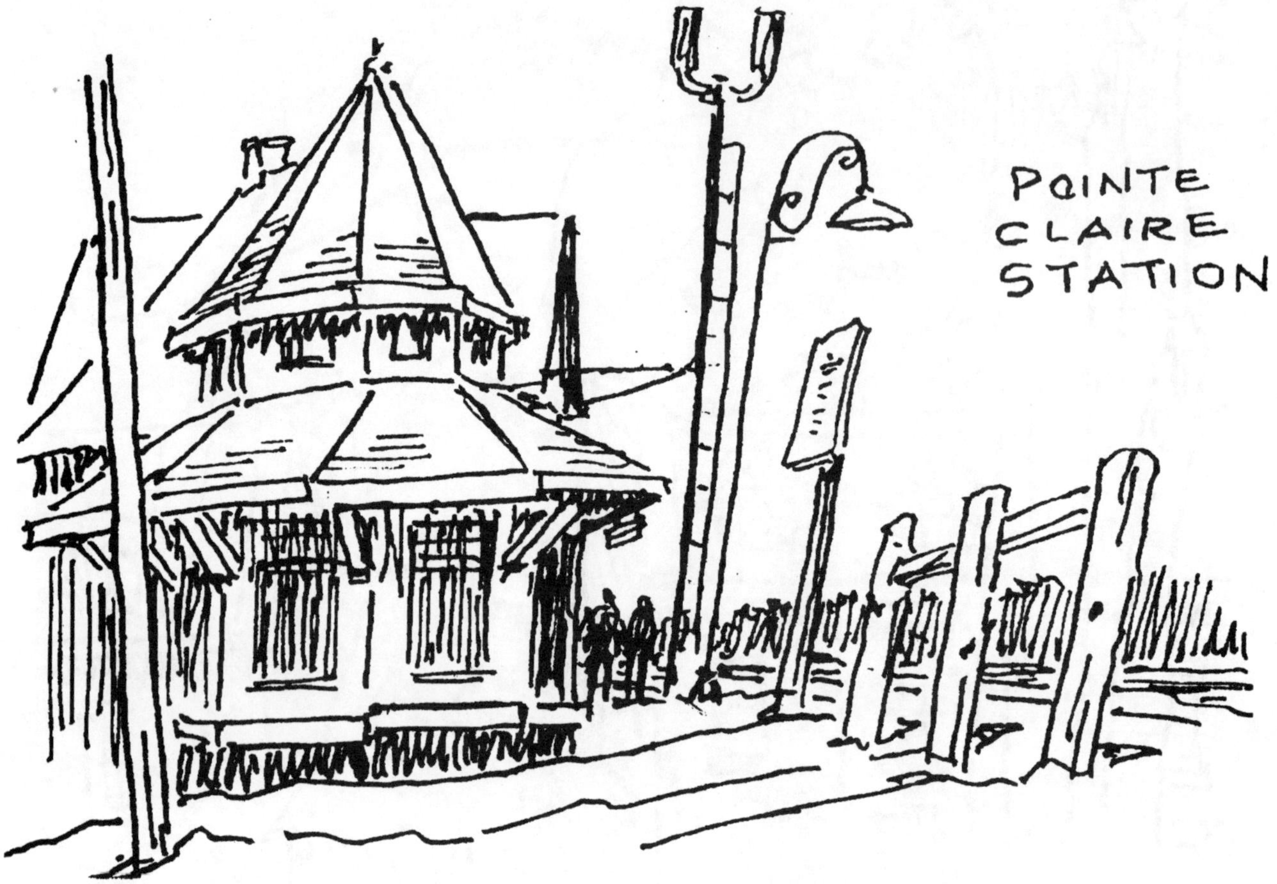


Lakeshore commuters had a good opportunity to study railroad activity while waiting for their trains - the CNR and CPR rails ran side by side. Before the days when air travel made worldwide name-dropping the thing to do, watching trains and hearing the locomotive whistle was the basis of our dreams of roving and exploring. Names of the railroad painted on the sides of boxcars had a romantic ring to them. Names like Atcheson, Topeko & Santa Fe, Southern Pacific, Union Pacific, The Rock Island Line, the mighty Pennsylvania and the New York Central conjured up visions of faraway places and strange and exciting regions.

You could read names like Pittsburgh & Lake Erie, Illinois Central, and "Chessie," the symbol of the Chesapeake and Ohio. Canadian Pacific, Northern Pacific all conjured up rich images of the daring dreams of ambitious men who opened up a continent. The names of places beyond the horizon spurred imaginations in a way VIA, Amtrak or Conrail cannot. But we still have our memories of standing on the platform and watching the world go by.

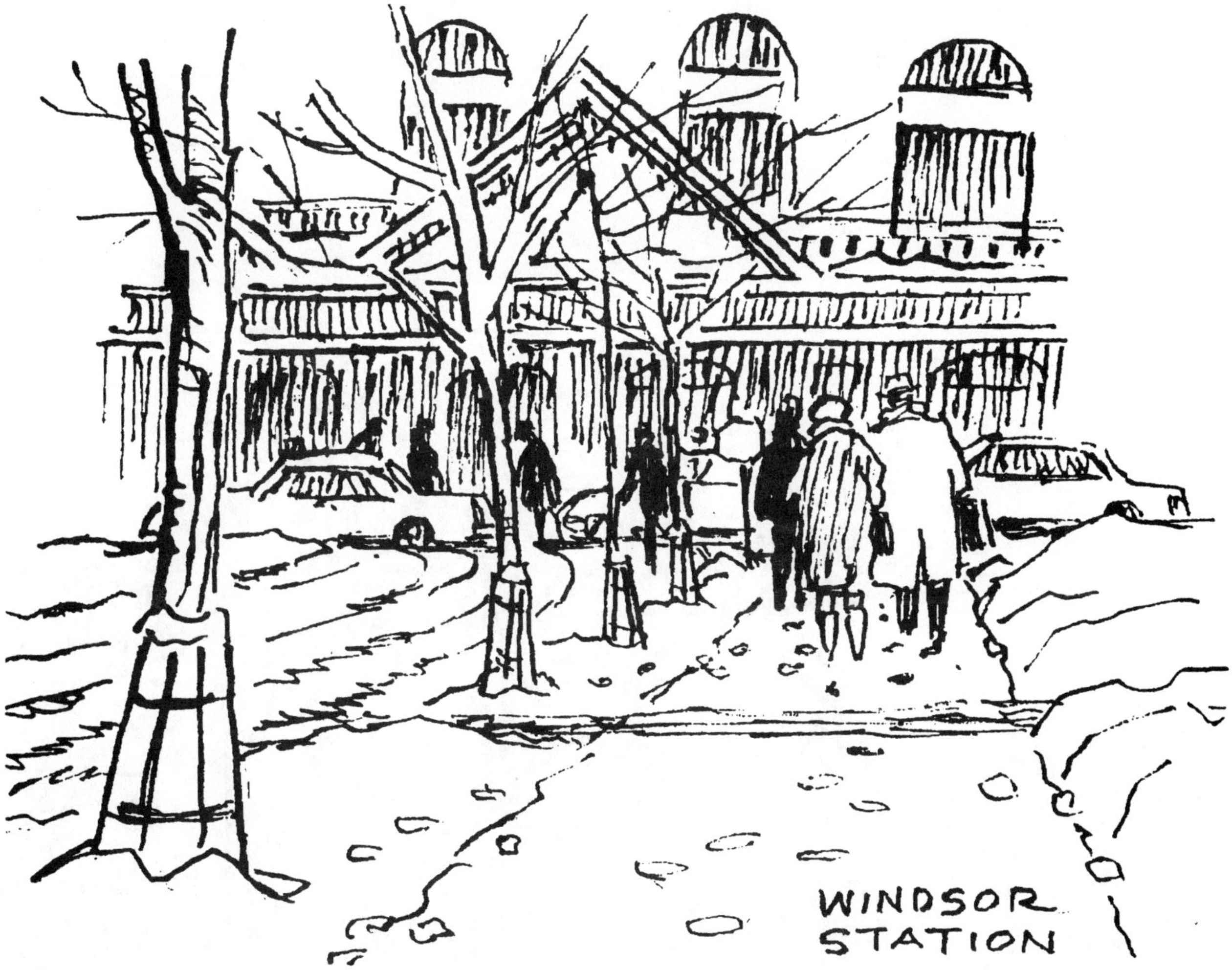
WINDSOR
STATION

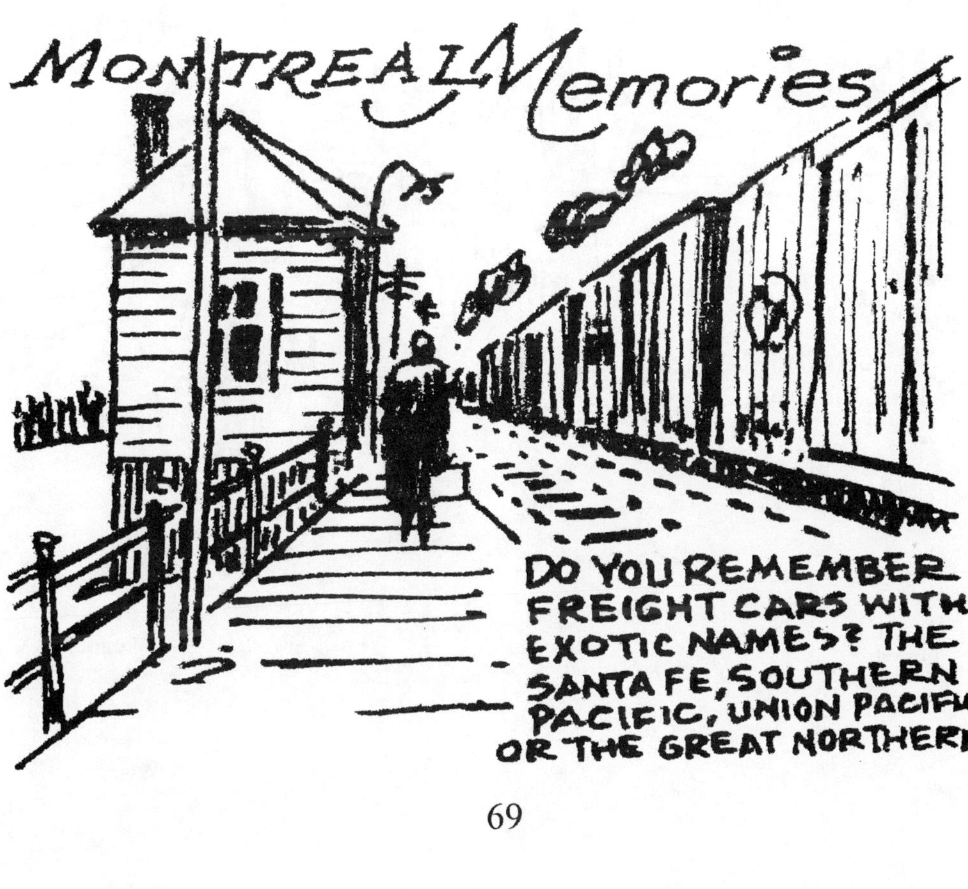
MONTREAL Memories
DO YOU REMEMBER FREIGHT CARS WITH EXOTIC NAMES? THE SANTA FE, SOUTHERN PACIFIC, UNION PACIFIC OR THE GREAT NORTHERN

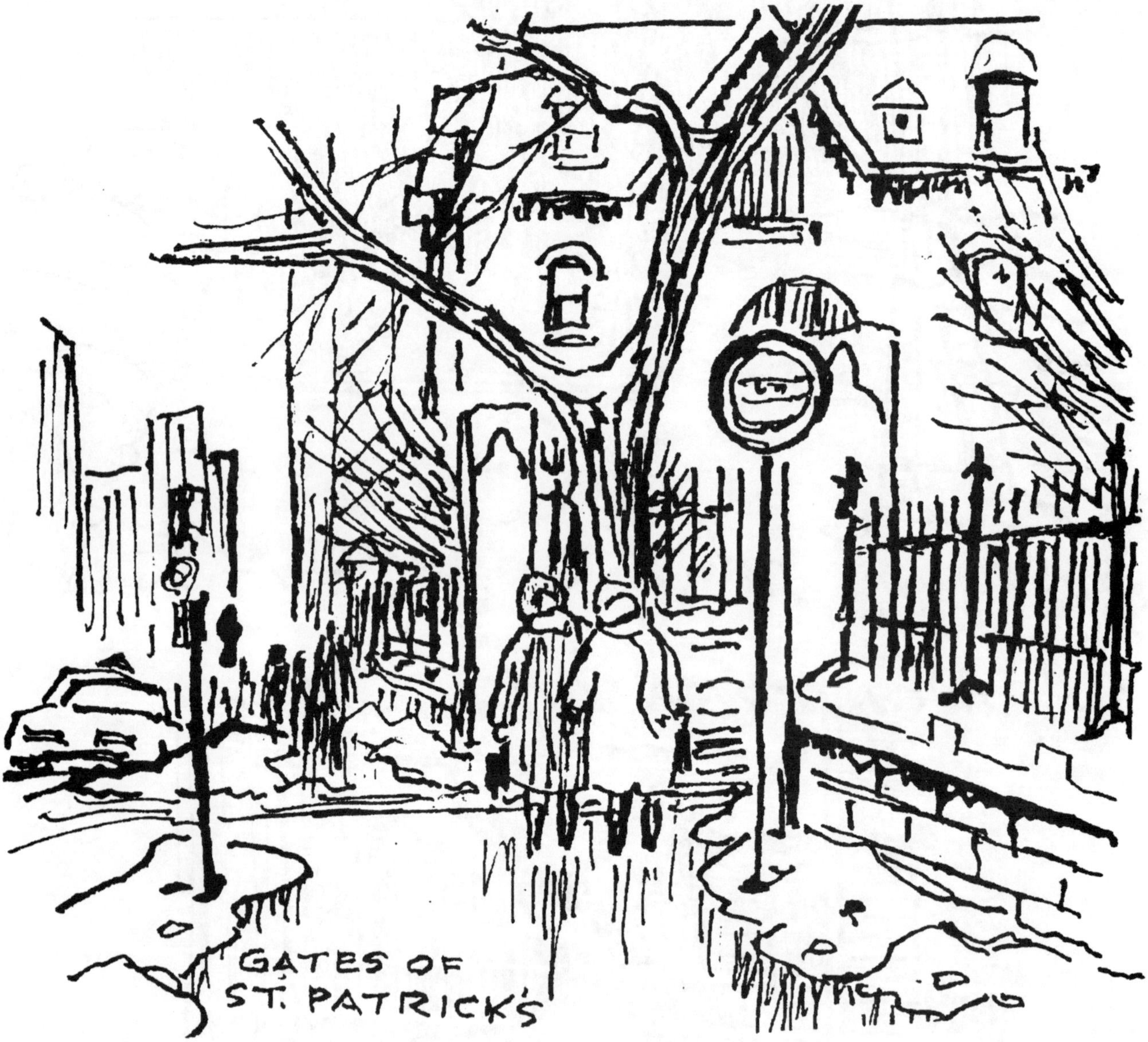
GATES OF
ST. PATRICK'S

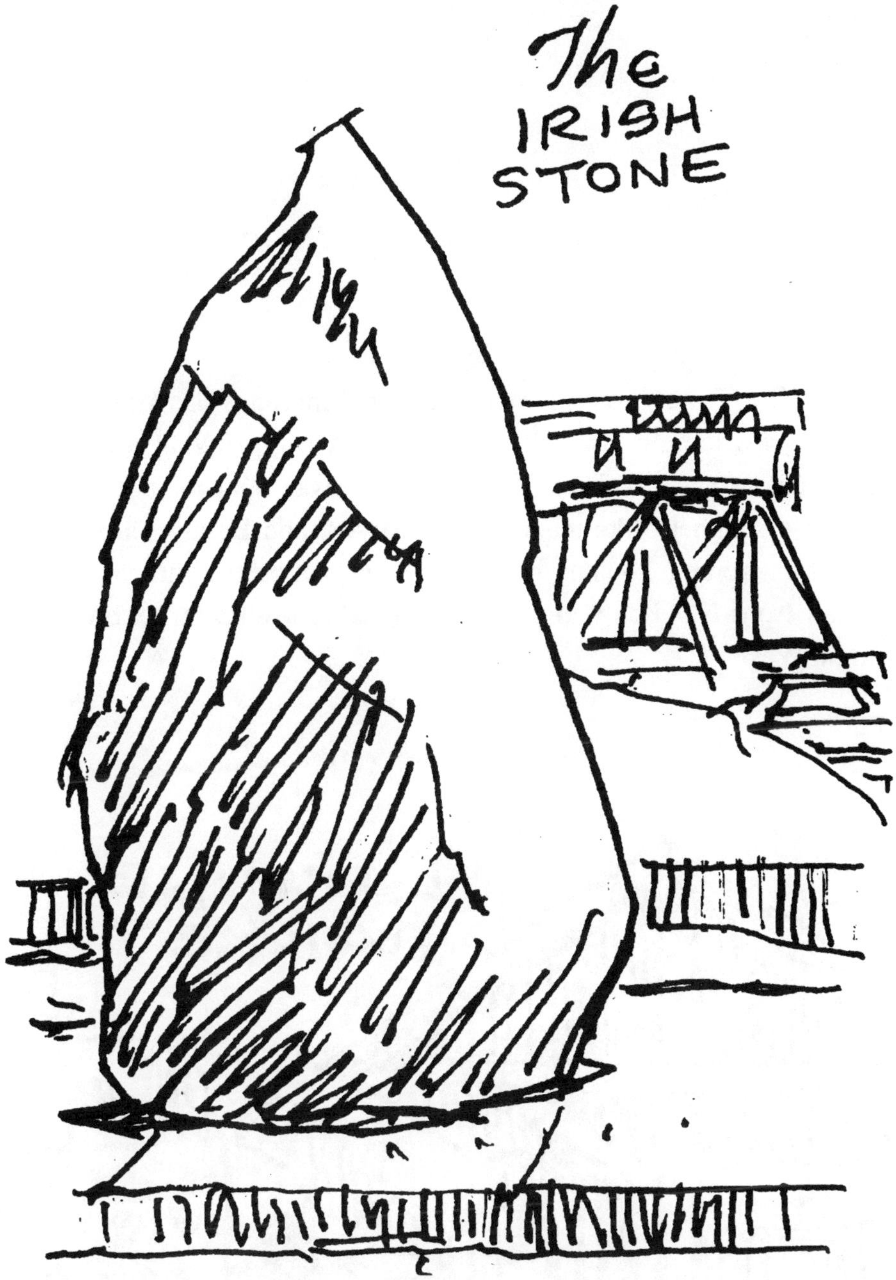


The Irish Stone stands as a grim monument to a grim time. Located at the entrance to the Victoria Bridge - built to provide railway service to the South Shore - the stone recalls the tragedy of these early Irish immigrants. The inscription reads:

TO PRESERVE FROM DESTRUCTION
THE REMAINS OF 6000 IMMIGRANTS
WHO DIED OF SHIP FEVER
A.D. 1847-48

THIS STONE IS ERECTED BY THE WORKMEN OF
MESSERS. PETO, BRASSEY AND BETTS
EMPLOYED IN THE CONSTRUCTION OF THE
VICTORIA BRIDGE
A.D. 1859

You have to be a real "Old Timer" to remember Montreal melons. Grown on Montreal Island, they were famous for their sweetness. A big growing area was Notre Dame de Grâce (NDG), back when Decarie was a farm, not a sunken expressway or a spaghetti-like maze of overpasses, and Benny Farm was really a farm, not a veterans' housing project. On hot summer nights you could feel the cool air from NDG as you passed along Sherbrooke Street on your way to Montreal West.

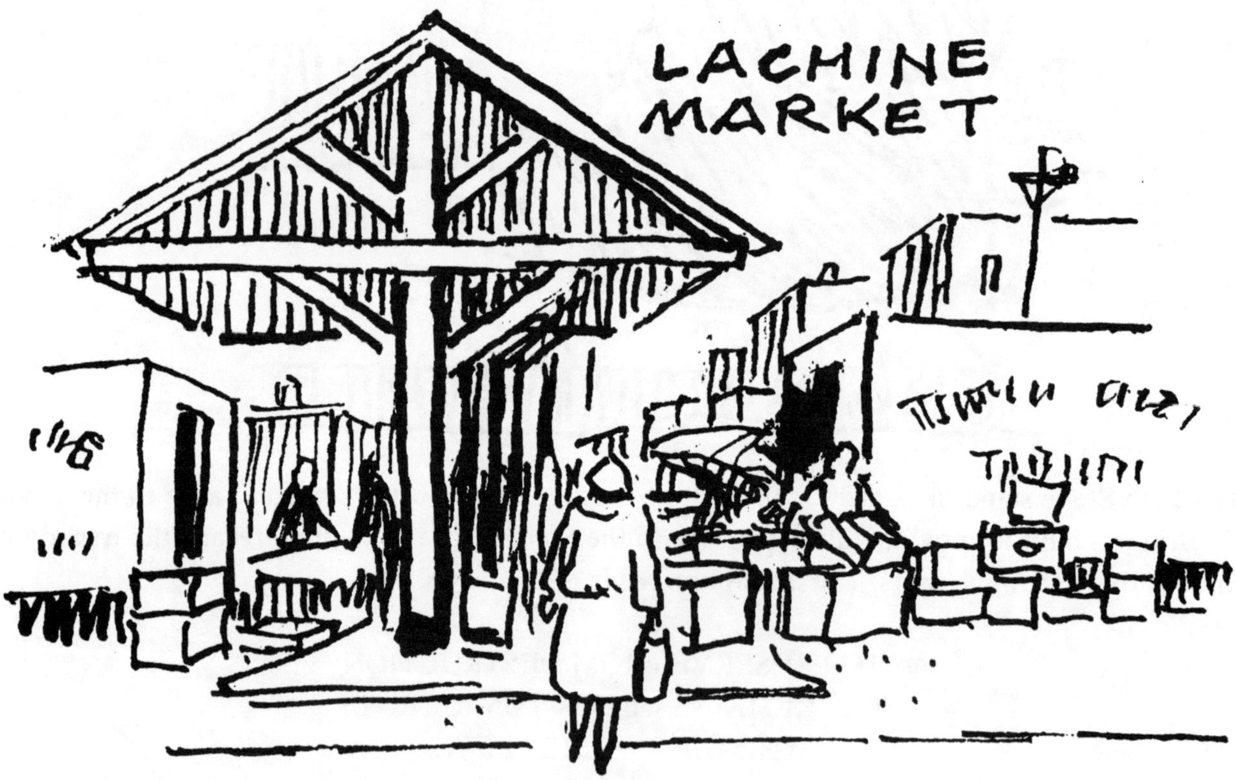

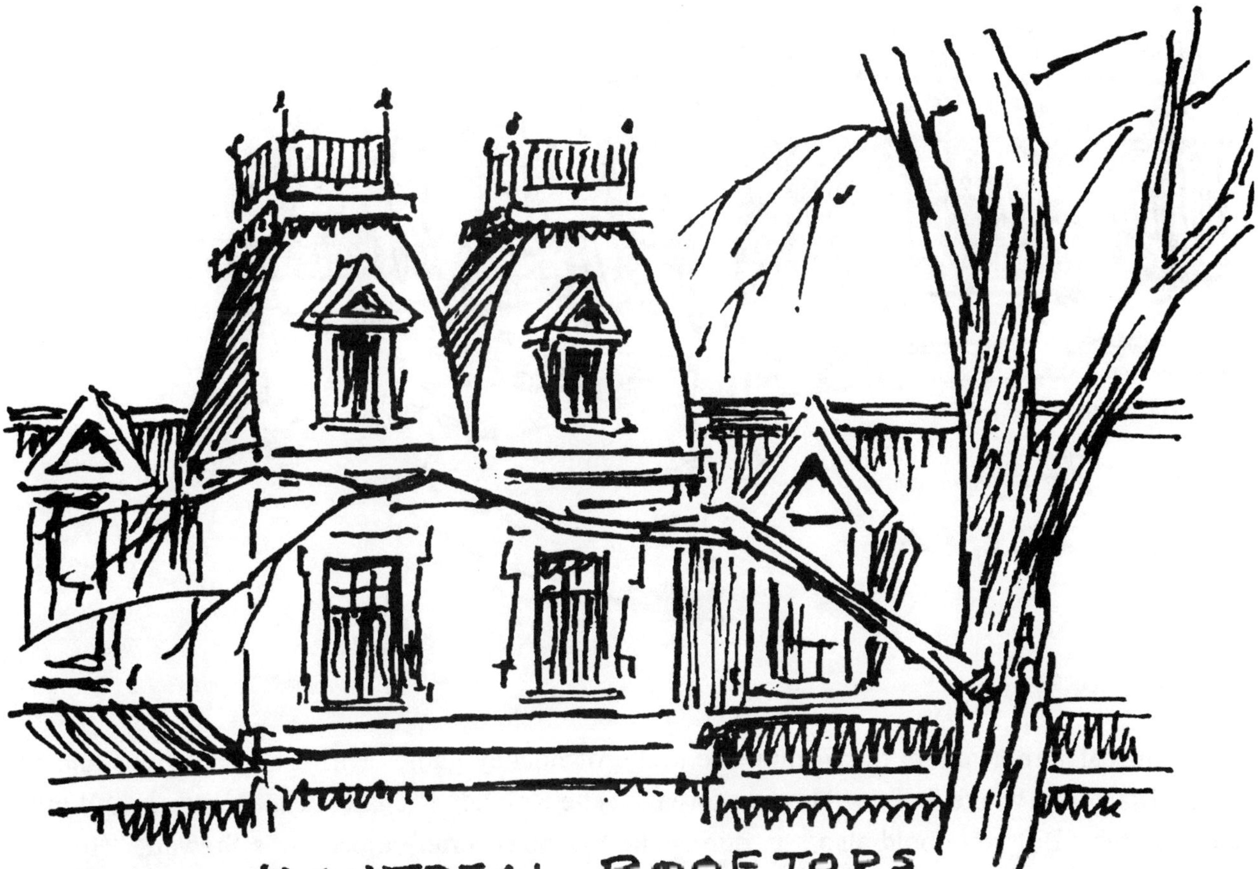

MORE MONTREAL ROOFTOPS

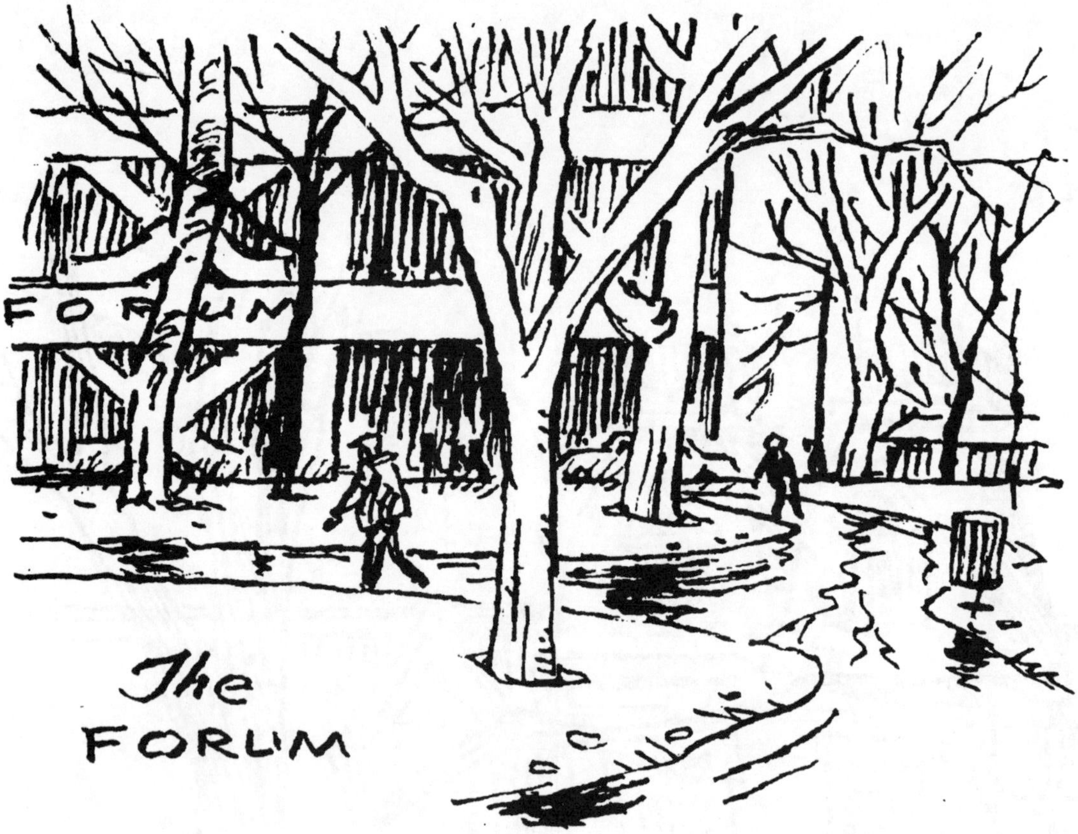


Every Montrealer remembers the Forum: the scene of hockey games with Les Canadiens and the Montreal Maroons, where we saw Howie Morenz, "The Rocket" Richard, Jean Beliveau, and other Canadiens stars. But you could also see, during the Maroons' brief career, Nels Stewart, "Hooley" Smith and "Babe" Siebert, as they, too, won a Stanley Cup. There were also other attractions at the Forum: the circus, wrestling, boxing, and the Six-Day Bike Race. Youngsters listened to the radio where Beehive Golden Corn Syrup promised admission to the bike races for a syrup label. Remember the crowd that jammed the Forum for the funeral of Howie Morenz in 1937?

Montreal has always been a hockey-loving town. But there have been other sports attractions - baseball, football, golf, swimming. We watch today's Expos, but we also watched the old Royals in Delorimier Park. Are you old enough to remember Jimmy Ripple, Bob Seeds or "Rocky" Nelson, those stars of the future that the Brooklyn Dodgers sent here, or Jackie Robinson, who led the Royals to a Little World Series win? And there was Montreal West's "Shag" Shaughnessy, who went from managing the Royals to President of the International Baseball League. Surely you can't have forgotten the Alouettes' glory days with Hal Patterson, Sam Etcheverry, and the coaching of "Pea Head" Walker, or do you still wince at remembering the Hunsinger Grey Cup fumble?

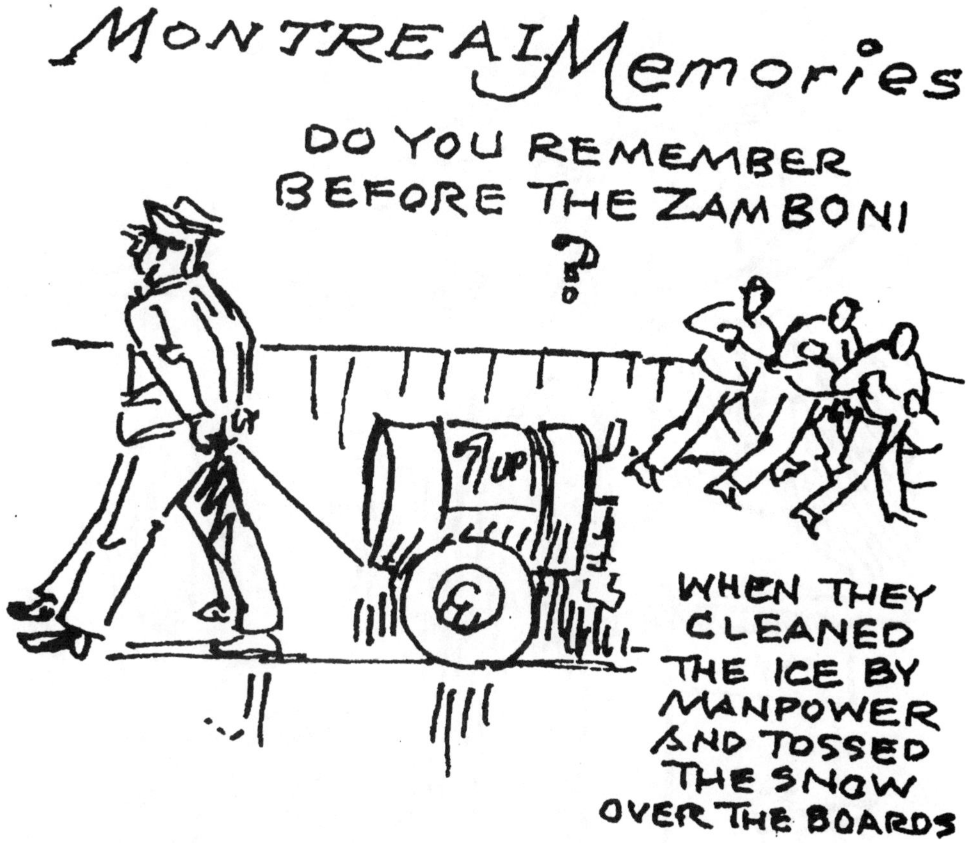
MONTREAL Memories
DO YOU REMEMBER
BEFORE THE ZAMBONI
?
7UP
WHEN THEY
CLEANED
THE ICE BY
MANPOWER
AND TOSSED
THE SNOW
OVER THE BOARDS

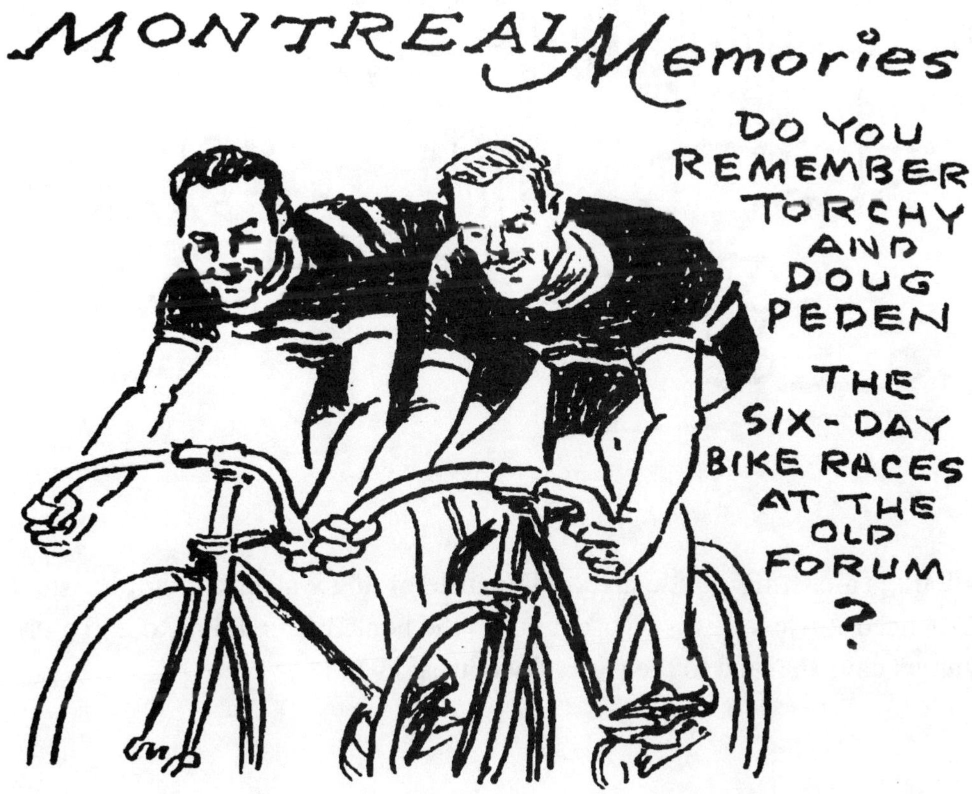
MONTREAL Memories
DO YOU
REMEMBER
TORCHY
AND
DOUG
PEDEN
THE
SIX-DAY
BIKE RACES
AT THE
OLD
FORUM
?

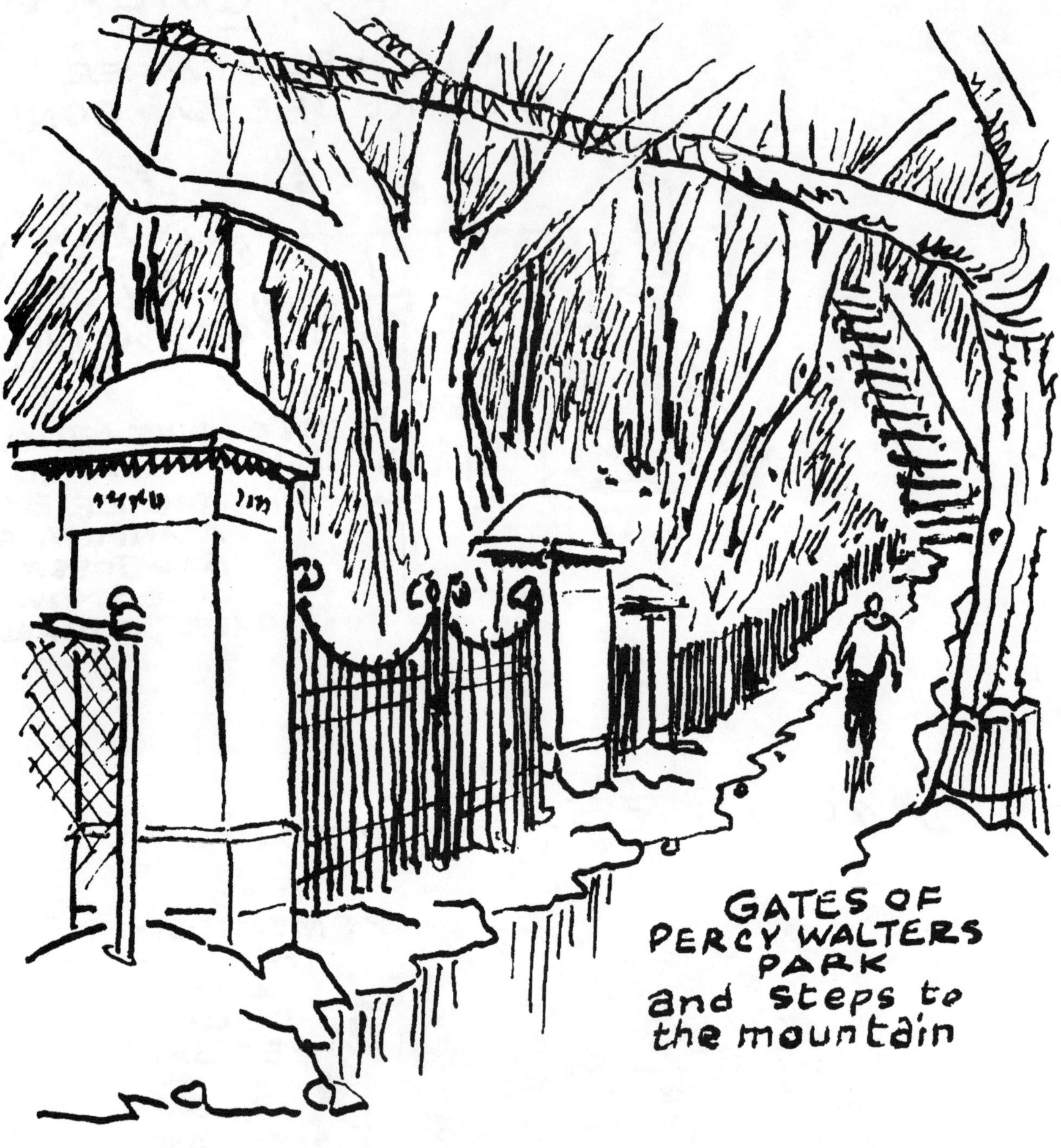


Percy Walters Park is a charming little area, a favourite of dog walkers. It still boasts the gates and fences that surrounded it when it was "Rosemount," the home of Sir John Rose. To preserve it as a park, Percy Walters gave the land to the City of Montreal in 1943.

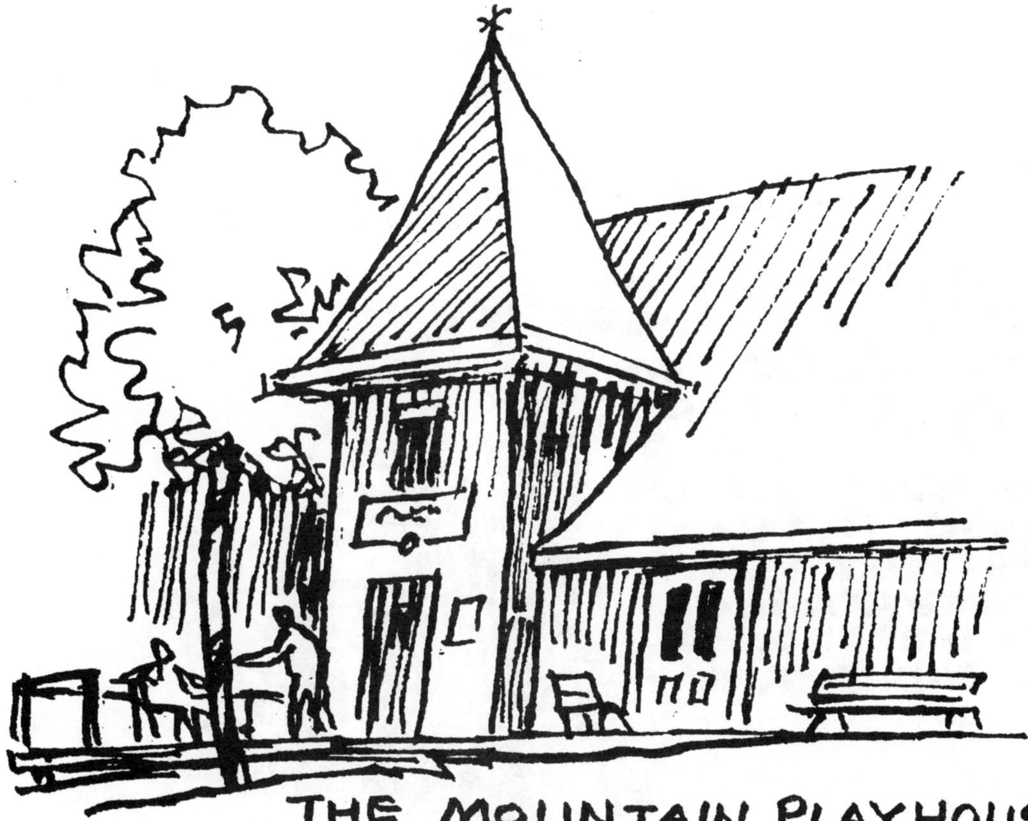


The Mountain Playhouse is long gone from Mount Royal - just a memory to many of us. Do you remember when it was the clubhouse of the Park Toboggan Club? Did you ever go on one of their toboggan rides? Gone with the Mountain Playhouse are many other recreation spots. Let's test your memory a bit.

Do you remember the old Gayety, Lili St. Cyr or "Peaches"? Maybe the Bellevue Casino rings a bell, or the Mount Royal Hotel's Normandy Roof. How about Chez Maurice or Rockhead's Paradise? There was His Majesty's Theatre, Martha Allan's Montreal Repertory Theatre (MRT), and Vaudeville at Loews Theatre with Red Skelton or Blackstone the Magician. And over the years there was the piano playing of "Mr. Fingers," Billie Eckstein, at the old Strand Theatre.

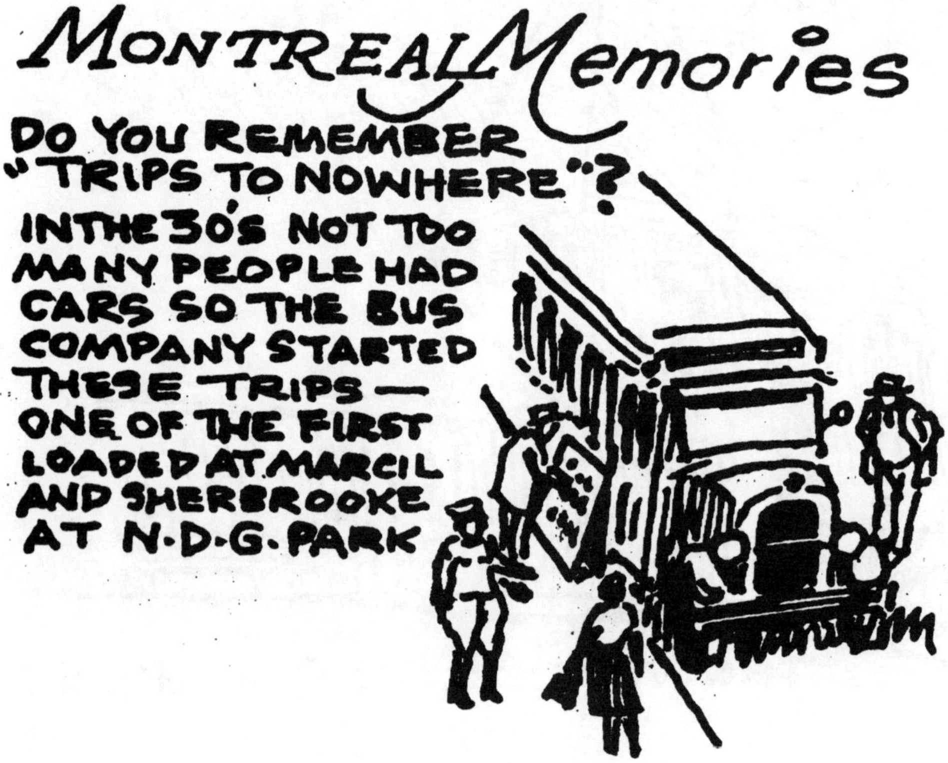


Do you remember "Trips to Nowhere"? These were bus trips, usually on summer evenings, that took you for a ride through the country around Montreal, with a stop at a refreshment stand. In the '30s there weren't too many automobiles about, so people jumped at the chance for a pleasant ride away from the city's heat.

# MONTREAL Memories

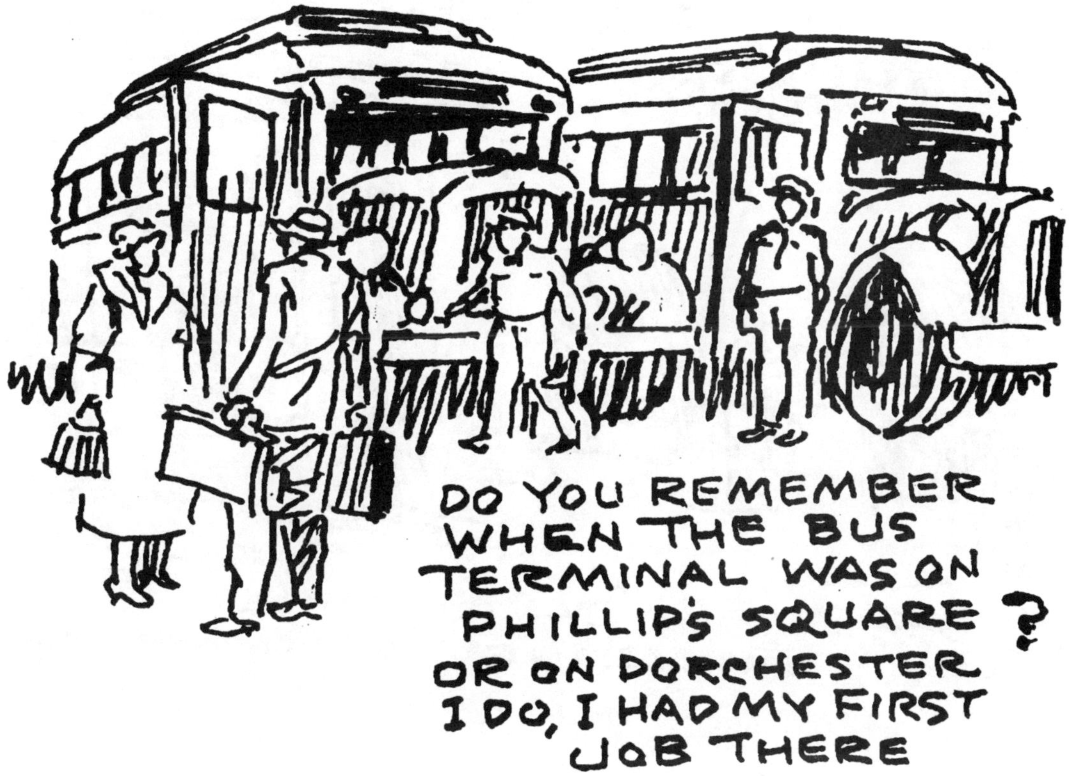


The terminal for inter-urban buses was first on Phillips Square. Then it was moved to Dorchester between Drummond and Stanley Streets before its present location on Berri. Many Montrealers visited New York City in the '30s: it was *the* place. Radio programs featured roadway bands and doings. There were local newspaper columns about the city: *The Gazette* had a "Lights and Shadows of Manhattan" column by Lionel Shapiro

So people headed for New York on buses with engines in the front and baggage loaded on the roof under a tarpaulin - to be unloaded and reloaded at the border. I remember it well: for four summers I was a teenage "steward" on the New York Express, an extra-fare bus with rest and meal stops. I loaded and unloaded baggage, announced towns we went through, and rounded up passengers at stops. But what better way to get to New York and the Metropolitan Museum, the original Whitney and the Museum of Modern Art.

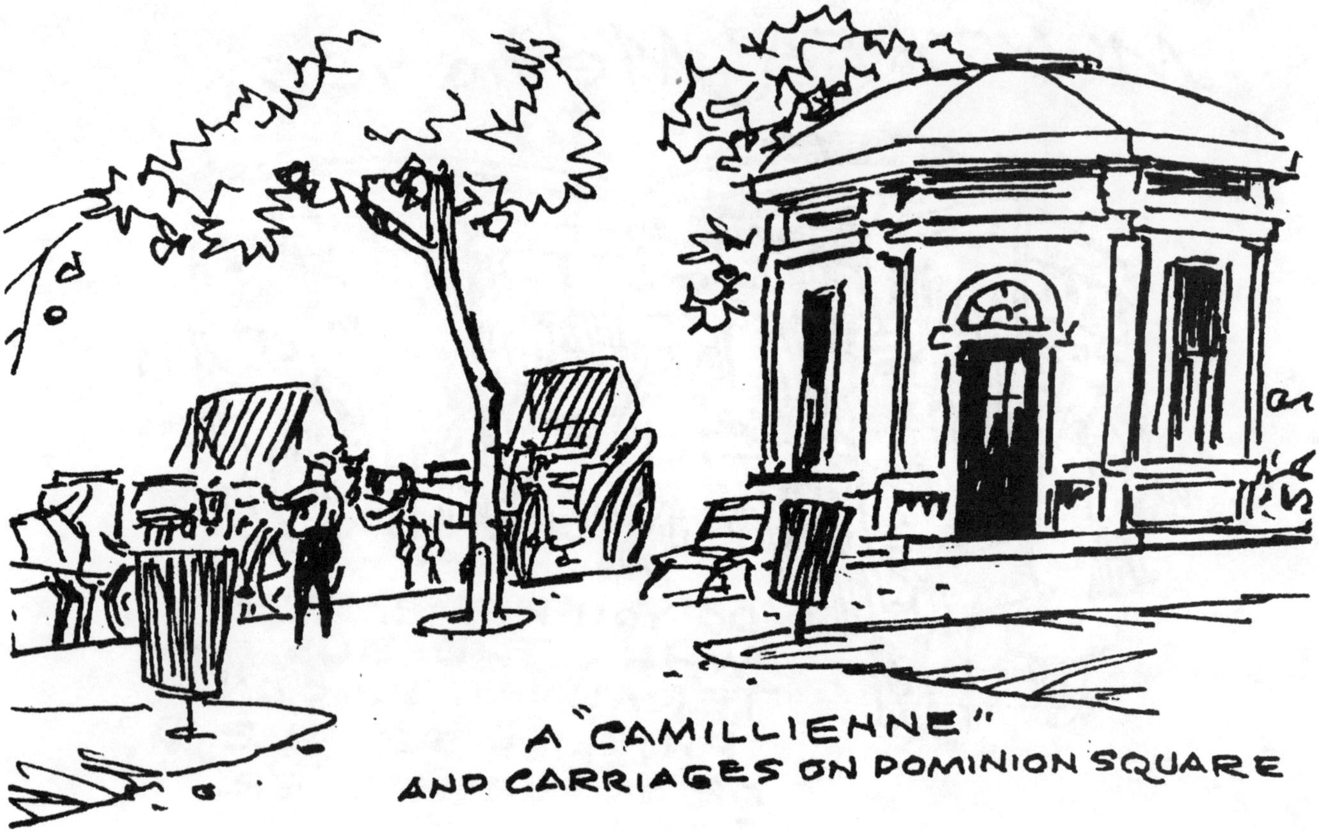

A "CAMILLIENNE"
AND CARRIAGES ON DOMINION SQUARE

The Depression had a big effect on 20th century society. Fathers lost jobs and money was scarce in most households. To combat unemployment, Mayor Camillienne Houde created a public works program, which produced the Chalet on Mount Royal, the Verdun Boardwalk and the "Camilliennes" - public toilets built in city parks. They were very welcome: I remember using the one on Dominion Square when I was hustling sightseeing trips. Now they are used as ice cream stands or for flower sellers.

Once a man came into an art gallery to buy one of my paintings for his daughter. They showed him a painting of a park with one of Mayor Houde's edifices. "I wouldn't give her that," said he, knowing its original purpose. Later, the daughter came in and made her selection. Guess what she chose?!

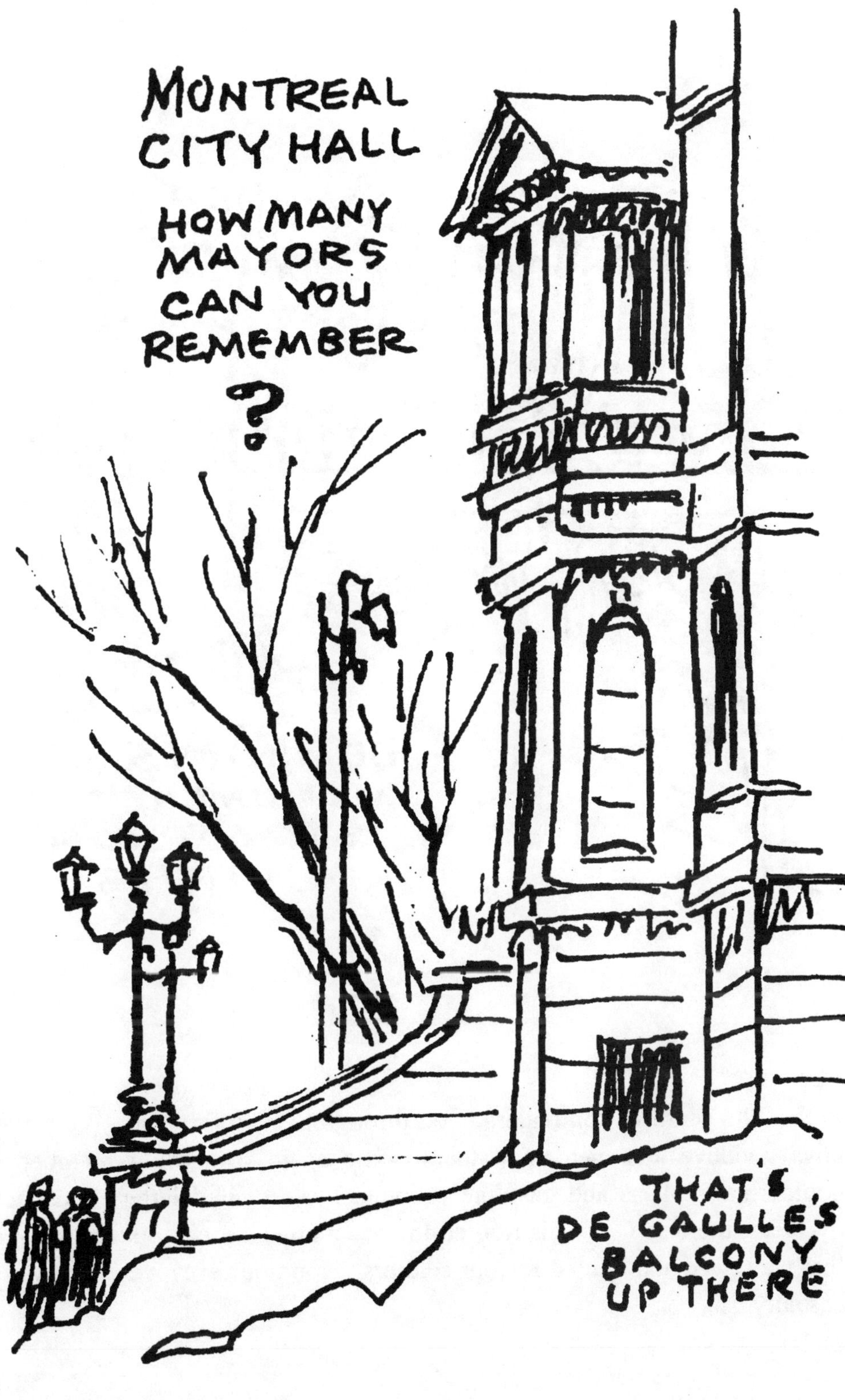
MONTREAL CITY HALL
HOW MANY MAYORS CAN YOU REMEMBER ?
THAT'S DE GAULLE'S BALCONY UP THERE

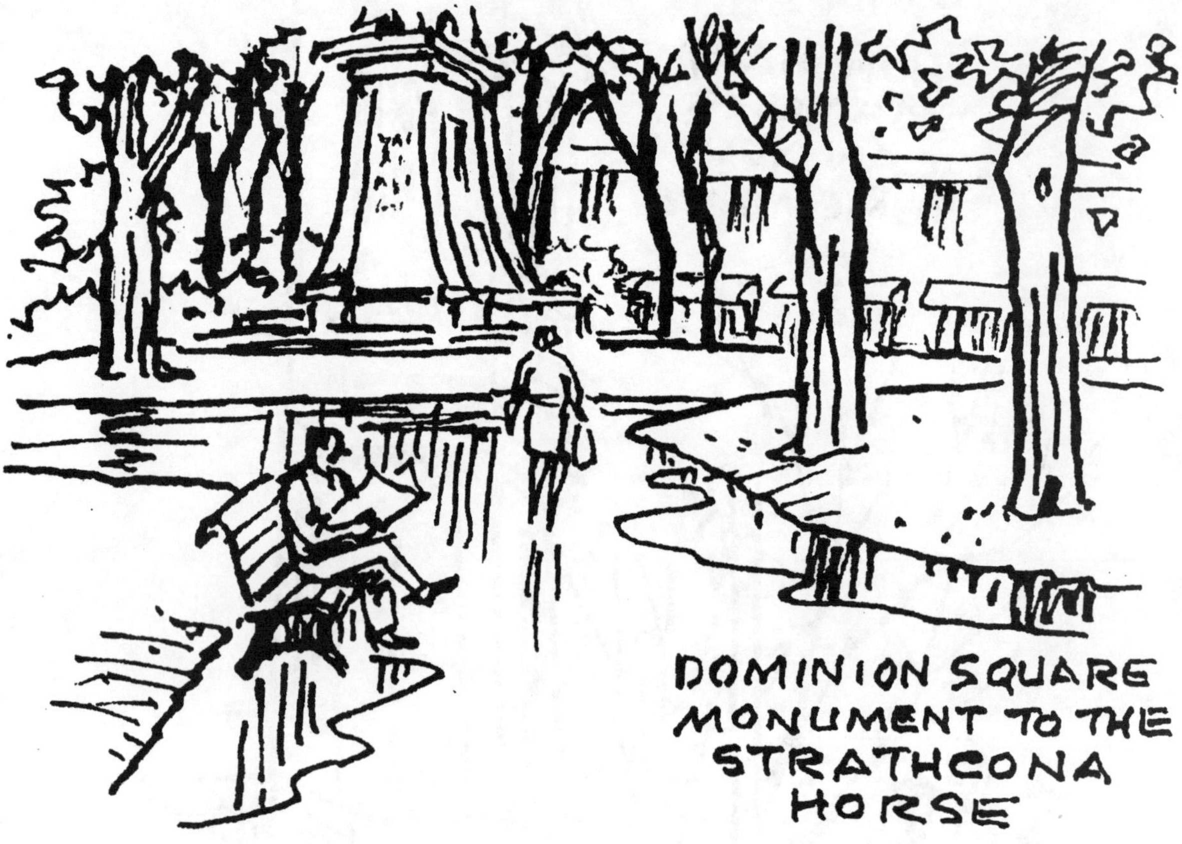


In the 20th century Montrealers lived through two World Wars. We waved the boys goodbye and welcomed them home again. Do you remember ration books, meat tokens and gasoline rationing? We mailed letters and packages overseas, the Red Cross distributed the necessities - socks, tuques, bandages - that we sewed and knitted for our soldiers … and our eyes were always on the casualty lists.

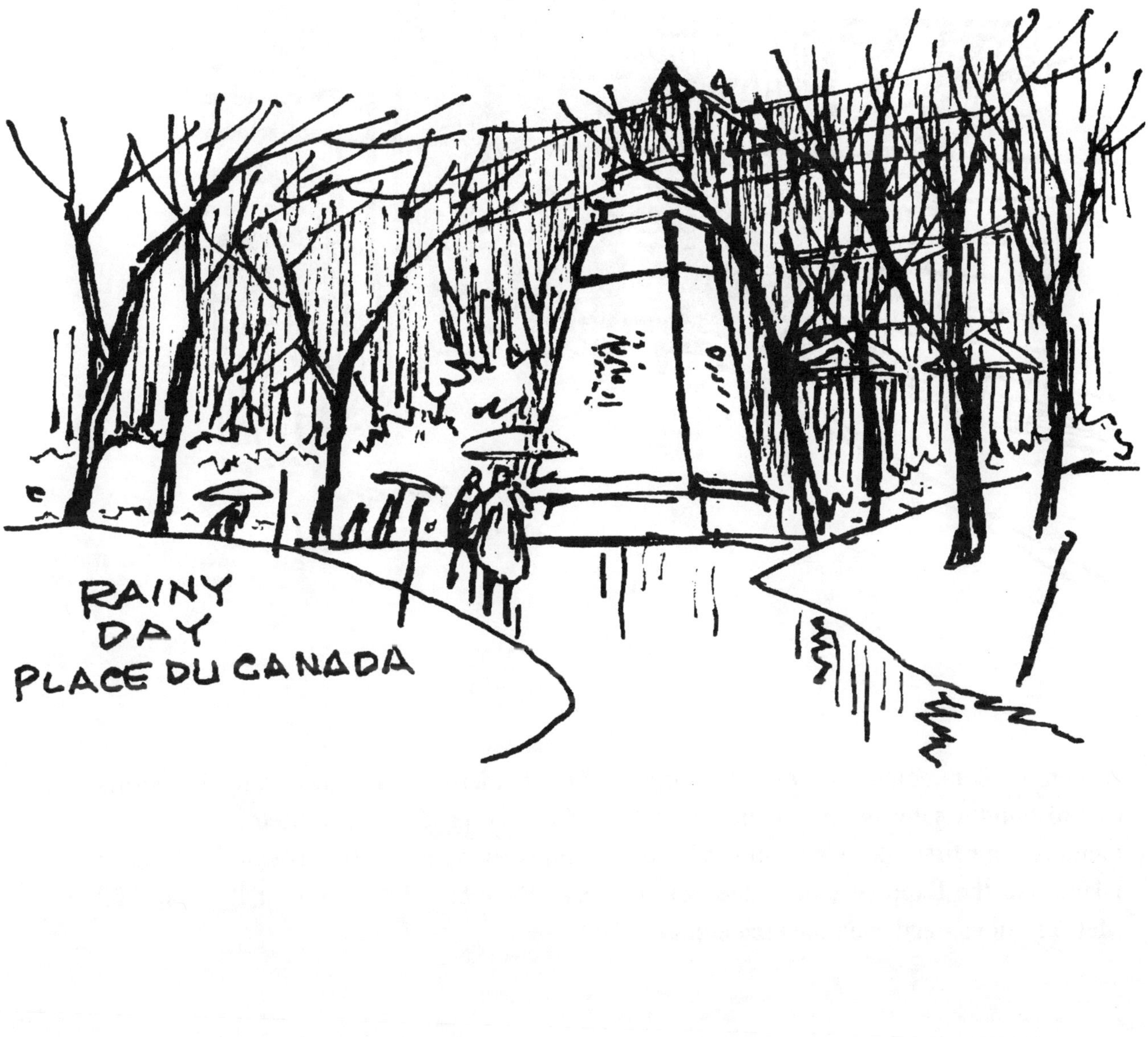
RAINY
DAY
PLACE DU CANADA

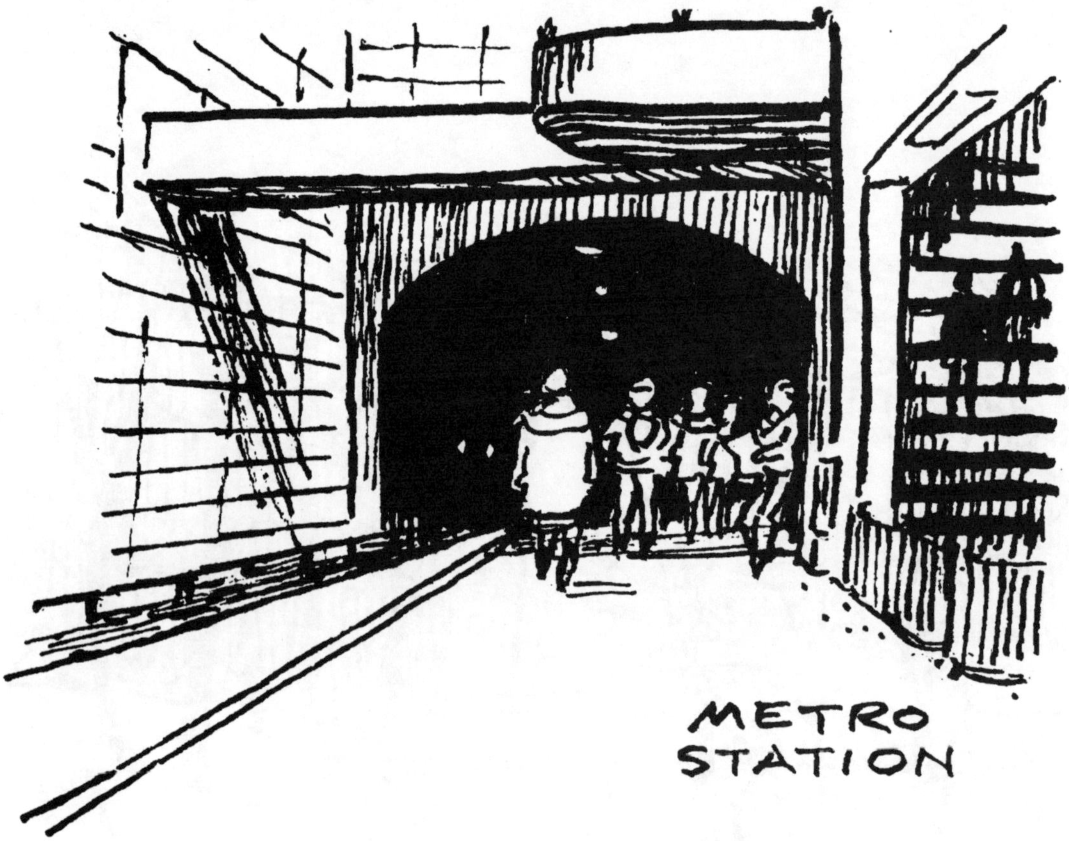


A memory common to many Montrealers is of the numerous mayoralty campaign promises to build a subway. When, finally, Mayor Drapeau produced the Metro, do you remember your first ride? Can you recall your feelings riding under the river to St. Helen's Island and the Expo site, or to the South Shore? How proud we were of the colourful Metro stations - and even the escalators worked.

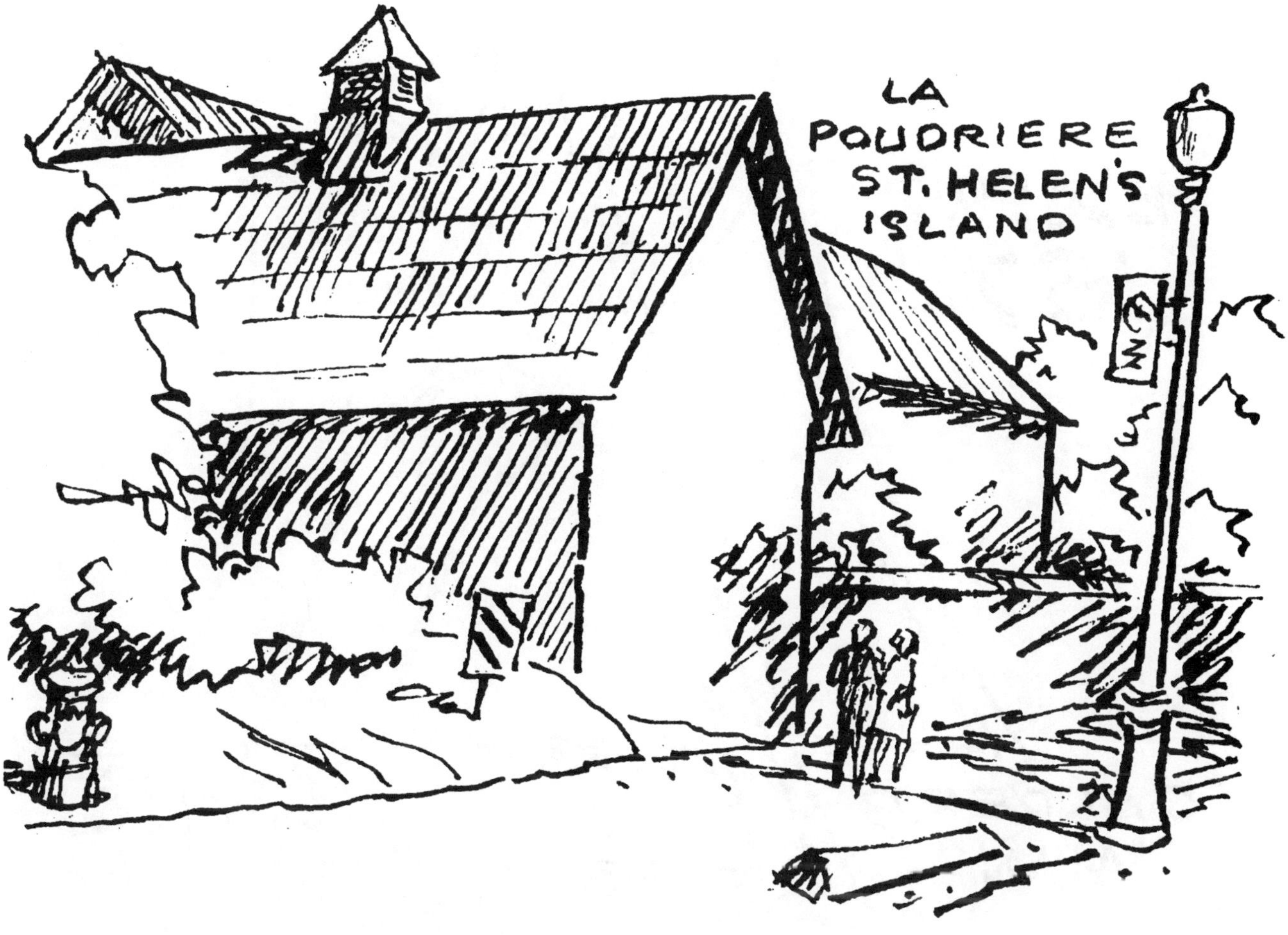


After it ceased to be a garrison for the British troops, the fort on St. Helen's Island was given to the City of Montreal for a park, and became a favourite playground for Montrealers. Maybe you are old enough to remember taking the ferry to the island for Sunday School picnics (before the Jacques Cartier Bridge was built). Later, the powder magazine became for a time La Poudriere, a small theatre among the trees.

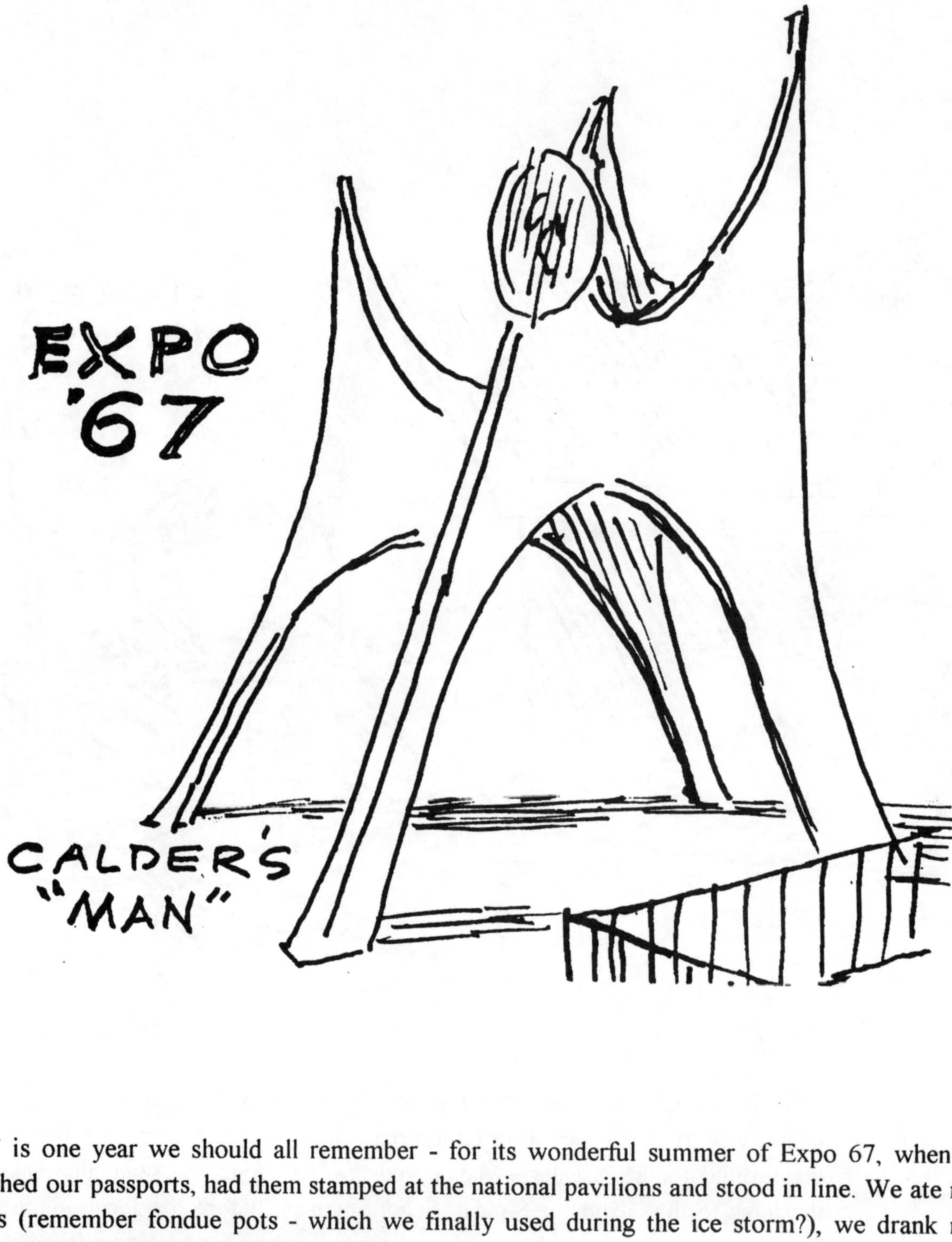


1967 is one year we should all remember - for its wonderful summer of Expo 67, when we clutched our passports, had them stamped at the national pavilions and stood in line. We ate new foods (remember fondue pots - which we finally used during the ice storm?), we drank new drinks, and watched acts from all over the world.

And do you recall the anxiety before opening day? Would it be ready or would those islands just sink into the river? But it all worked to give Montreal its best summer in history. As an encore, in 1976 we were given the Olympic Games - a brief excitement, and the Big Owe - one long headache.

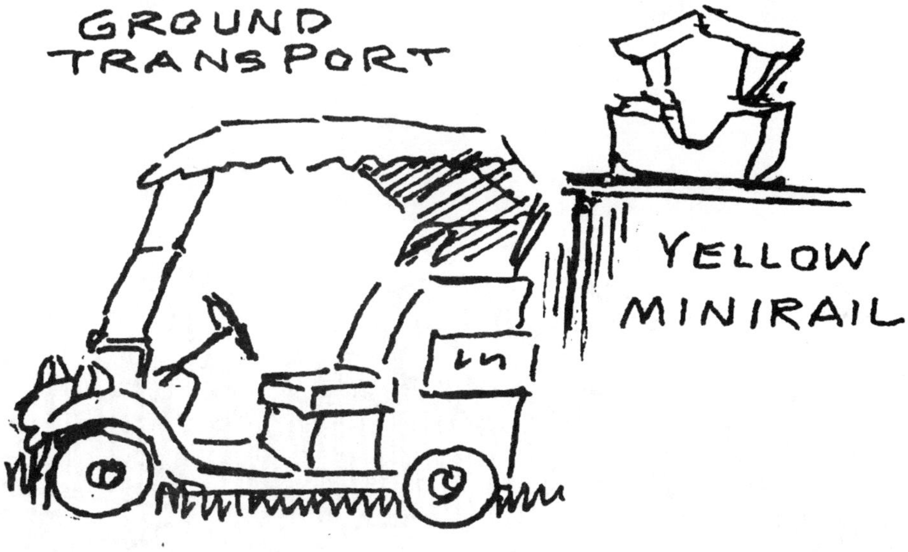
GROUND TRANSPORT
YELLOW MINIRAIL

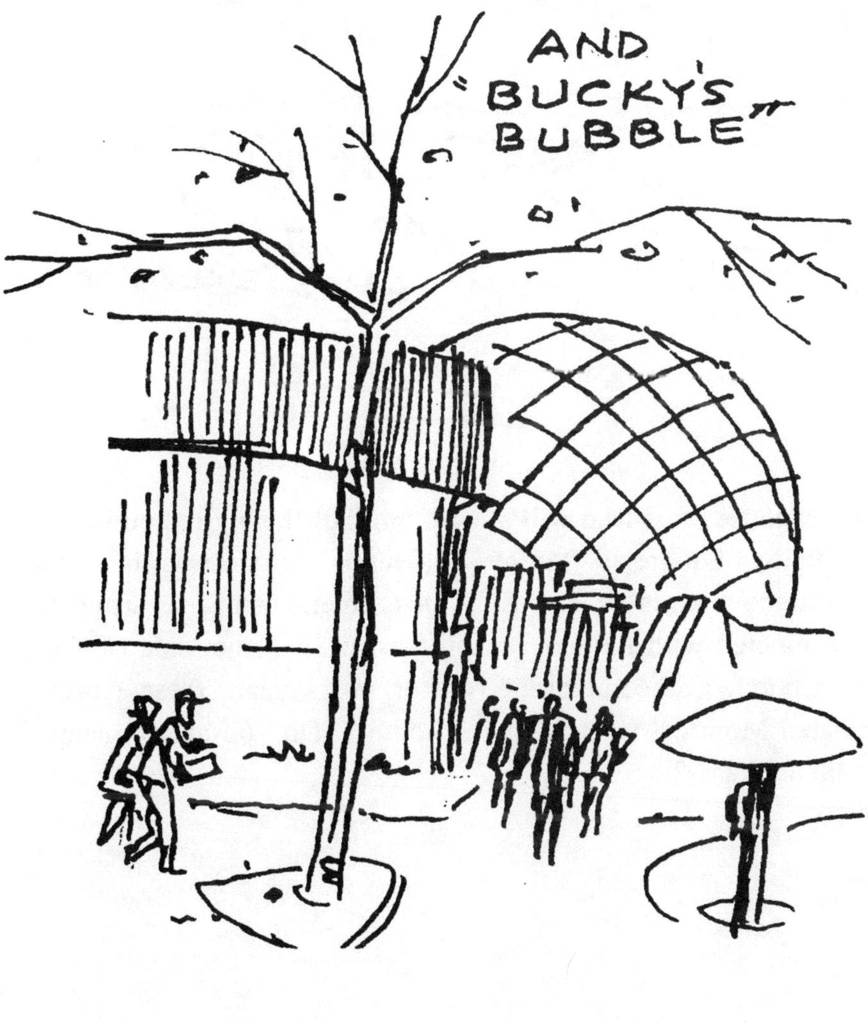
AND "BUCKY'S BUBBLE"

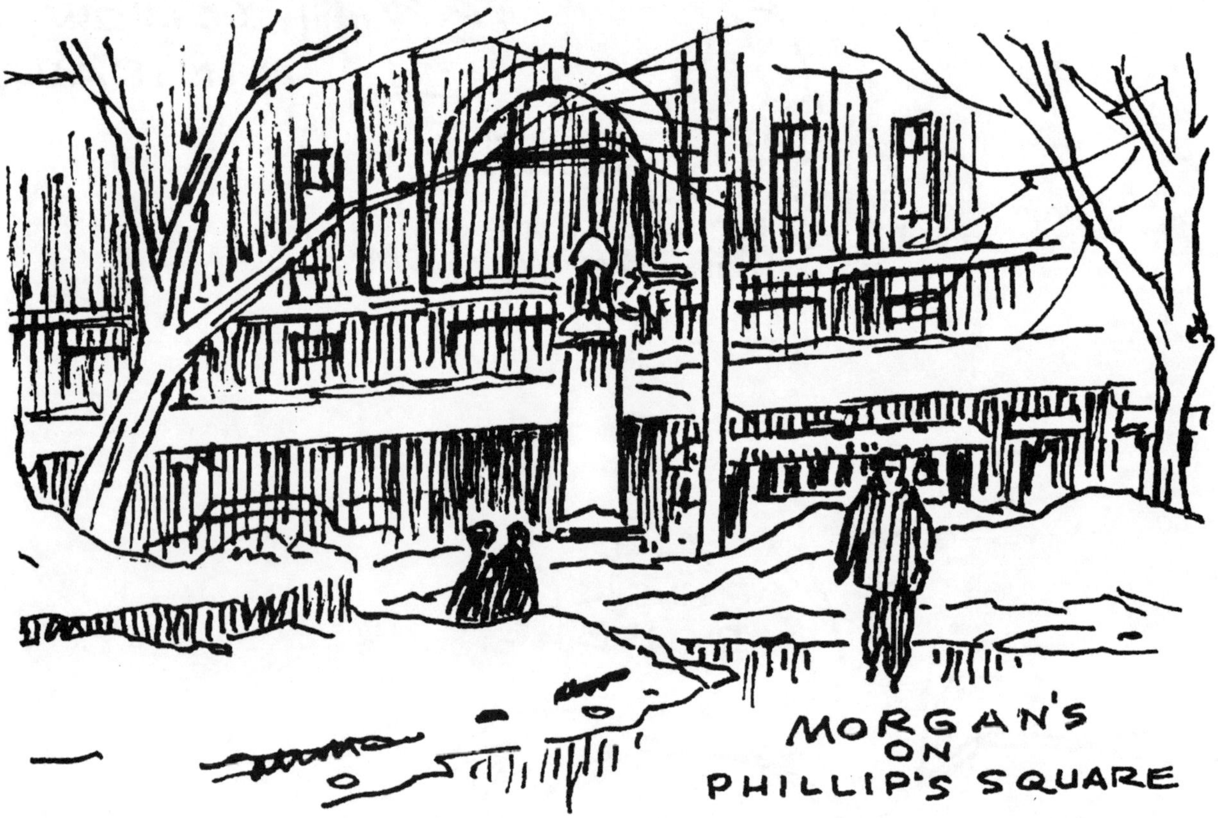


There are those of us who will always think of the big red building facing Philips Square as "Morgan's." Henry Morgan was the first retailer to move up town from St. James Street. His big department store competed with Eaton's, which was on the other side of the Christ Church Cathedral property. For many years these stores dominated Montreal merchandizing activity. Do you also remember Dupuis Frères?

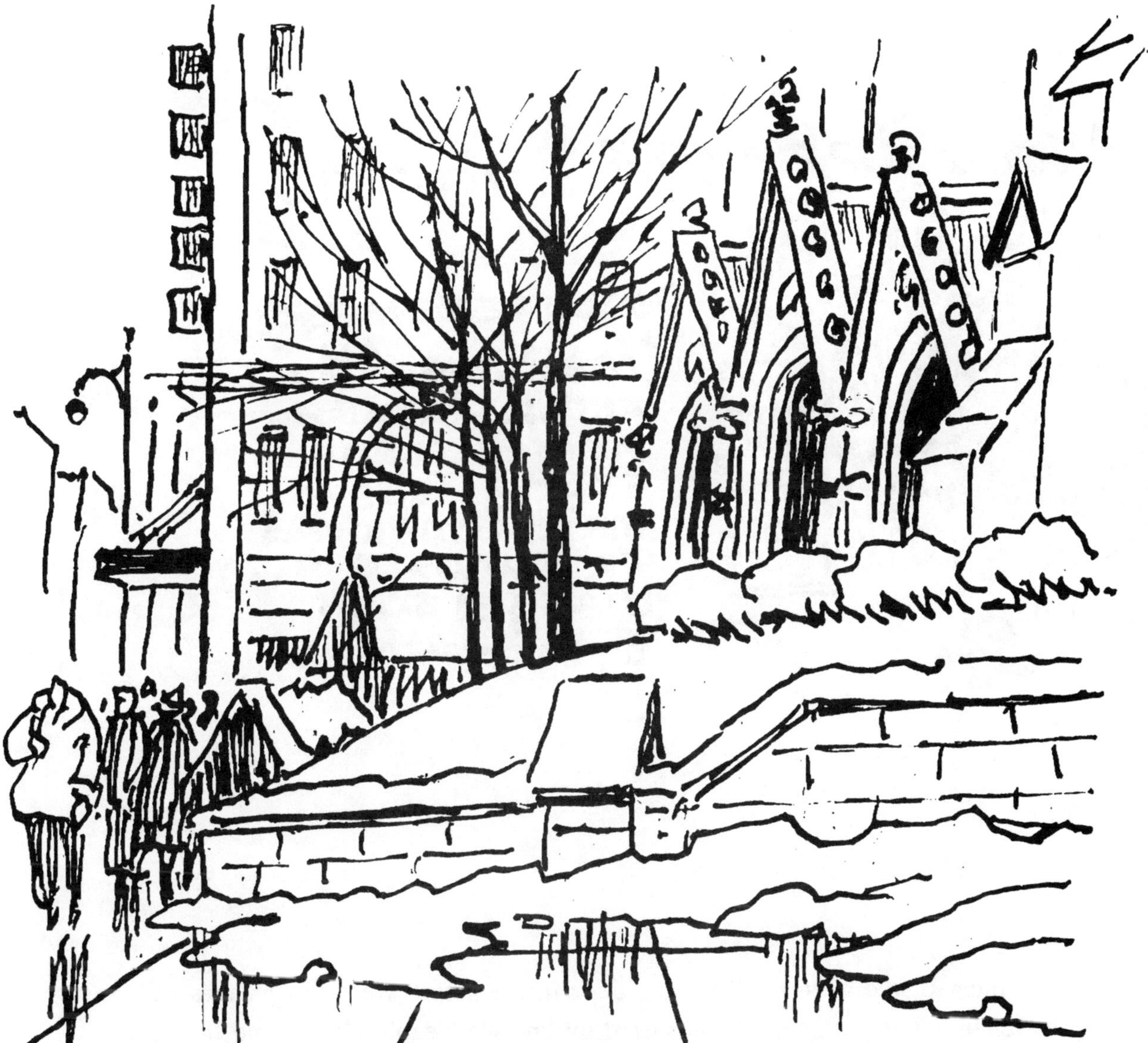

EATON'S ON
STE. CATHERINE STREET

FOR MOST OF THE CENTURY EATON'S WAS THE SHOPPING MECCA FOR MANY MONTREAL WOMEN. THE BIG BUILDING NEXT TO CHRIST CHURCH CATHEDRAL DREW THEM FOR SATURDAY AFTERNOON SHOPPING VISITS

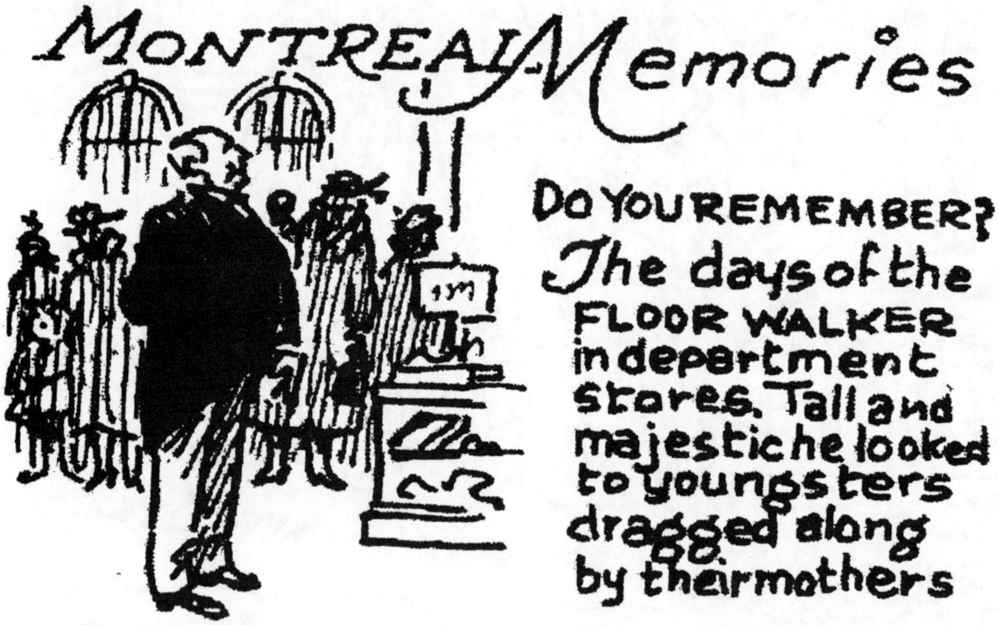


For most of the century, the great department stores were the palaces of merchandizing. Counters were staffed by knowledgeable clerks, and in the early days there were “floorwalkers.” To little children accompanying their mothers, the towering floorwalker in Eaton’s was an awe-inspiring sight as he directed customers to the elevators or an appropriate sales counter. This is quite a contrast to current conditions when sometimes you can wander through many departments without finding an open cash register or a clerk to question.

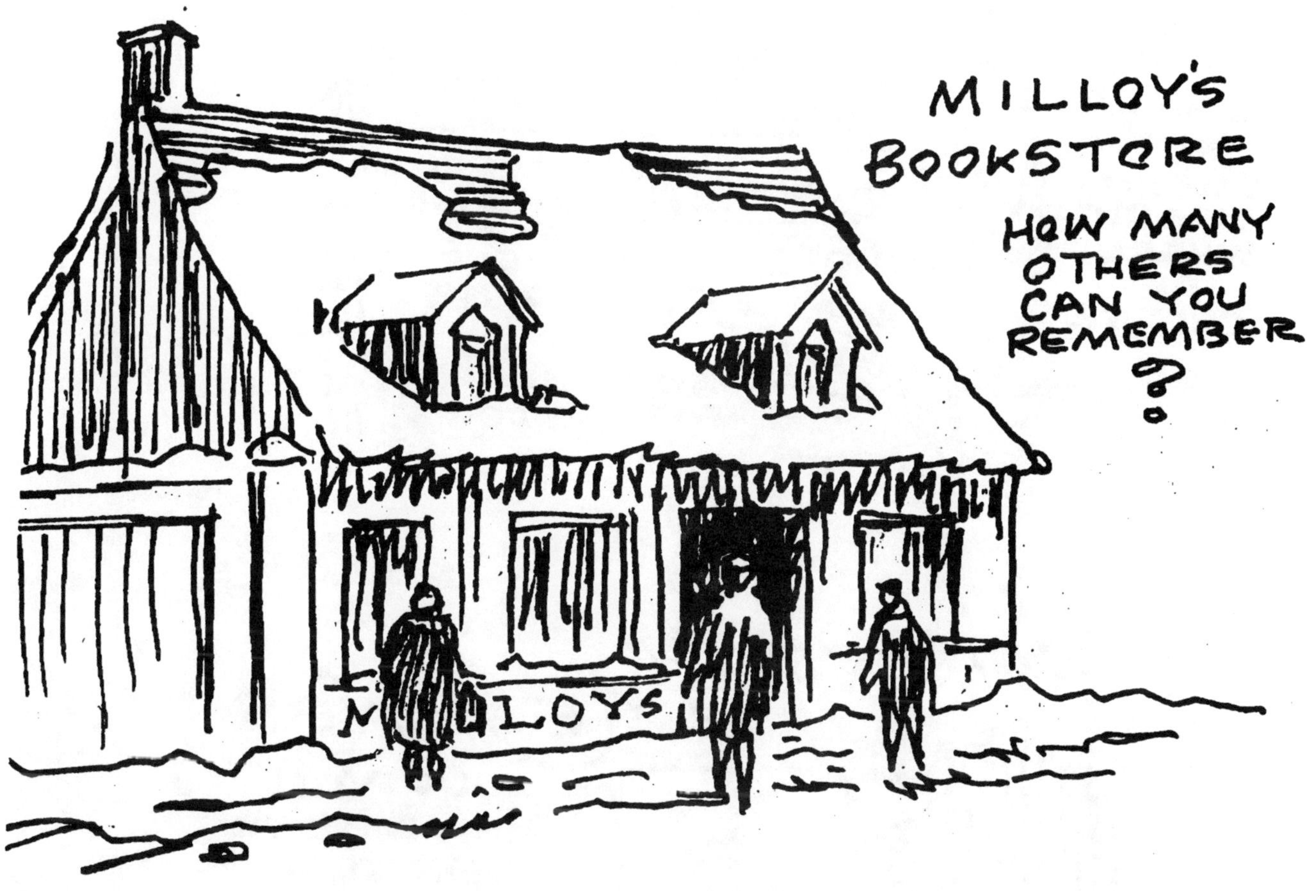


Milloy's Bookstore was located on St. Catherine Street and would only be remembered by Old Timers. It was one of many small bookshops that have come and gone in our town. You must have memories of a few, such as Everyman's on St. Catherine Street and Roddick's just opposite. Remember the splash Classics made? They come, they go, and now even Russell's has been chased away by developers.

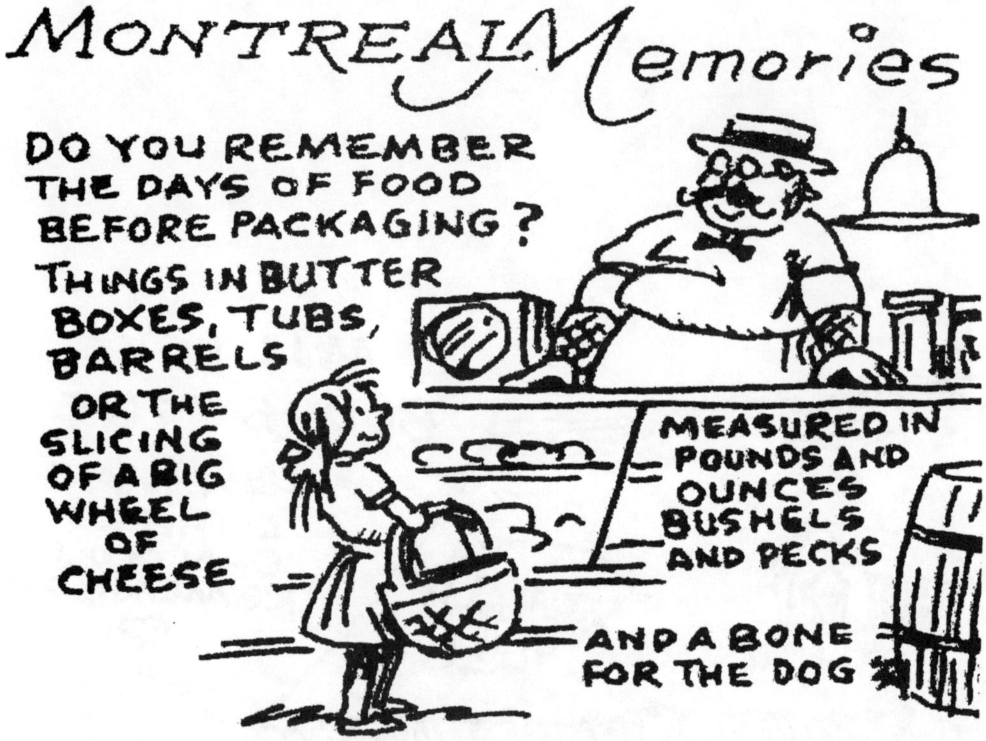


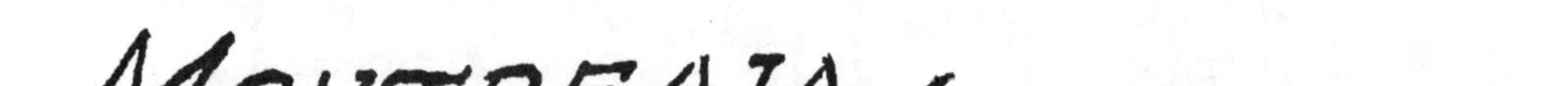


The Old Soda Fountain

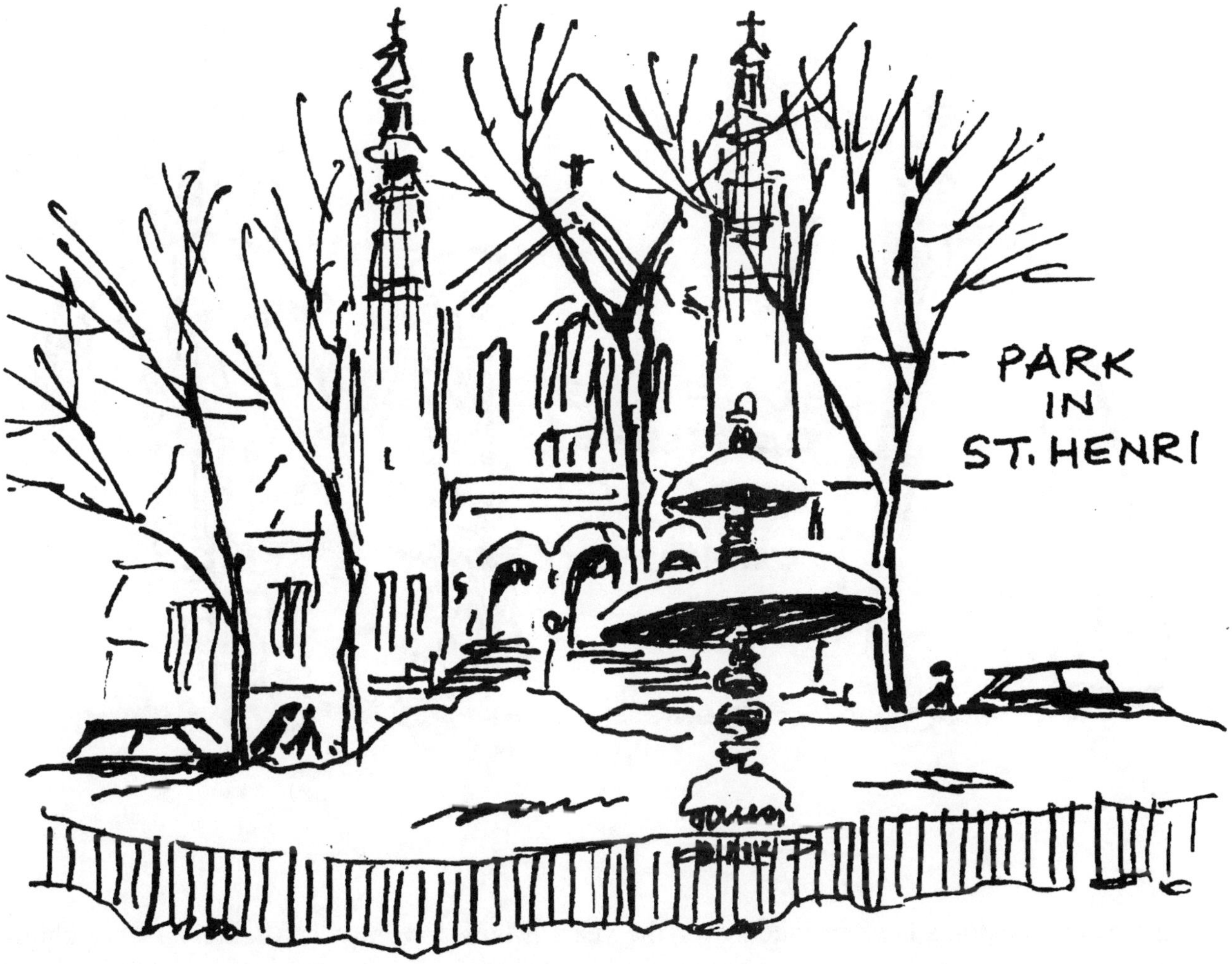
PARK
IN
ST. HENRI

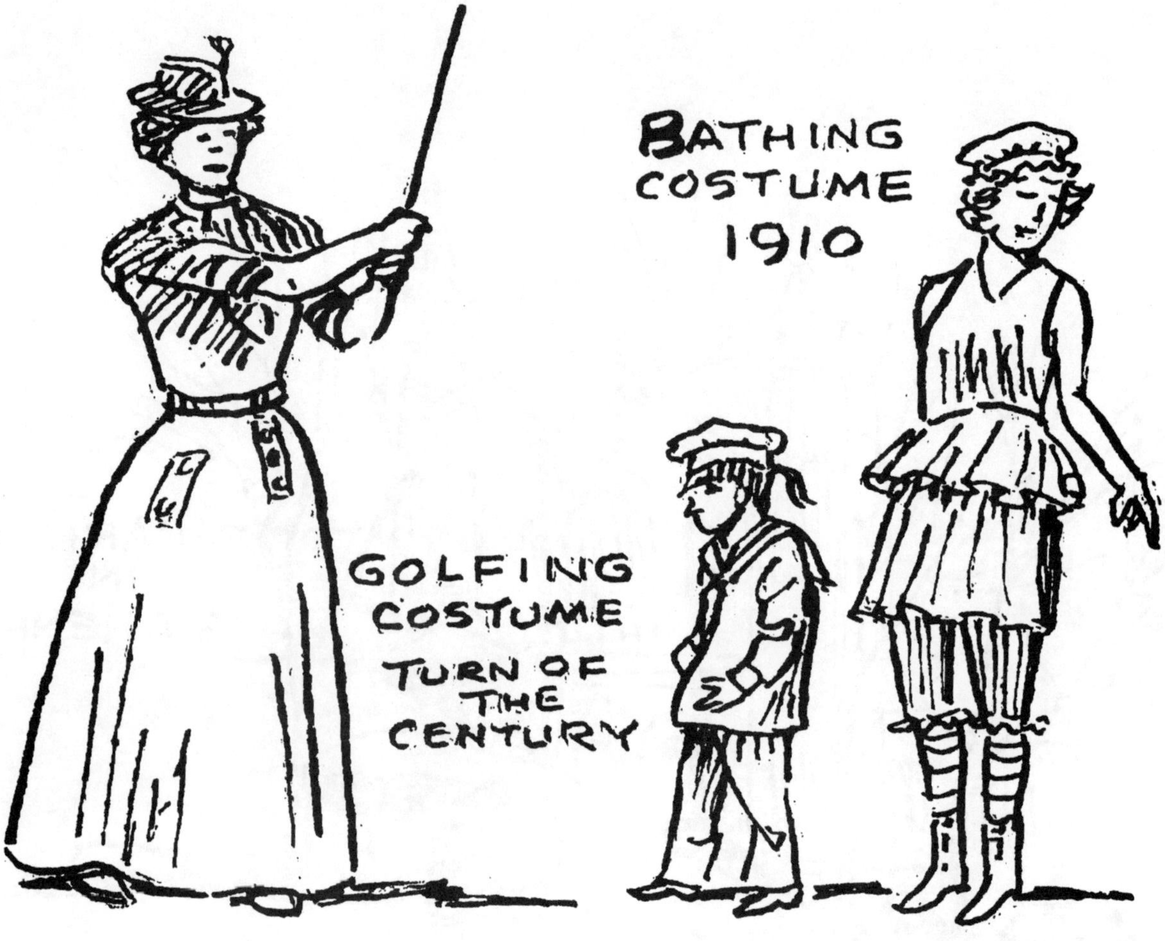


Costumes and customs have changed over the years. Many a woman can remember her childhood winter outfit of overshoes and Red River coat. Boys' clothing was more nondescript. Sweaters were usually in weird combinations of colours, but if you were lucky you had one in the colours of the Canadiens or the Maroons. Remember "breeks" - britches, quite often of corduroy, which dried stiff as a board.

Of course, in winter everyone wore overstockings, and tuques pulled down low over your ears. Sometimes you got away with wearing moccasins or ski boots. In summer, girls wore dresses and played hopscotch and jacks or skipped rope. Boys, before the age of the T-shirt, wore shirts, shorts and running shoes. They spun tops, played marbles or baseball. Remember "scrub" or being in the "cow"?

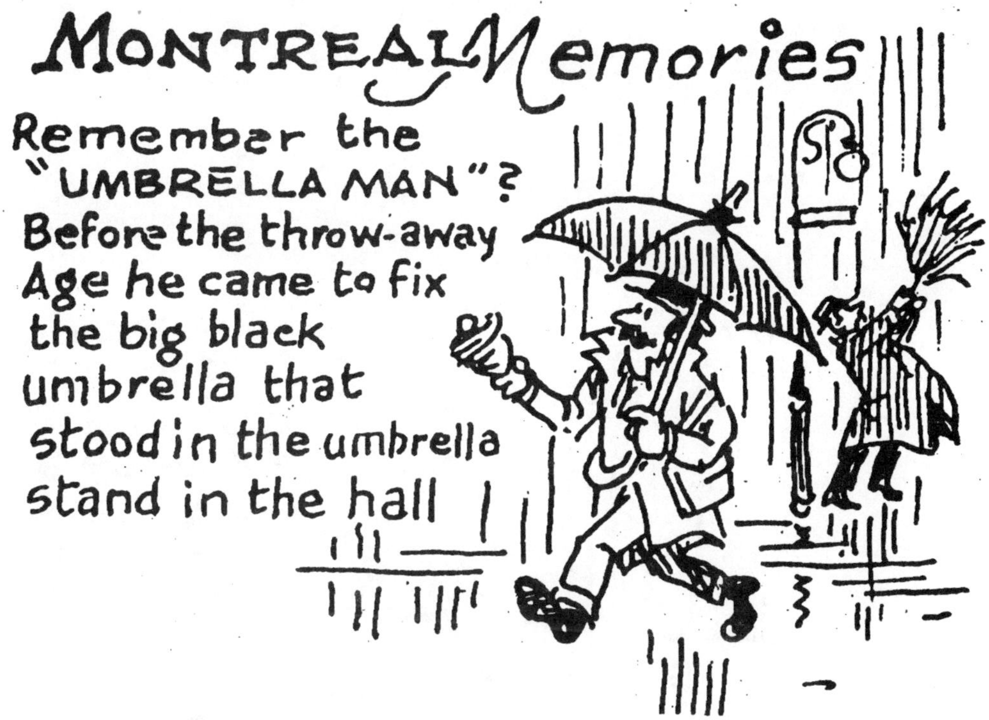


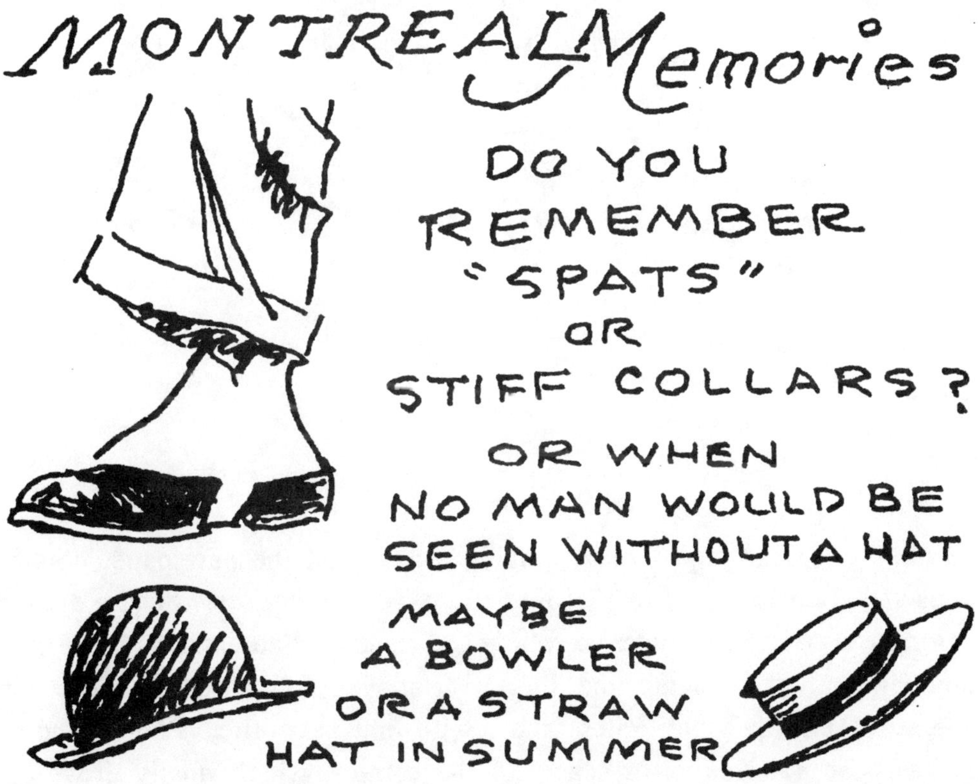


Have you seen anyone wearing spats lately? But you remember them, surely. Toe rubbers, too - the things tossed on the ice at the Forum after a Canadiens' victory. Also, stiff collars and hats that all men had to wear, even to a picnic in summer. It was a more formal world, with offices insisting on proper dress during business hours - and all this without air-conditioning!

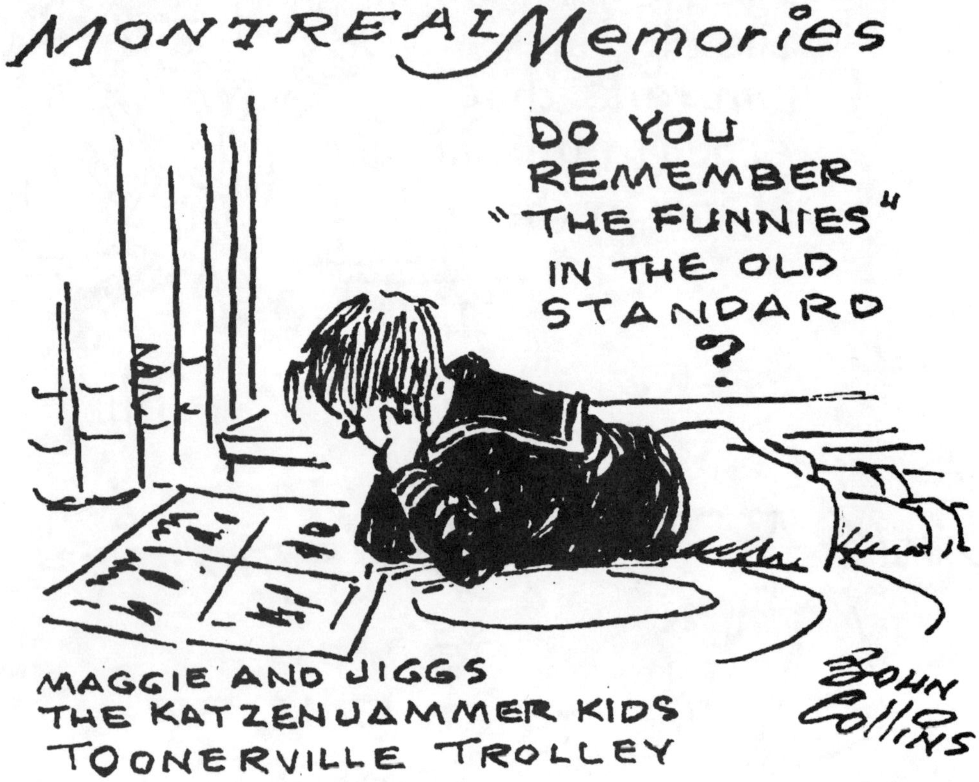


Most Montreal children's first exposure to graphic art was on the newspaper comic pages. *The Standard* gave us weekly helpings of this visual delight, while *The Herald* had a daily display. *The Star* and *The Gazette* were much slower to follow the trend. In the early days we had "Mutt and Jeff," "Bringing Up Father" (Maggie and Jiggs), "Happy Hooligan," and "The Katzenjammer Kids." Later we had "Terry and the Pirates" and my all-time favourite, "Pogo." The only problem over the years has been a shrinking of space for the comics, which finally drove the creator of "Calvin and Hobbs" out of business.

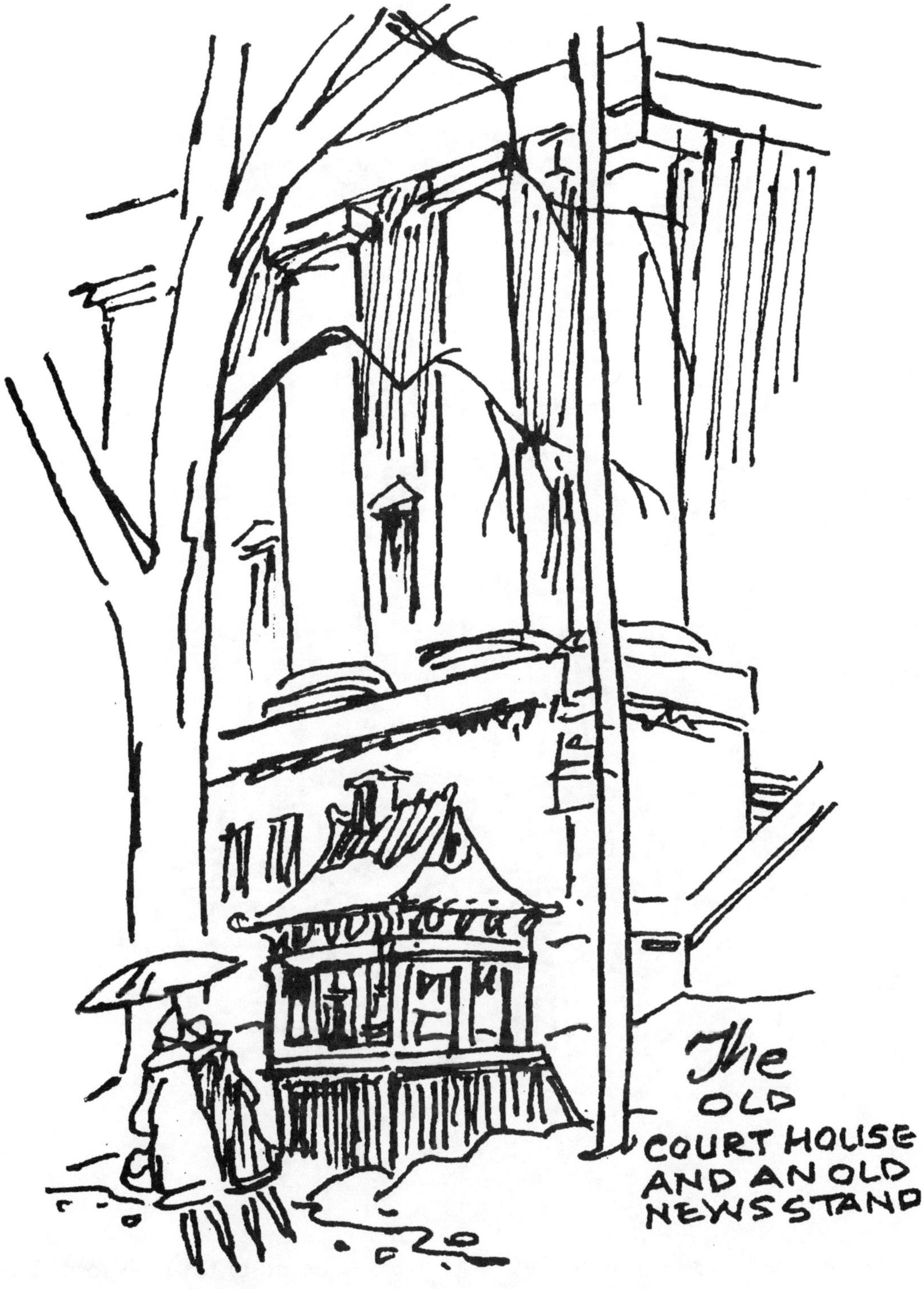


The old newspaper kiosks were among the many little shacks where vendors huddled inside in winter. Later these shacks disappeared as City Hall's "beautification plans" drove the vendors off our streets. Do you remember all the papers that have gone? *The Standard, The Star, The Herald, Le Canada, La Patrie,* Jean Charles Harvey's *Le Jour* - where I saw my first cartoon in print, and *The Witness* - for whose last issue I was asked to draw a cartoon of my own.

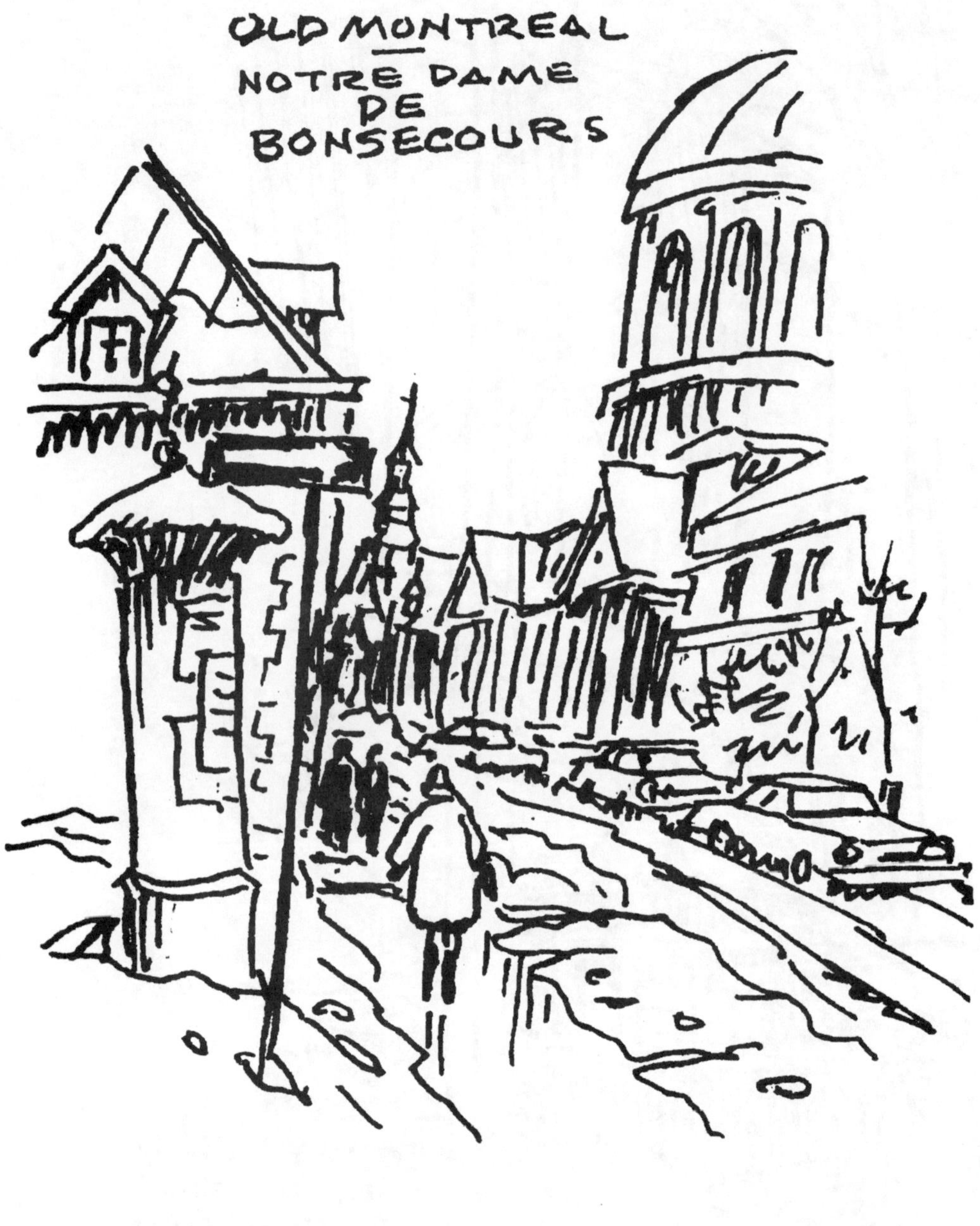


Do you remember the tours of Montreal we used to give our out-of-town visitors? We would begin in Old Montreal at Notre Dame de Bonsecours Church. This old "Sailors' Church," with its tiny boats hanging from the ceiling, was especially appealing. The tour usually included visits to the "Midgets' Palace" and the Wax Museum or maybe a look at the coloured fountains in LaFontaine Park. Mount Royal with its spectacular view of the city would be the grand climax.

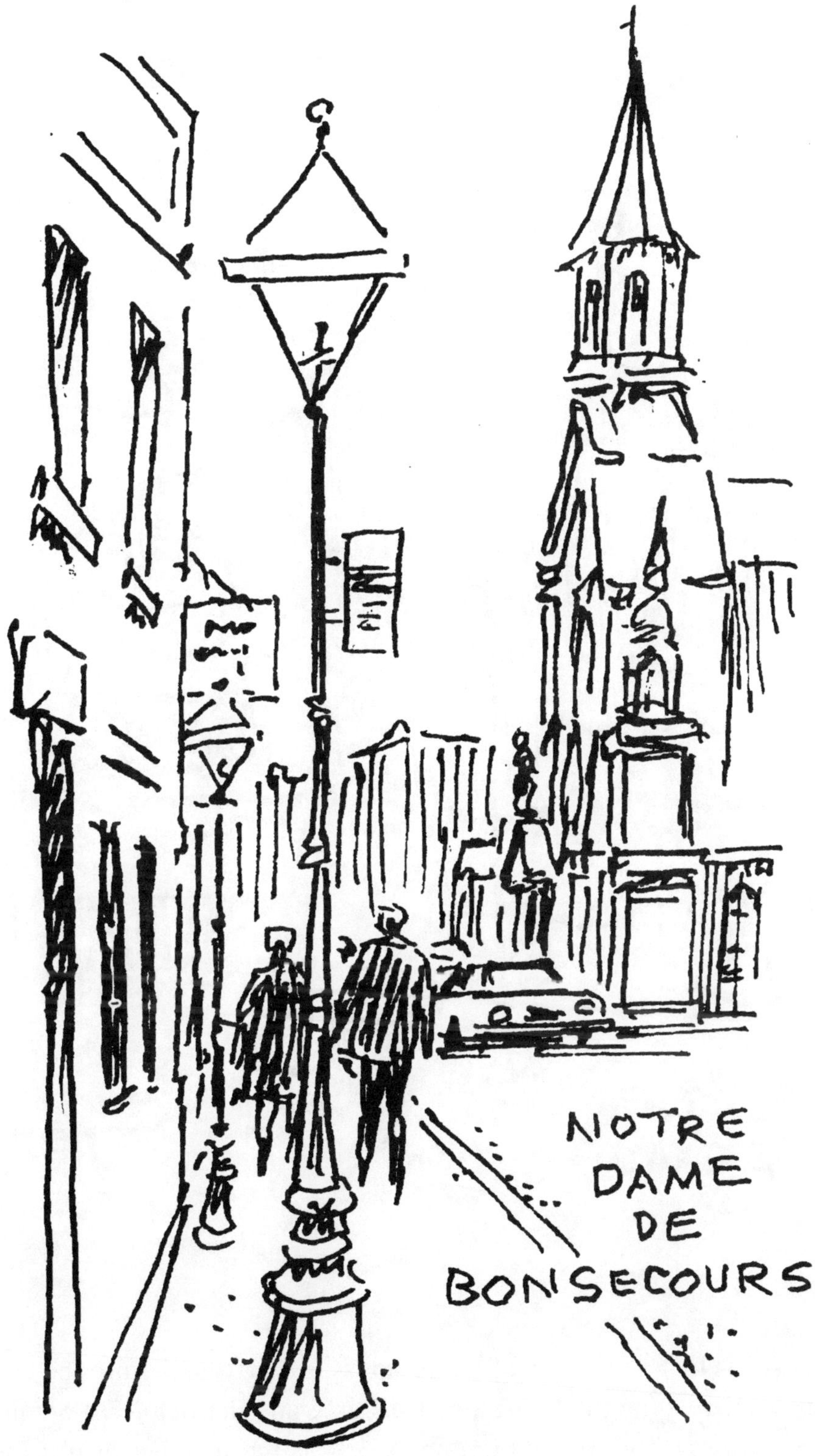
NOTRE
DAME
DE
BONSECOURS

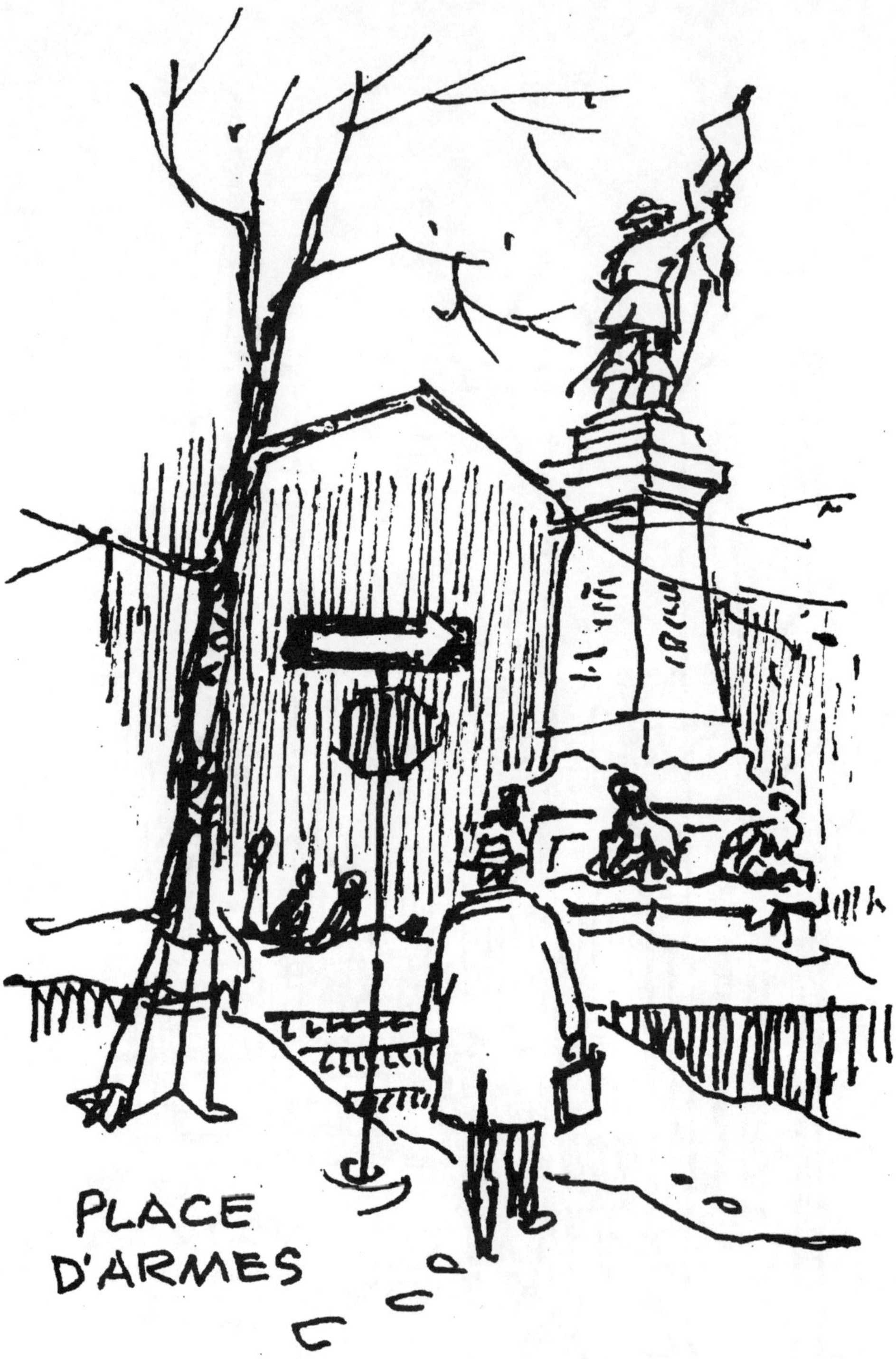


Place d'Armes was long the centre of big business in Montreal before the banks and investment houses moved up town. With Notre Dame and the Sulpician Seminary on the south and the Bank of Montreal on the north, it was the meeting of history and commerce. Do you remember hurrying across the square to catch a streetcar? It was a junction spot for streetcars, where winter or summer, office workers squeezed onto the back of trams at rush hours.

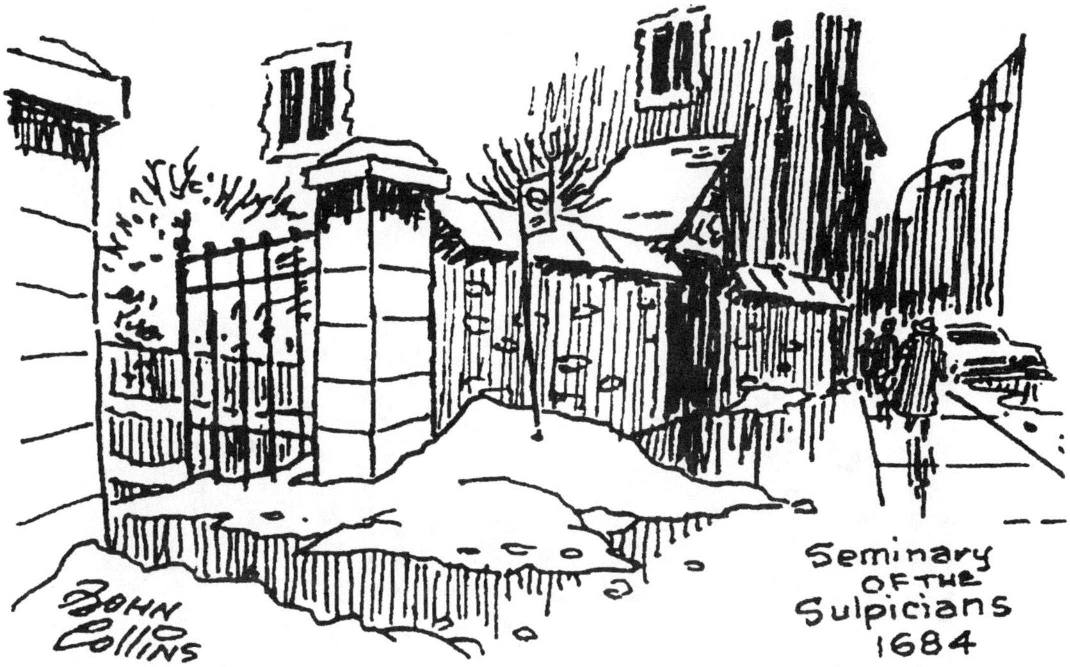
John Collins
Seminary of the Sulpicians 1684

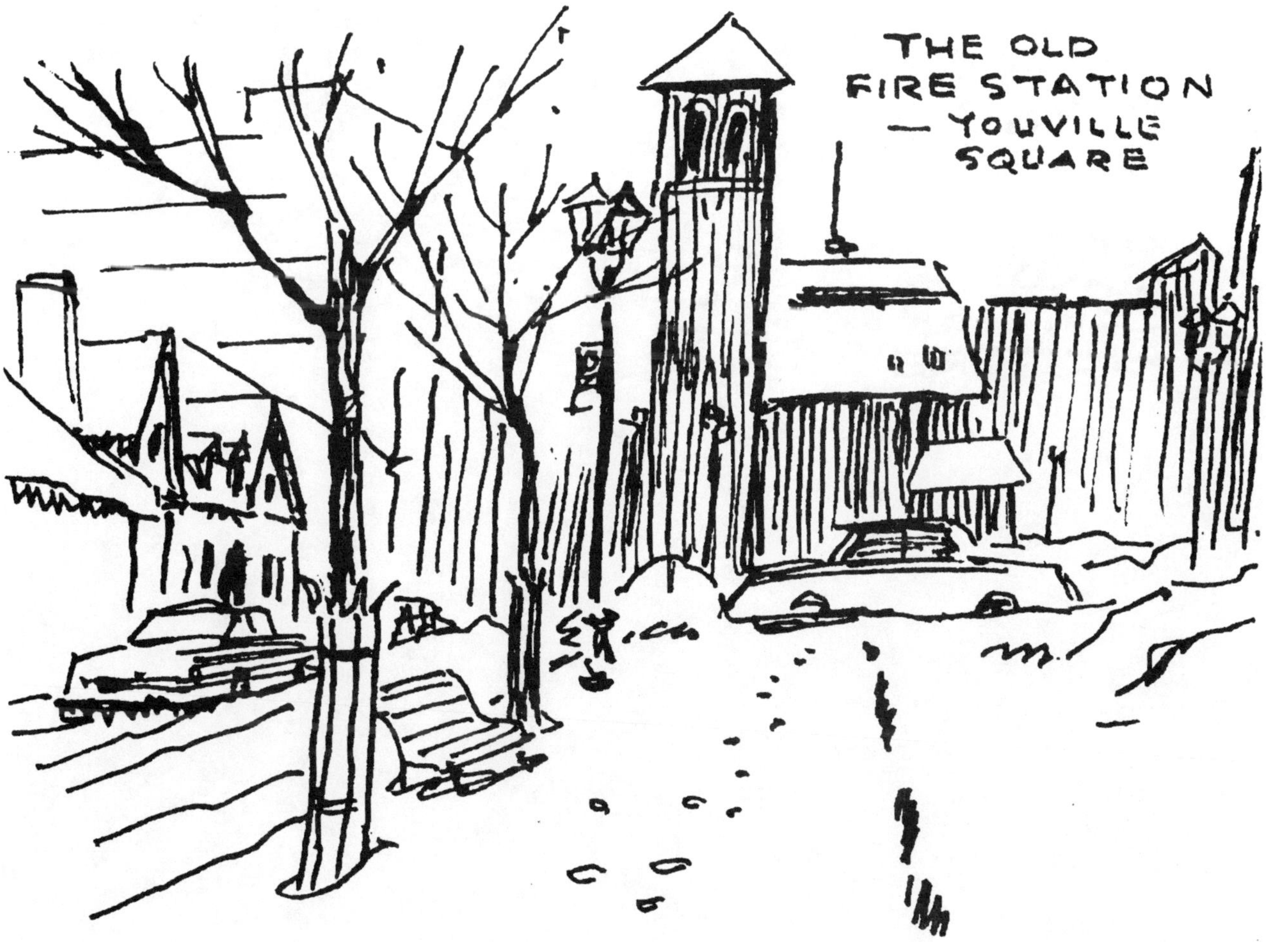
THE OLD FIRE STATION — YOUVILLE SQUARE

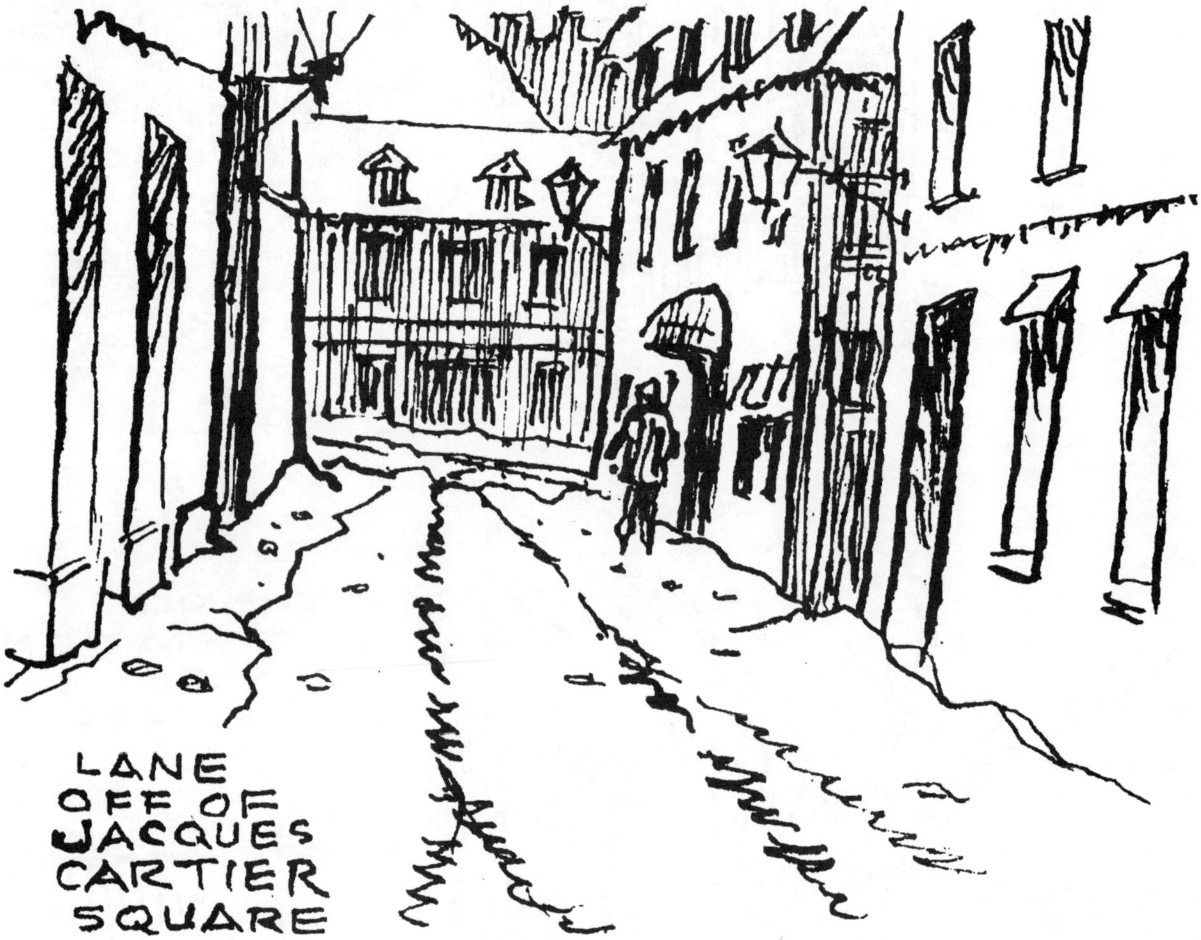
LANE
OFF OF
JACQUES
CARTIER
SQUARE

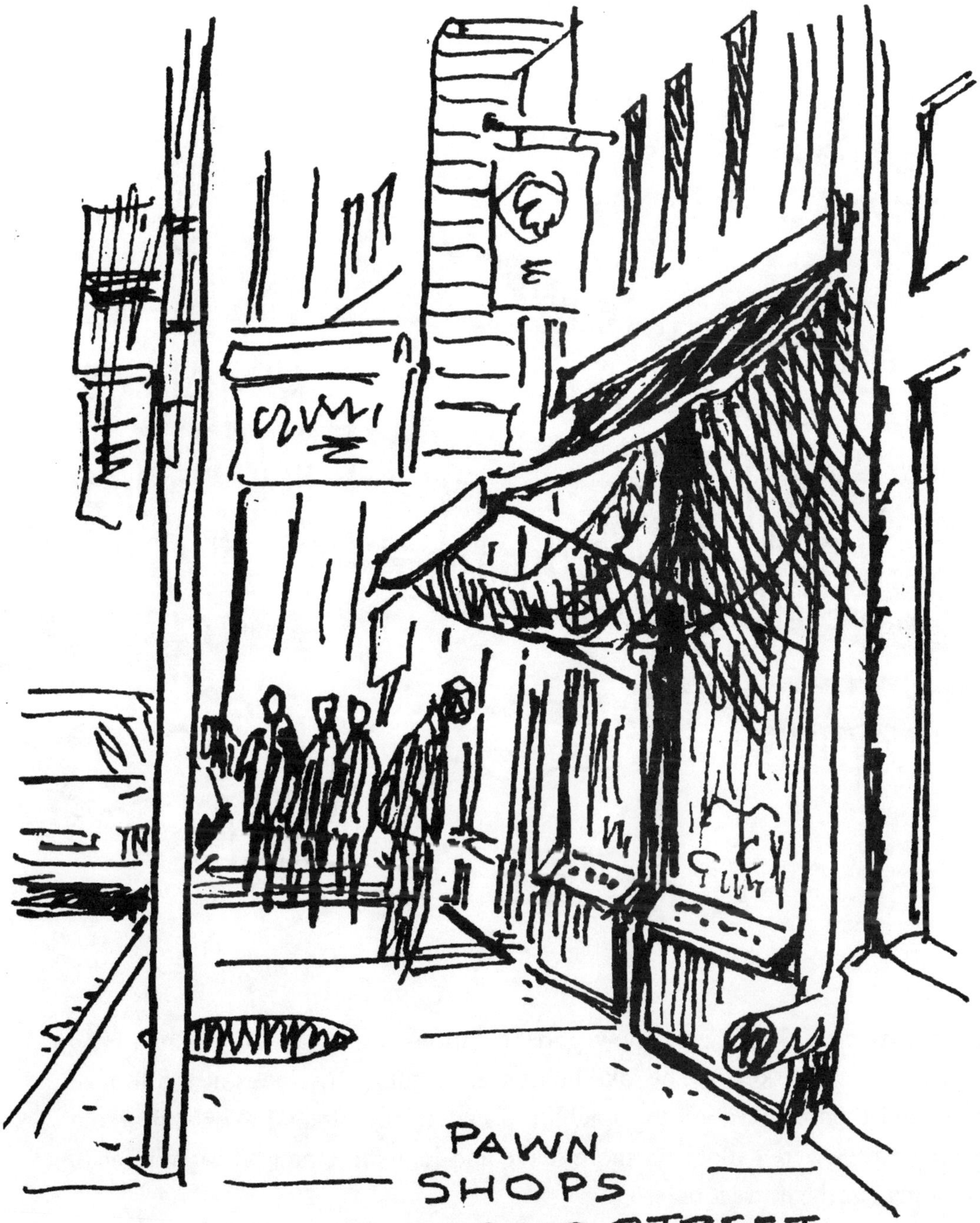

PAWN SHOPS ON CRAIG STREET

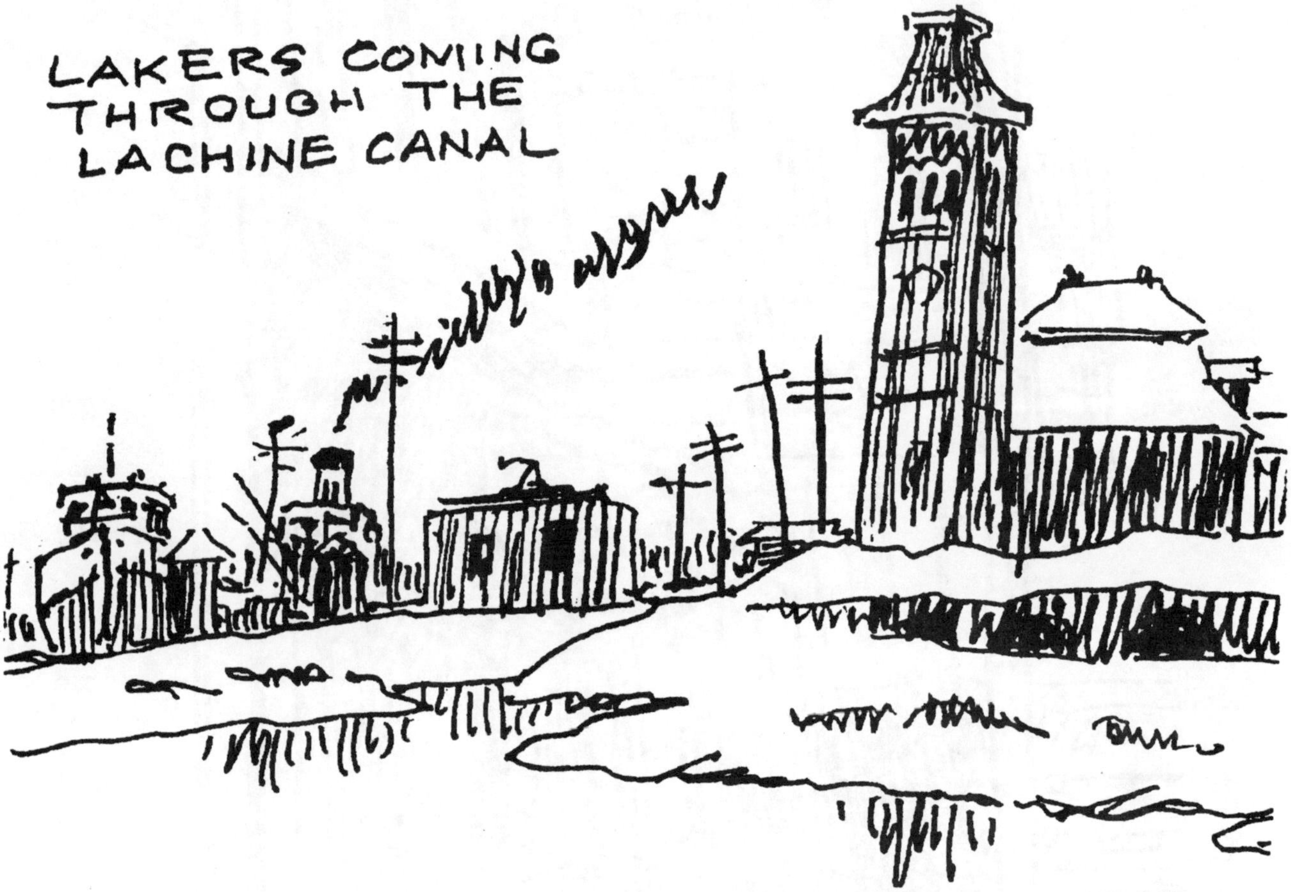


Before the St. Lawrence Seaway and new port operations, our waterfront was a busy place and a great place to sketch. The lake boats went through the locks at the foot of McGill Street and then on through the Lachine Canal to the Great Lakes. Crowding Commissioners Street were sailors on shore leave and longshoremen with their cargo hooks, all looking for the nearest tavern.

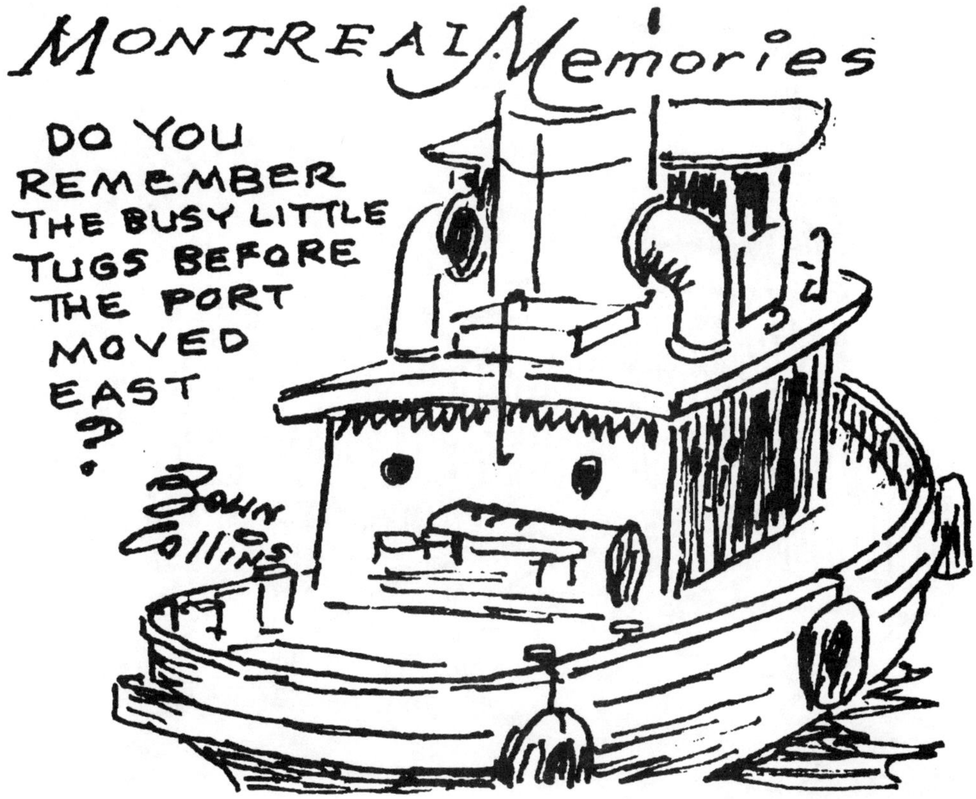
MONTREAL Memories
DO YOU REMEMBER THE BUSY LITTLE TUGS BEFORE THE PORT MOVED EAST ?
Bown Collins

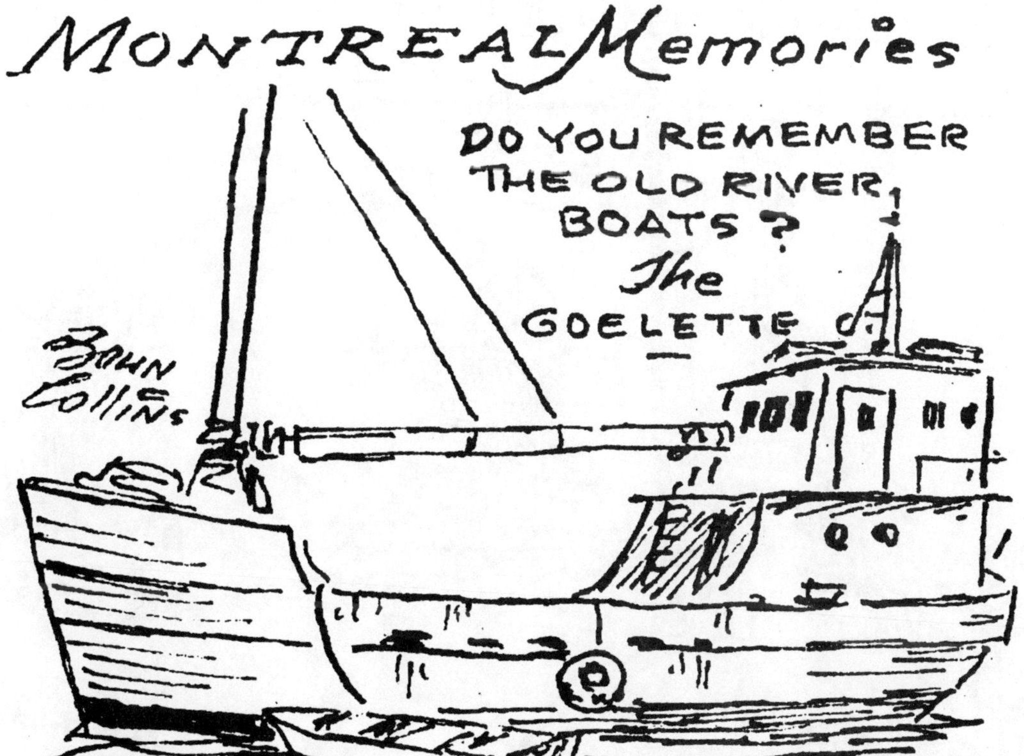
MONTREAL Memories
DO YOU REMEMBER THE OLD RIVER BOATS ?
The GOELETTE
Bown Collins

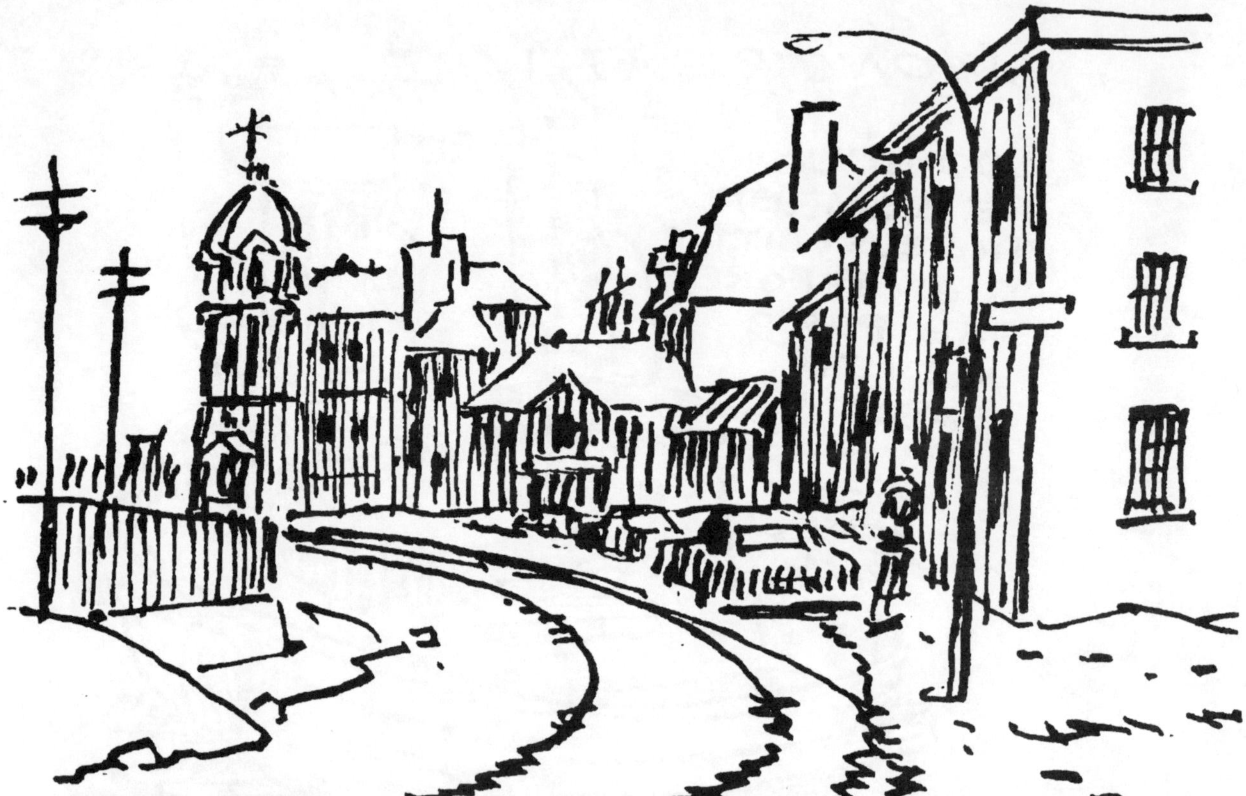

THE OLD HARBOR COMMISSIONERS BUILDING

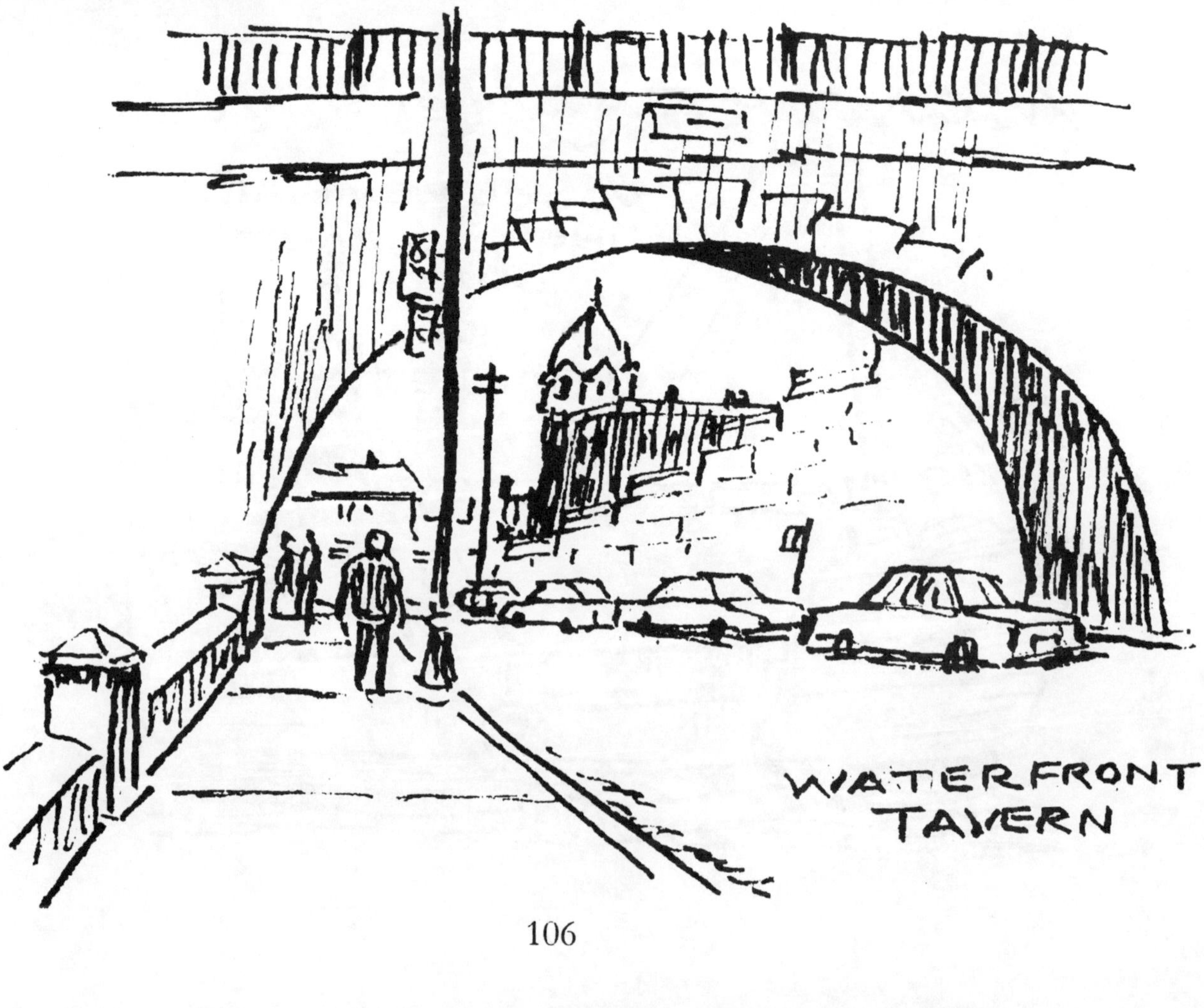

WATERFRONT TAVERN

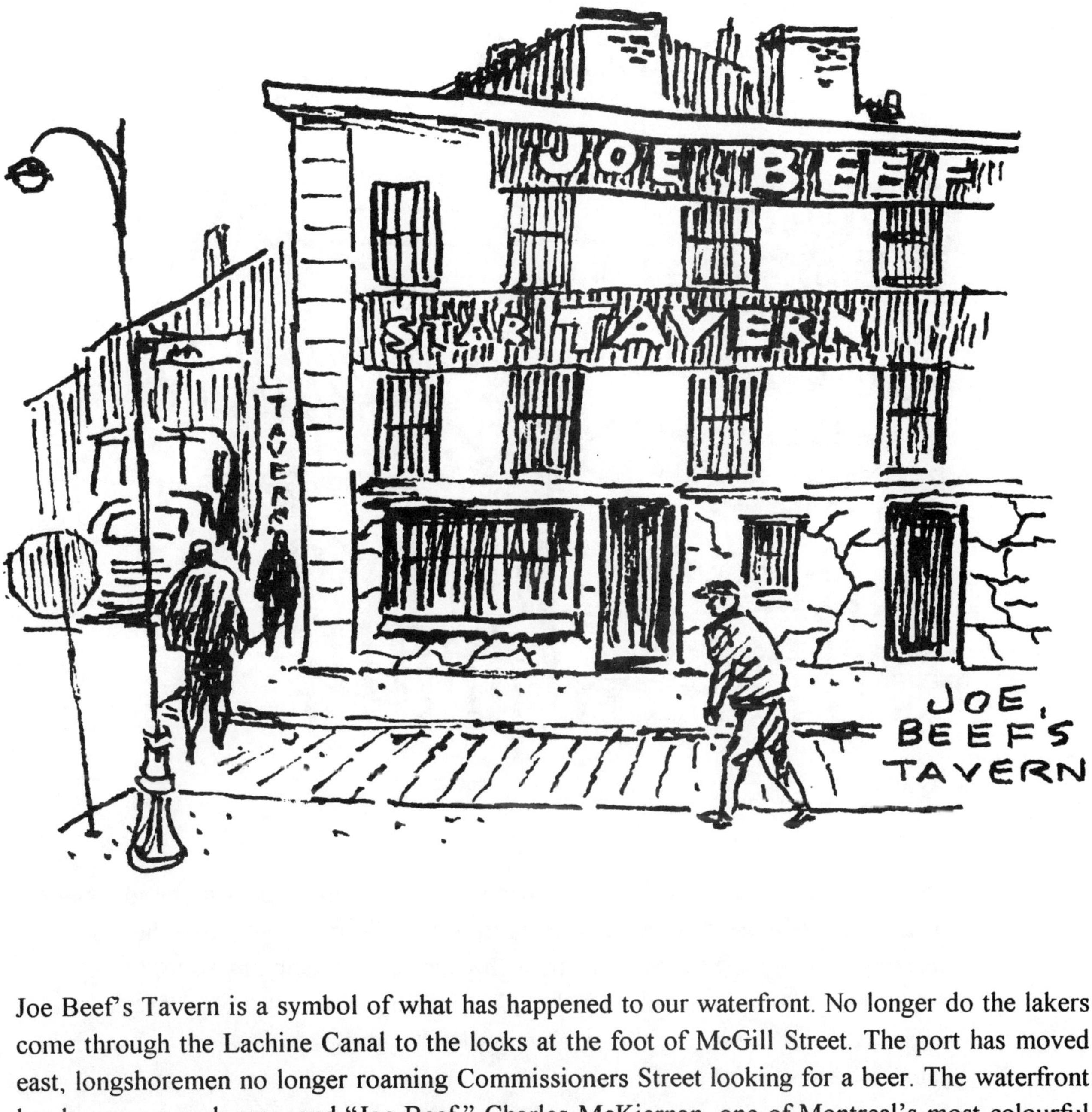


Joe Beef's Tavern is a symbol of what has happened to our waterfront. No longer do the lakers come through the Lachine Canal to the locks at the foot of McGill Street. The port has moved east, longshoremen no longer roaming Commissioners Street looking for a beer. The waterfront has become a park area, and "Joe Beef," Charles McKiernan, one of Montreal's most colourful characters of the 19th century, is all but forgotten.

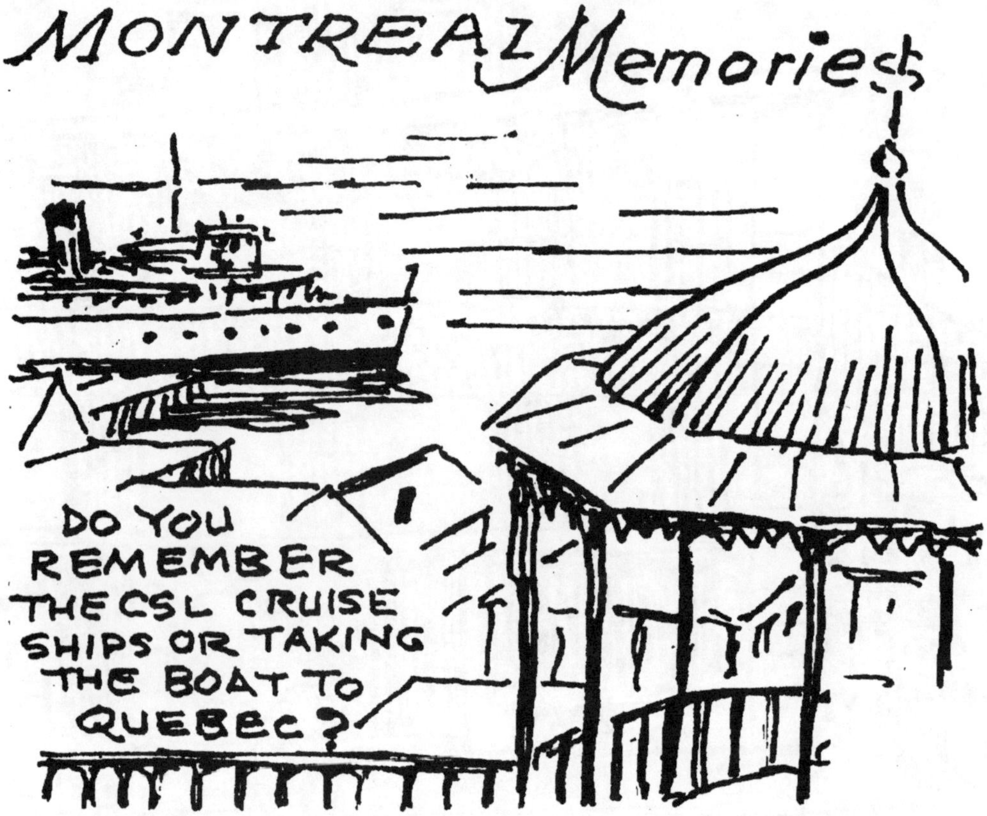


Do you remember the CSL cruises down the river to Murray Bay and Tadoussac? The big white vessels attracted tourists from the US and would give them a picturesque trip on the Saguenay River, with good food, dancing and shore trips. Or you could just take the boat to Quebec City. The big wooden ships were taken out of service after a fire on a ship in Ontario. Many young Montrealers had summer jobs on these ships of fond memory.

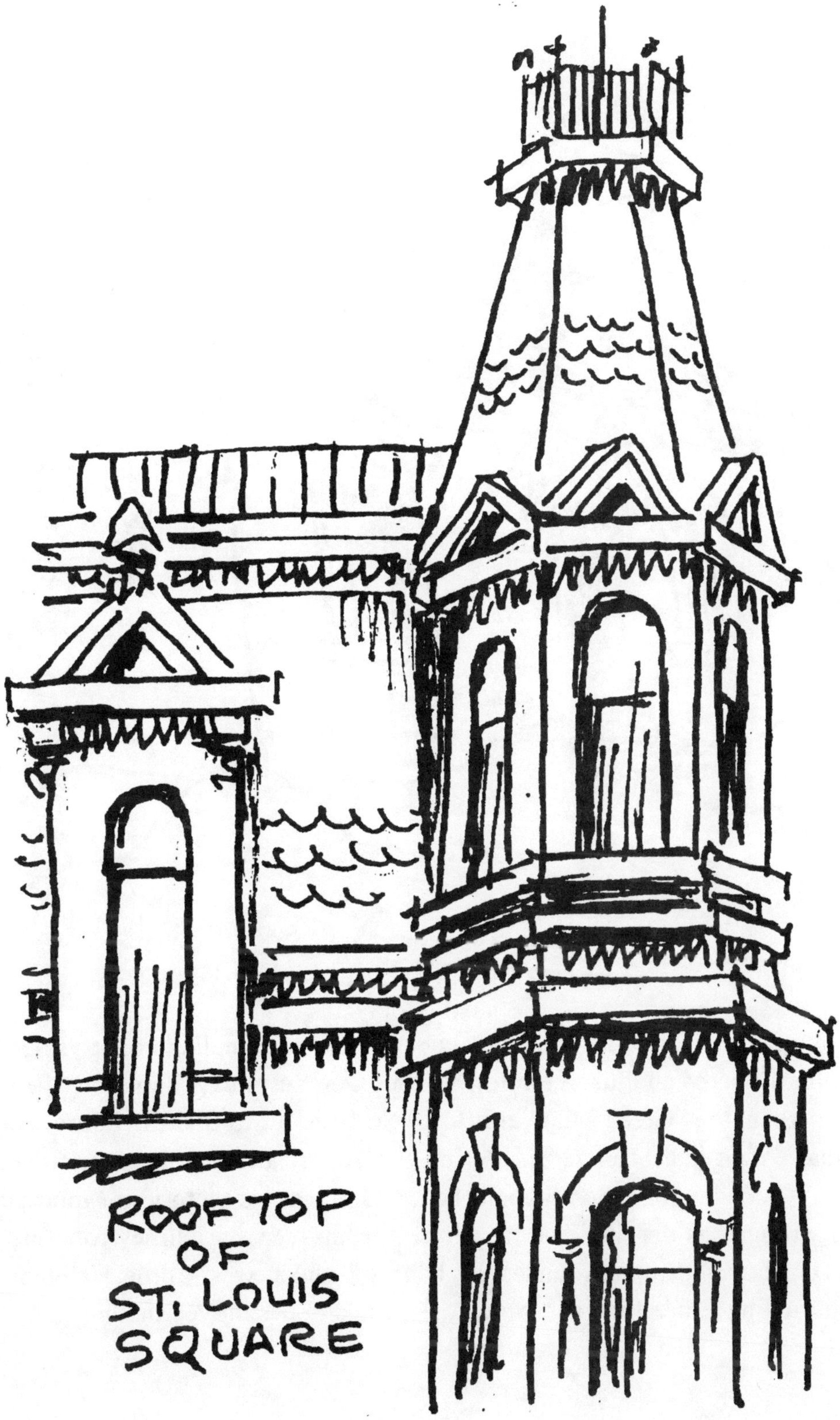
ROOF TOP
OF
ST. LOUIS
SQUARE

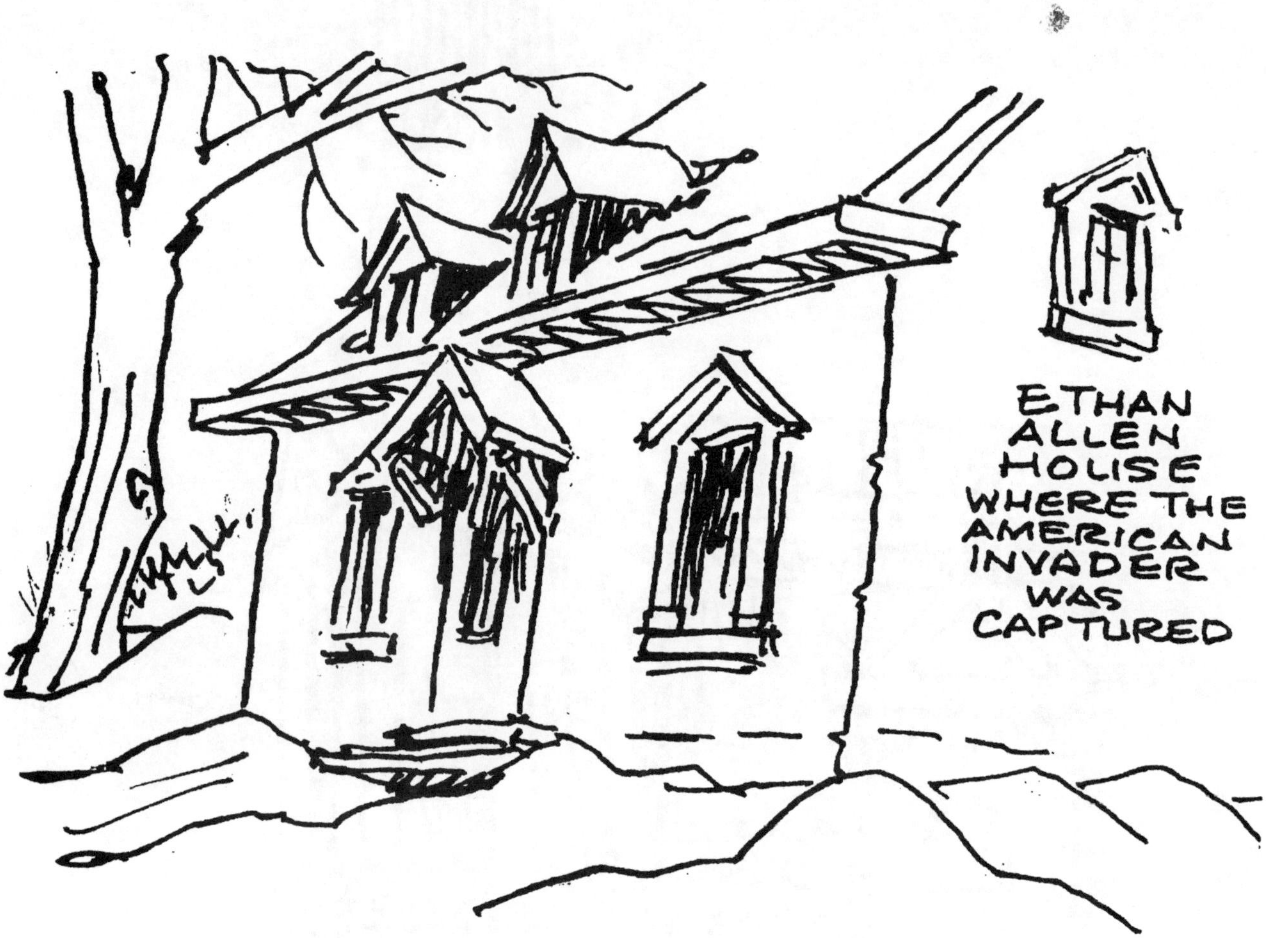


The story of any city is growth - how it takes over the surrounding countryside. Edgar Andrew Collard wanted an illustration for his "All Our Yesterdays" column: the subject being Ethan Allen, the "Green Mountain Boy." So I set out to find the house where allegedly Ethan Allen had been seized during the American Revolution. After having captured Fort Ticonderoga, Allen thought he could repeat his victory in Montreal - but he guessed wrong, was defeated and he, himself, captured. My journey took me along rue Notre Dame and there, surrounded by huge oil tanks, was a little Habitant farmhouse, identified by a metal marker. Since then, the city has moved the house to a park further east.

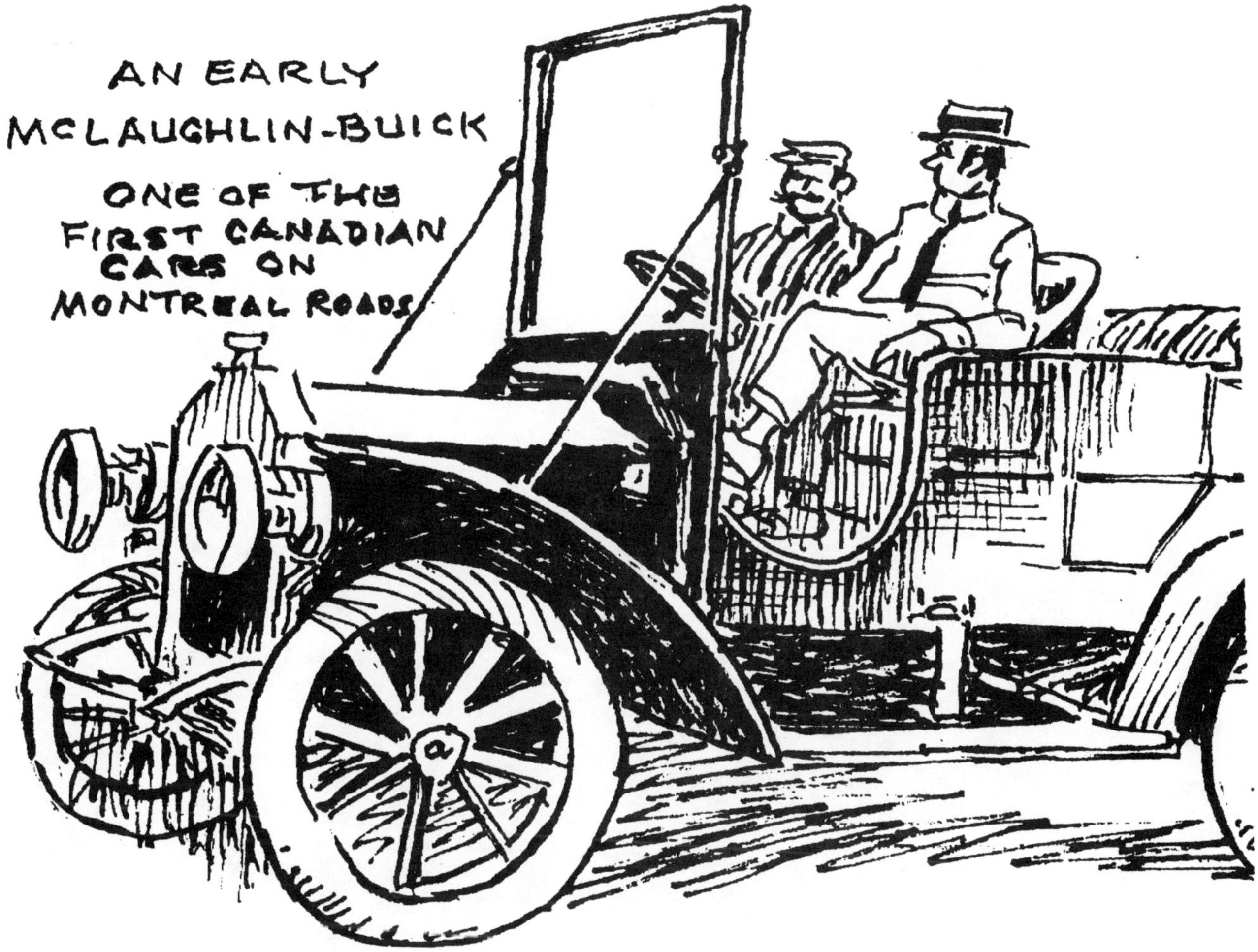


We started this book with the automobile, and even after a century of invention it is probably still the biggest influence in most people's lives. It has enabled us to travel more easily and widely than man could ever go before. We'll end our sketchbook tour with an old McLaughlin Buick, a big name when I was young. In spite of technological advances, we're going into the new century still behind the wheel, still cursing at traffic tie-ups and road construction, and still looking for a place to park.

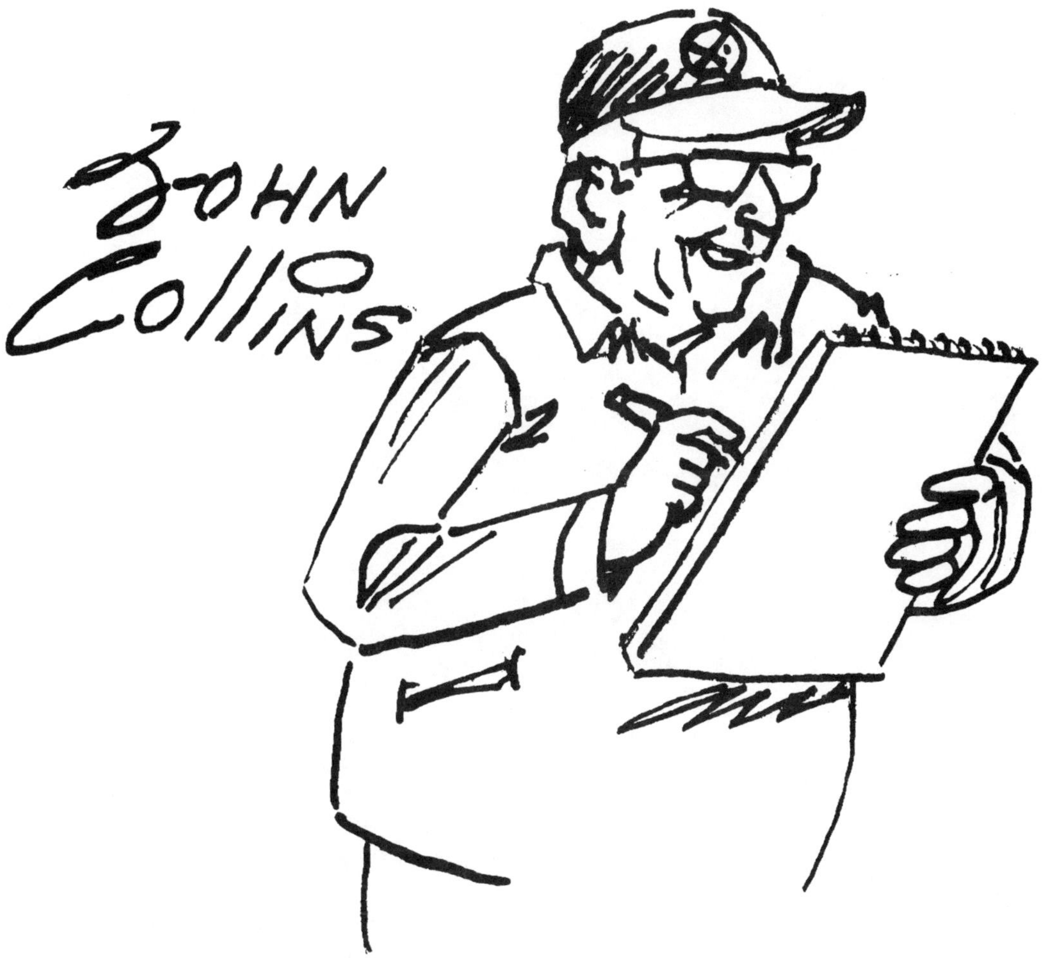


John Collins was born in 1917 in Washington, D.C. He came to Montreal at the age of two and has lived there ever since with a brief interlude of three years in Florida. He attended schools in Montreal including art training at L'Ecole des Beaux Arts and Sir George Williams College. For over forty years he was editorial cartoonist of *The Montreal Gazette*, where he also illustrated editor Edgar Andrew Collard's historical column "All Our Yesterdays." His sketches have illustrated five of Mr. Collard's books.

Canadian honours have come to John Collins in the form of two National Newspaper Awards for cartooning and two national watercolour awards. He is a past-president of the Association of American Editorial Cartoonists and an honourary member of the Canadian Association of Editorial Cartoonists. A member of the Lakeshore Association of Artists, he has works in private collections in Canada and the United States and in private collections of The Sun Life Company, *The Gazette*, Avmor and the cities of Dorval and Pointe Claire. Mr Collins, a long-time exhibitor at Artlenders Gallery, is now represented by West End Gallery of Westmount.

AGMV
MARQUIS
Québec, Canada
2000